Situations and Syntactic Structure

Linguistic Inquiry Monographs
Samuel Jay Keyser, general editor

A complete list of books published in the Linguistic Inquiry Monographs series appears at the back of this book.

Situations and Syntactic Structures
Rethinking Auxiliaries and Order in English

Gillian Ramchand

The MIT Press
Cambridge, Massachusetts
London, England

This book was set in Nimbus Roman by Westchester Publishing Services. Printed and bound in the United States of America.

Library of Congress Cataloging-in-Publication Data

Names: Ramchand, Gillian, 1965- author.
Title: Situations and syntactic structures : rethinking auxiliaries and order
    in English / Gillian Catriona Ramchand.
Description: Cambridge, MA : The MIT Press, 2017. | Series: Linguistic
    inquiry monographs; 77 | Includes bibliographical references and index.
Identifiers: LCCN 2017042768 | ISBN 9780262037754 (hardcover : alk. paper) |
    ISBN 9780262535038 (pbk. : alk. paper)
Subjects: LCSH: English language--Syntax. | English language--Auxiliary
    verbs. | English language--Aspect.
Classification: LCC PE1361 .R36 2017 | DDC 425--dc23 LC record available at
    https://lccn.loc.gov/2017042768

10 9 8 7 6 5 4 3 2 1

Contents

Series Foreword

We are pleased to present the seventy-seventh volume in the series *Linguistic Inquiry Monographs*. These monographs present new and original research beyond the scope of the article. We hope they will benefit our field by bringing to it perspectives that will stimulate further research and insight.

Originally published in limited edition, the *Linguistic Inquiry Monographs* are now more widely available. This change is due to the great interest engendered by the series and by the needs of a growing readership. The editors thank the readers for their support and welcome suggestions about future directions for the series.

Samuel Jay Keyser
for the Editorial Board

Preface

In some ways I have been writing this book in my head for twenty years, working on various aspects of the syntax and semantics of the verbal extended projection in English and other languages. The immediate impetus came from the collaborative paper I wrote with Peter Svenonius on reconciling Minimalist and cartographic approaches to phrase structure (Ramchand and Svenonius 2014), and I knew that the compositional semantics component of that paper was a huge promissory note that had to be redeemed if the enterprise were to succeed. The present monograph is motivated by a conviction about what the relationship between phrase structure and semantic interpretation should look like, a conviction I found that many shared, but which was rather difficult to actually implement. Implementing the intuition required some radical changes to the assumed semantic ontology for natural language, changes that I believe are more in line with internalist intuitions (see Chomsky 1995, Pietroski 2005), without giving up on a system that grounds interpretation in truth. The formal semantic framework I have in mind to underpin the kind of system I propose is a version of Kit Fine's truthmaker semantics (Fine 2014), using situations as exact verifiers for natural language clauses. The system is quite different from the kind of semantics that takes worlds as its foundation and in which, instead, possible and impossible situations are *primitives* of the ontology. The intuition that is important to me is that the syntax of natural languages gives evidence on the meaning side for a natural language ontology that might be quite different from the one that seems most compelling from a purely metaphysical point of view. Like Fine (and Moltman 2018), I am more concerned with *how* language puts meaning together than with how truthmakers are connected to a metaphysics of the real world (if indeed such a thing is even possible).

One crucial innovation in the system requires reifying the linguistic symbol itself as an object in the ontology. I do not think this is a "trick"; rather, it simply acknowledges a feature of the natural language system that is very important—self referentiality and a deep indexicality (relativization to the particular speaker)—that I believe has desirable consequences that extend far beyond the scope of the present monograph.

The first few chapters of the monograph were written while I was on sabbatical at the University of Edinburgh in the second half of 2015. I thank the University of Tromsø for its generous sabbatical provision and its support of pure theoretical research, and the University of Edinburgh for being a welcoming host. In the early stages of writing, I benefited a great deal from correspondence with Lucas Champollion and from discussions with Ronnie Cann, to whom I am very grateful. I would also like to thank audiences at the LOT Winter School in Nijmegen in January 2017 and to audiences at a mini-course at the University of Budapest in February 2017. I would like to thank Marcel den Dikken and Eva Dekány for inviting me to teach at the latter event. I also benefited from discussion and feedback at Daniel Altshuler's UMass semantics seminar in the spring of 2017. I would further like to thank Daniel Altshuler and Miriam Butt for very useful detailed comments on an intermediate draft, and Sergey Minor for invaluable and detailed feedback on the whole prefinal manuscript. Special thanks go to Robert Henderson for turning up in Tromsø in late 2016 and giving a talk at our colloquium series on ideophones, which contributed the final piece of the puzzle. I remember that eureka moment very well when I realized that the exoticism of ideophones was just "the truth standing on its head to get attention." A big thank-you goes to my colleagues at the University of Tromsø and in particular the CASTLFish milieu (Tarald Taraldsen, Antonio Fábregas, Sergey Minor, Peter Svenonius, and Björn Lundquist deserving special mention in this regard), for reacting to and commenting on all things related to syntax and morphology, for providing the intellectual frame for the kinds of questions I find myself asking, and for providing standards for the kinds of answers that satisfy.

Finally, even though this book did not benefit from any direct or detailed discussions with Angelika Kratzer, she is in many ways the forerunner and inspiration for the research agenda here. Her work on the syntax-semantics interface is interwoven with these pages, and this particular monograph would have been impossible without her research as backdrop and standard.

I thank Anne Mark and the team at MIT Press for their engagement and professionalism in bringing this work to publication.

1 Introduction to Events and Situations in Grammar

The primary reason for the use of events in the semantics of natural language is empirical. Starting with Davidson 1967, a large body of evidence has shown that they are necessary ingredients in the most empirically adequate descriptions of the way language works. The obvious application is in the semantics of verbs, a class of words found in every natural language we know of (see Baker 2003). What has been more controversial, and what still engenders open and lively debates, is the exact nature of the interpretational ontology and how it connects to the compositional semantics of natural language.

This monograph does not argue for the existence of verbal events per se, or particular details concerning their nature and internal structure (for the state of the art, see Truswell to appear). It *does*, however, relate directly to issues of semantic ontology, and the way we set up our compositional semantics so as to properly integrate it with robust facts about the syntax and morphology of natural language.

Verbal meanings are remarkably diverse, albeit within certain constrained abstract limits.[1] At a very basic level, we need a placeholder variable as the unity to which the different core properties of an event description can be ascribed. This is what I take to be the fundamental insight of Davidson 1967. We also need, at the end of the day, to be able to construct arbitrarily complex, coherent, and unified descriptions of the world, and assert their existence. These coherent, unified situations are built up cumulatively from a combination of the verb and its arguments (intuitively, the "core" Davidsonian event) *together with* all the adverbial, prepositional, and modificatory devices at a language's disposal.

Now, while full propositional content at the sentence level can indeed be modeled by situations (as Barwise and Perry (1983) initially argued in their pioneering work), it is a separate step to say that situations should be given status as part of our object language in semantic description. This step does appear to me to be warranted, and the evidence for the ontological reality of situations is persuasive. As Kratzer (2014) notes, "[E]xamples can be constructed to show that natural languages have the full expressive power of object language quantification over situations." Situations and Austinian "topic situations" (Austin 1950) seem to be needed to account for (i) truth conditions in context and (ii) tense marking (Klein 1994), and (iii) they are necessary in a variety of ways for quantifier domain restriction (see Kratzer 2014 for details).

I will take it, then, that we have linguistic evidence for the reality of event descriptions from the core properties of verbs and verbal meanings, and we also have evidence from a wide variety of discourse-level effects for the reality of situations. But are Davidsonian events and situations the same thing? And what is the relationship between the verb denotation and the rich situational description that eventually gets established at the sentence level?

According to Kratzer (2014), the answer is that events and situations are indeed exactly the same ontological type, but that events are minimal situations. In her view, the notion of exemplification mediates the relation between propositions and Davidsonian events, and makes explicit how the latter relate to situations more generally. As she puts it:

(1) *Exemplification*
    A situation s exemplifies a proposition p iff whenever there is a part of s in which p is not true, then s is a minimal situation in which p is true.
    (Kratzer 2014)

The intuition is that a situation is something that propositions can be "true in," but a situation *exemplifies* a proposition if it is the minimal such situation, with no extraneous, unnecessary parts. It is the "minimal" situation that makes the proposition true.

If we incorporate Davidsonian event semantics into situation talk in this way, we get (2b) as the representation of a sentence such as (2a) (taken from Kratzer 2014).

(2) a. Ewan swam for 10 hours.
    b. $\lambda s[\text{past}(s) \land \exists e[e \leq_p s \land \text{swim}(\text{Ewan})(e) \land f_{\text{hour}}(e) = 10]]$

So sentence (2a) is a property of situations such that the situation is "in the past" and there is an event that is a subpart of it that is the exemplification of Ewan swimming. The temporal measure of the exemplified event in hours is 10. Here we see that both situations and events can be arguments of temporal modifiers. One could also break down events/situations into their temporal run-times and explicitly predicate the temporal predicates of these intervals instead, *or* one could allow temporal predicates to pick out this aspect of the event description, as in (2b). The important point here is that in this system, events/situations have temporal parameters, and temporal properties can be ascribed to them.

According to Kratzer (2014), formula (2b) "incorporates the usual notation for Davidsonian event predication. Within a situation semantics, this notation is just a convenient way to convey that *swim*(*Ewan*)(e) is to be interpreted in terms of exemplification: we are not talking about situations in which Ewan swims, but about situations that *exemplify* the proposition 'Ewan swims' " (my emphasis).[2]

For Kratzer, an event is ontologically the same kind of animal as a situation, but it is one that stands in the exemplification relation to a particular kind of atomic proposition (namely, the ones that we usually assume are the introducers of Davidsonian events). In this way, then, Kratzer is in fact relating the use of the term *event* to something independent *about the syntax*. In effect, if a proposition comes from the interpretation of vP, then it corresponds to *event*, while if it comes from the interpretation of a larger syntactic phrase, then it corresponds to *situation*. However, this has no real effect on the *semantic* ontology.

The problem with the standard view as described above is that it underplays the differences between the semantics of the inner vP (what I have elsewhere called the *first phase*; Ramchand 2008) and the semantics of higher parts of the clause. To explain what I mean by this, I must briefly discuss certain typological patterns in linguistic forms.

1.1 Linguistic Generalizations and Constraints on the Syntax-Semantics Mapping

It is perhaps a truism that the syntactic representations of natural language need to be given a compositional interpretation (see Heim and Kratzer 1998). However, the standard mechanisms used in formal semantics for modeling compositional interpretation are in fact extremely powerful. The unfettered lambda calculus, endowed with abstraction over predicates of higher types, can put any jumble of words or structures together to deliver the final desired output reflecting our description of the intuitive truth conditions (see Higginbotham 2007). In the absence of explicit constraining principles, the notation itself overgenerates. After all, formulating explicit constraining principles is the job of linguists, not of the notation.

So what constraining principles do we need? Ideally, in my view, we need to build a compositional semantics of the clause that makes the deep and uncontroversial generalizations about verb meaning fall out as a natural consequence. In Ramchand to appear, I argue that we need the compositional semantics of the vP to reflect the universal hierarchical structuring of causal embedding. In this monograph, I pursue the logic further and take seriously the typological fact that natural languages universally encode temporal information hierarchially *outside* of the causal and force-dynamical content of the event itself. This universal fact about semantics is rarely perceived as such because it has already been reified as syntactic fact in the form of a phrase structure template: CP > TP > VP. The template consisting of these three zones is as much a template as any more articulated cartography (see Ramchand and Svenonius 2014 for discussion), and at this stage of our understanding it must simply be stipulated. It follows from nothing else. Unfortunately, it also does not fall out immediately from event semantics, under any current understanding of the term. This is because, on current understanding, events (and situations)—besides trafficking in notions such as causation and agent—also have properties related to time because they are particulars with a specific time course.

Consider a hypothetical language spoken on the planet Zog. The planet Zog is a world very different from our own, inhabited by many strange creatures, one species of which has acquired symbolic thought and speaks its own form of language: Zoggian, which has properties found in no human language. In particular, Zoggian displays the bound morpheme /fub/,[3] which denotes roughly 'the process of dissolving into a green slimy puddle'. In addition, it includes the bound morpheme -*ax*-, which has the semantics of PAST, and the bound morpheme *ilka*, which has the semantics of CAUSE. Like human languages, Zoggian works by generating hierarchical symbolic structures with predictable interpretations. However, unlike the Human PAST morpheme, the Zoggian PAST morpheme always occurs hierarchically closer to the conceptually rich part of the verbal meaning than the CAUSE morpheme does. The relevant sentences of Zoggian are given in (3) and (4). (Note also in passing that Zoggian's basic word order is OSV.)

(3) Blixa   fub-ax.
    the.house dissolve.green-PAST
    'The house dissolved into a green slimy puddle.'

(4) Blixa   marrg   fub-ax-ilka.
    the.house the.zog dissolve.green-PAST-CAUSE
    'The zog dissolved the house into a green slimy puddle.'

The tree structure for sentence (4) is given in (5).

(5)

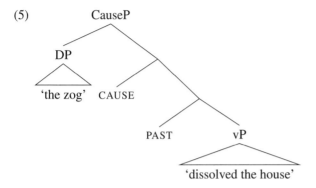

'dissolved the house'

Suppose further that there are many Zoggian language families but that, with very few exceptions, CAUSE appears external to temporal information. This is no problem for a compositional semantics. Indeed, it is no problem for the semantics developed for Human languages either. For example, simple denotations for the Zoggian verb and for the PAST and CAUSE morphemes could be given as in (6).

(6) a. $[\![vP]\!] = \lambda e[fub(e) \wedge \text{UNDERGOER}(e) = \text{'the house'}]$
    b. $[\![\text{PAST}]\!] = \lambda e[\tau(e) <_t \text{'now'}]$ (where τ is e's temporal trace function)
    c. $[\![\text{CAUSE}]\!] = \lambda x \lambda e[\text{CAUSER}(e) = x]$

The vP combines with the PAST morpheme by argument identification to give (7).

(7) $\lambda e[fub(e) \wedge \text{UNDERGOER}(e) = \text{'the house'} \wedge \tau(e) <_t \text{'now'}]$

This then combines with the CAUSE morpheme, again by argument identification, to give (8).

(8) $\lambda x \lambda e[fub(e) \wedge \text{UNDERGOER}(e) = \text{'the house'} \wedge \tau(e) <_t \text{'now'}$
$\wedge \text{CAUSER}(e) = x]$

Note that the denotation I have given for CAUSE is essentially identical to the compositional system assumed by Kratzer (1996) for the folding in of the external argument by argument identification. The only difference is that for Zoggian, I have folded in the meaning of past tense first, also by argument identification.

To return to English, the analogous case would be verbs that looked like *slimed/slimedify*, instead of the more natural *slimify/slimified*.

(9) (*Zoggified English*)/*Zoggedify English*
    a. The house slimed.
    b. The man slimedify the house.

It is important to understand why the semantics works. The trick is not the use of argument identification itself (what Heim and Kratzer (1998) call "predicate modification"). As Heim and Kratzer (1998) demonstrate, argument identification can always be rewritten as some form of function composition, although the formulas look less transparent. The reason for the commutability of PAST and CAUSE is that the new information is added by a simple conjunction. Argument identification is not sensitive to what it is being added to, as long as it is also a legitimate predicate over events. This means that regardless of the order in which we combine CAUSE and PAST, we end up with the same representation. And regardless of how we tweak the subtle details of the CAUSE and PAST denotations, this will always be the case just as long as *both of those predicates manipulate semantic factors that are properties of events*. If events are temporal entities, then CAUSE and PAST both denote properties of some aspect of the event. The only way to enforce one ordering over another would be to stipulate a presupposition for CAUSE, for example, that it can only combine with event descriptions that have not yet been located in time. While lexically specific information like this is certainly attested in natural language, it seems preferable to have a more general way to approach a human language universal.

Semantic theory can do a bit better if it imposes a different structural type on tense predicates. We could stipulate that even though events have temporal properties, the semantic type of functional tense is always such that it relates constituents that are properties of times directly, and that this switch comes after the lower vP domain. This would be a way of ensuring that grammaticalized tense formally composes semantically *after* cause, as indeed in much recent semantic work (Klein 1994, Kratzer 2000). The point I am making here is only that there is nothing about the internal logic of events that makes this stipulation natural or obvious. It can be made, but it is the equivalent of the syntactic stipulation, achieving the ordering by fiat. We could *imagine* things to be otherwise, but they never are. The current ontology, which utilizes events that are full-blown temporal (and even worldly) particulars, does not naturally underwrite the ordering facts we find in the *syntaxes* of human languages. Something needs to be stipulated on top of this system in any case, and the question is exactly what. Basically, I am not satisfied with a templatic approach to the problem as delivered by the functional sequence, or by the semantic correlates in terms of stipulated distinct types. The functional sequence (even in the form of the very pared-down CP > TP > VP template) is a convenient descriptive device that should be anchored semantically in some deeper way, ontologically. Stipulated semantic orders also seem to me to not go deep enough, and are also essentially templatic. I would like to use the robust empirical facts about ordering to motivate a restructuring in the semantic system of composition from the inside, one that actually does have the well-known templatic facts about sentence semantics and hierarchical ordering as a consequence. I am looking for an explanation of the templatic effects from the semantic and cognitive primitives that form the basis of natural language. My hope is that by being explicit about how the semantics needs to be structured, we make a start on filling in one side of the equation for communication with the conceptual-intentional system, the more general cognitive mechanisms of the mind/brain.

Note also that I will be essentially reversing the normal methodology found in much work on the syntax-semantics interface, which starts with establishing the explicit and precise representation that has the correct truth conditions (since this is something that is accessible to verification by intuitions) and *then* partitions those contributions among the elements of the sentence in some kind of function-argument notation. Instead, I will start with the individual building blocks and come up with a reasonable description of their contribution to the sentence meaning. I will then try to build up gradually to a final semantic representation that has the right truth conditions. The two strategies should in theory give rise to the same syntactic-semantic analysis, but in practice they do not. This is because the one strategy (my own) places more weight on the integrity of different lexical items and their constancy across instances of use, and the other (the standard semantic methodology) places more weight on expressing the full precision required for determinate truth conditions.[4]

As part of this agenda, I take seriously the robust crosslinguistic generalization that when they appear (and they seem to in over 80 percent of the world's languages[5]), tense and aspect inflection are hierarchically *outside* the core verbal description (including the description of cause, process, and result in the verb). Note that the existence of a template in this sense is not falsified by languages that do not have the appropriate inflection (since there is no claim of universal overtness here); rather, it would be falsified by a language that had morphemes with the relevant semantics but in the wrong order. So although one *could* imagine the reverse (and we would be able to build a compositional semantics to describe it, as we saw for Zoggian), this does not actually seem to happen in the world's languages. In other words, verbs do not share stems for tense specification, with suffixes and/or prefixes indicating the specifics of the description for the dynamic process or stative situation involved.

Robust generalizations of this type, at such a basic level of language structuring, are impressive and need to be taken seriously. At present, the use of situations to model propositions does not give us any purchase on why the template should be the way it is. However, situations are an important step forward because they have the right structure to subsume the kind of information and modifications that we find in the verbal extended projection: namely, reference to times, worlds, locations, and ultimately the speaker.

1.2   Event Properties and Event Instantiations

To summarize, the Kratzerian notion of situation has the following definitional characteristics (see Kratzer 1989 for detailed exposition).

- Situations are particulars that exist in worlds and at times.
- Situations stand in part-whole relationships to each other (they form a mereology). In other words, situations can be temporal or spatial subparts of other situations. (I will use the notation $\leq_s$ to express the notion "situational subpart.")
- Situations grow deterministically into a particular possible world, in the sense that there is a unique maximal element in the mereology. So situations are just instantiated world parts, and the maximal element in a situational mereology is a particular world.

  So every s is related to a unique possible world w. We can then say that situations have world parameters, since they are deterministically related to a particular world. They also have time properties, or parameters, and in this sense they can also be "proposition exemplifiers"; more complex situations can be related to simpler Davidsonian atomic exemplifying situations via the subpart relation. I will largely stick to this view of situations as worldly particulars located in time, and I will also have use for the intuitive correspondent to Kratzer's notion of "exemplifying situation" at the level of the vP.

  Within the vP, however, I will argue that we need a rather different sort of beast than (even a minimal) situational description. Intuitively, we will need representations that express force-dynamically relevant descriptive content and relationships to participants, but do not have temporal (or worldly) information. But how can we even formalize what it means to be an event without making reference to being in the world, and therefore being part of a particular world and time?

1.2.1   Philosophical Antecedents

There is a long tradition of formal semantic work that grounds all semantic definitions in objective particulars. This work leads up through Quine and Carnap and culminates in Lewis, perhaps the most influential of the analytic philosophers on modern semantic thinking. In this tradition, atemporal and aworldly statements are built from the mundanely worldly ones, by generalizing over times and "possible" worlds. This hugely successful and productive intellectual tradition lies at the heart of our classical semantics of propositions and modality.

However, there is an alternative strand of thought that is troubled by the feeling that this method often simply doesn't adequately render our intuitions about linguistic meaning. For example, Fine (2005) argues that we need to make a distinction between facts that are always true as a matter of contingent circumstance and facts that are *essentially* true.

Empiricists have always been suspicious of modal notions. For them, the world is an on-or-off matter—either something happens or it does not; and there appears to be no room in their on-or-off world for a distinction between what happens of necessity and what only happens contingently or between the essential features of an object and those that are only accidental. (Fine 2005, 1)

Here, Fine is interested in the fact that certain inherent or essential properties of an object are there in a logically prior way, not as "contingent" facts about how the world is. Although in the end the possible-worlds way of expressing the idea of essential properties in terms of "*all* possible worlds" gives technically the right results in many cases, it also seems to obscure the difference that we intuitively feel between the essential truth and the contingently universal truth. Fine claims that semanticists in this case have been willing to sacrifice this intuition in the service of an idea that is more tractable formally and mechanically. He continues:

For empiricists, in so far as they have been able to make sense of modality, have tended to see it as a form of regularity; for something to hold of necessity is for it always to hold, and for something to hold possibly is for it sometimes to hold. But if there is not enough going on in the actual world to sustain the possibilities that we take there to be, then one strategy for the empiricist is to extend the arena upon which the possibilities are realized to include what goes on in each possible world. Of course, such a view is compatible with a moderate realism in which possible worlds, and what goes on in them, are taken to have a different ontological status from the actual world and what goes on in it. But combine the regularity view of modality with a nominalism about what there is and we end up with a position very like Lewis's. Indeed, it might be argued that, *au fond*, Lewis is as sceptical of modal notions as Quine. Neither can understand modality except as a form of regularity; and the only difference between them lies in the range of the regularities to which their respective ontologies allow them to appeal. (Fine 2005, 1)

As we will see more directly in chapter 5 on modality, the correspondence between quantification and modalized propositional meaning is very seductive. There is clearly something deep at stake here, and logical quantification is one way of getting at the mystery of hypothetical reasoning. However, it might not be the only way. In the case of "essential truths," we might decide to begin with these as primitives instead of recasting them in extensional notations. Fine in particular argues that transcendental essences in his sense must exist in a *basic* form, in a separate dimension of existence not derived from or defined in terms of worldly instantiations (both real and possible). As Fine puts it:

> Finally, it will be suggested that the identity of an object—what it is—is not, at bottom, a worldly matter; essence will precede existence in the sense that the identity of an object may be fixed by its unworldly features even before any question of its existence or other worldly features is considered. (Fine 2005, 321)

I will argue that what we need here in the representation of events is similar in that *essence* must precede *existence* in the cumulative building up of a natural language proposition. Fine's own arguments concern objects and identity, and he explicitly does not carry those arguments over to the discussion of events as objects. Empirically, I think the arguments can be made for the event domain on the basis of phenomena like the imperfective paradox and resultative participles. I also think that the linguistic evidence from verbal templates complements the philosophical arguments from Fine. Under plausible assumptions about the mapping between syntax and semantics, the cumulative hierarchical complexity of syntactic structuring should be paralleled by increasing semantic complexity. I think the evidence suggests that semantically also, at least for the human mind, the verbal concept, along with its arguments, is conceptually prior to its embedding in time and world. Across human populations, linguistic facts paint a consistent picture to this effect, and it would be nice if the semantic ontology reflected this consistent picture.

To put the argument another way, the grounding of *all* denotational types in worldly meanings (by which I mean particulars in worlds and times) by using worldly events/situations at every level of the clause seems to make it impossible to derive the layering of syntactic structure by purely semantic means. Specifically, the fact that time reference provides the *outer clothing* of verbal meaning in language after language, and never the other way around, is something that would have to be stipulated as a universal syntactic fact. If we wish to reduce syntactic stipulation and see explanations for deep typological generalizations in facts about cognition, then we need to adopt a semantic framework that is more sensitive to the patterns that syntax gives us. Only then will we have a vocabulary that is commensurate with the primes of psycholinguistic and neurolinguistic investigation, and that we can use to address the interface questions. At the very least, I think it is worthwhile to approach the problems of meaning and the interface with cognition from the inside out, by looking at the ways in which language structures the way meanings are built up.

This also returns us to an old debate concerning internalist vs. externalist theories of meaning. The debate has already been won by the externalist camp on the entirely reasonable grounds that there is a crucial "aboutness" to language and that if we attempt to ground our theories in internalist notions, then we are condemned to theories that make no sense of the interusability of language and that end up being at best unfalsifiable and at worst mystical. For this reason, our theories are grounded in notions of reference to individuals in the world, and to truth. However, I find myself in agreement with Chomsky (1995) (see also Pietroski 2017), who convincingly shows that reference and truth are themselves mystical notions, and that the quest to fill out some materialist agenda closing the gap between mind and body in itself presupposes an unwarranted dualism. Quoting from Nagel 1993, 37, Chomsky argues:

[It is a] hopeless task to "complete the materialist world picture" by translating accounts of "mental phenomena" in terms of a "description that is either explicitly physical or uses only terms that can apply to what is entirely physical", or perhaps give "assertability conditions" on "externally observable grounds". (Chomsky 1995, 4)

Instead, Chomsky advocates a naturalistic internalist view—naturalistic in the sense that we attempt to study humans just like anything else in the natural world, but internalist because we are attempting to understand the internal states of an organism. This is not to say that we could not and should not have a methodologically naturalistic approach to what we think of as "external" and "objective." Here is Chomsky again:

One branch of naturalistic inquiry studies common sense understanding. Here we are concerned with how people interpret object constancy, the nature and causes of motion, thought and action, and so on ("folk science", in one of the senses of the term). Perhaps the right way to describe this is in terms of beliefs about the constituents of the world (call them "entities") and their organization, interaction, and origins. ... It is an open question whether, and if so how, the conceptual resources of folk science relate to those involved in the reflective and self-conscious inquiry found in every known culture ("early science"), and to the particular enterprise we call "natural science". For convenience, let's refer to the study of all such matters as "ethnoscience". It is also an open question how the conceptual resources that enter into these cognitive systems relate to the semantic (including lexical) resources of the language faculty. ... The ethnoscientist seeks to determine what people take to be constituents of the world, however they may talk about it. A different inquiry seeks the best theory of language and its use, and the states, processes, and structures that enter into it. (Chomsky 1995, 28–30)

I consider this book to be part of the second line of inquiry described by Chomsky. It takes seriously the idea that natural language symbols correspond to mental representations (formed and codified through experience of the "world"), which are then deployed by human beings in a particular context to help describe other particular things they take to exist in the world.

Neurologist Rodolfo Llinás (1987) puts the matter well when he describes perception as "a dream modulated by sensory input", the mind being a "computational state of the brain generated by the interaction between the external world and an internal set of reference frames". But the internal frames that shape the dreams are far more intricate and intriguing than often assumed, even at the level of the lexicon, still more so when we turn to expressions formed by the computational procedures. (Chomsky 1995, 23)

Peter Svenonius and I argued (Ramchand and Svenonius 2014), that a new ontology of sorts was required, one that contrasted atemporal and aworldly "event essences" with "situational" particulars. The new member of the ontology, intuitively the equivalent of essential conceptual events, or "event types," is a slippery notion that is difficult to make coherent without resorting to possible worlds themselves for its definition. A new ontological primitive for language and its integration into a compositional semantics that still grounds itself in the external significance of language, like the one we attempted to motivate in Ramchand and Svenonius 2014, poses problems of such foundational complexity that they are hard to solve. Fine (2000) takes a different approach and presents a formal semantics for his logic of essence that uses a special notion of truth with respect to a predicate F, $\Box_F$—that is, truth *in virtue of the nature of that predicate*.

Also relevant is current semantic research that pursues this kind of intuition in terms of event *kinds*: namely, recent work by McNally and Gehrke (Gehrke 2015, Gehrke and McNally 2015, Grimm and McNally 2015), who argue on the basis of certain kinds of nominalized and participial forms that the event kind actually forms the *basis* of all subsequent event-denoting forms. I consider this to be convergent research, albeit employing a more standard formal system. One difference between Gehrke and McNally's work and mine comes from the fact that I will claim that a "concept"-like notion operates in principle throughout the first phase (i.e., the lowest phase of the syntactic representation). Another difference is that, instead of invoking a primitive corresponding to event kinds, I will use an implementation in terms of "partial event descriptions" and link the nature of that partiality to the nature of the conceptual content of lexical as opposed to functional items, a move that will end up having its own technical consequences.

The solution to reconciling the intuition that natural language symbols denote essential mentalistic concepts (Fine, Chomsky) with the necessity of linking up with the ethnoscientific constituents of the "world" to convey aboutness and interdescribability will require a drastic change in the system. We must reify the contextual and self-conscious aspect of meaning and build it into the system of representation itself. I will propose an implementation of that intuition by using *words of the language as elements in the domain of individuals*—an implementation inspired by Potts (2007), who first proposed it for the analysis of metalinguistic comment, and used explicitly in the analysis of ideophonic elements by Henderson (2016).

The link between words of a language and their semantics is achieved in acquisition, mediated by perception/cognitive uptake of events in the external world. But word meanings are, crucially, generalizations across particulars that can then be deployed by a speaker. In this way, the lexical item is the codification of a certain implicit perceptual and cognitive generalization, *reusable* as a bridge between internal representations and external events.

It is inspiring also in this regard to recall that in their work on situations, Barwise and Perry (1983) cite the efficiency of language as one of its central design features. That is, alongside the external significance of language and its productivity and compositionality, we have the fact that words of a language are efficient members of the code in being able to be *reused in situation after situation*. To this, Barwise and Perry correctly add the perspectival relativity of language, its ambiguity, and its mental significance.

So, for human language to get off the ground, children need to be in possession of symbols that are *shape abstractions over the different actual situations encountered in the learning phase*, symbols they can then deploy as a means of characterizing new situations in the world as they come across them. The reusable, highly efficient part of semantics is what Barwise and Perry call "meaning." At this level, the symbols are compositional and efficient, but they greatly underdetermine the information conveyed by a sentence. To get from abstract and reusable meanings to actual information, we need to know facts about the user, the deployer of the meanings, and where the deployer is located in time and space. In turn, the information conveyed by a sentence is related to the actual situation by the description relation: a situation can be (partially) described by some information, or conversely, information can be supported by a situation.

In terms of implementation, my inspiration has come from the apparently extreme and exotic case of ideophones. Henderson (2016, 665) states that work on the formal semantics of ideophones is scarce because "it is not at all clear how to formalize the distinction between descriptive meaning ... and depictive meaning, which ideophones seem to traffic in." In giving his own account, Henderson explores a formal foundation for the notion of *demonstrations* from Davidson 2015 and extends it to account for the ideophonic data. According to Henderson, demonstrations are a special type of communicative event that stand in a similarity relation to the event demonstrated. Ideophones might seem like a curious and typologically rare corner of the semantics of human language, but in fact, I think that the problem they pose is perfectly general—it is just that it can be seen most clearly in this extreme case. In the general case, we need to link the properties of the communication/demonstration event with the symbols being actively deployed in order to achieve the description of a real-world particular.

The idea is this: The lexical predicates of a language are reusable symbols of event depiction encoding a cognitive/perceptual semantics, derived from experience of the world but involving primitive and natural generalizations over actual physical instantiations. Because these depictive semantic symbols are formed by learning and labeling *generalizations* over time and space, they are by definition silent about temporal and locational properties. They involve the recognition of specific causal and force-dynamical relationships among actants (see also Copley and Harley 2015), and the ability to ascribe basic cognitively apprisable properties to individuals.

In an actual proposition, a speaker *uses* these depictive predicates to abstractly characterize an actual existing event, only subsequently adding information about that event's temporal and locational properties. The latter properties are defined in relation to the speaker's own origo.

In short, the standard classical semantics involving event particulars does not do justice to the order in which natural languages build up propositions from linguistic symbols. In the semantics proposed here, lexical items need to be taken seriously as "individuals" deployed by a speaker. These lexical items are bundles of form and meaning that contain cognitive abstractions of event properties that transcend time and place. The choice of the primitives of these abstractions will be motivated by the data on verb meaning and classification. This way of doing things does not immediately improve on certain open questions concerning conceptualization, but it does offer a system that will be able to connect more systematically both with the syntax and with the units of cognition and language processing.

1.2.2   A Quotational Semantics for Natural Language

We will be building up representations of propositions in four stages:

1. The putting together of lexical items that encode certain event properties. This stage needs to be productive and compositional, but with no reference to temporal or worldly parameters.
2. The assertion by the speaker of the existence of an event in world and time with those properties.
3. The addition of specific temporal and worldly properties to the event.
4. The anchoring of the temporal and worldly properties via the origo (the speaker and her contextual coordinates).

To do this, we need to add to the usual model a domain D_μ, which is the domain of well-formed linguistic entities of type μ, after Potts 2007. These linguistic objects are triples, consisting of a <phonological string, **syntactic features**, SEMANTICS>. Full expressions of type μ will be written in sans serif type. For example, the verb run might have the denotation in (10).

(10) ⟦run⟧ = <run, <**Init, Proc**>, λe[run(e)]>

For convenience, I adopt Henderson's (2016) convention that uses the bottom corner notation to pick out the semantic part of the triple denoted by something of type μ. Thus:

(11) ⌞run⌟ = λe[run(e)]

We can think of the building up of a proposition as a deployment of something of type μ, to create a relationship between a (complex) event property and a demonstration event.

In Ramchand 2008, I argue that the compositional relationships among lexical items in this domain are restricted to certain basic relations of causation and result, and also to the HOLDS relation that relates subevents to their actants. The lexical conceptual content of verbs obviously varies without limit in other dimensions. Crucially, however, the lexical conceptual content of verbs cannot and does not include temporal information, since this content is a cognitive *abstraction over time and space*. Apart from this part of the claim, it is not the purpose of this monograph to investigate or argue for a particular view of the internal semantics of event descriptions. The way the system is set up here, it in principle allows readers to slot in their own denotations for lexical items and the functional projections within the first phase. The important part of the system for present purposes is that we need to have methods for composing elements of type μ, to create derived elements of type μ by the end of the first phase. The rule for composing μ entities will be as shown in box 1.1.

Box 1.1
Language symbols as objects in the ontology

1. Symbols of the language constitute the domain D_μ, which are triples consisting of a <phonological string, **syntactic features**, SEMANTICS>.
2. The semantics of a verbal lexical item is a partial description based on sensory and cognitive abstractions over experience.
3. The syntactic part of the information in a triple that is a member of D_μ is a subtree of the language. The merger of $u_1 \in D_\mu$ and $u_2 \in D_\mu$ creates a derived element of D_μ, u_3, whose syntactic representation is built by merging the syntactic representation of u_1 with the syntactic representation of u_2, and whose semantics is composed by ordinary argument identification of ⌞u_1⌟ and ⌞u_2⌟.

The linguistic unit so formed will also be an ordered triple, and its phonology will be formed by concatenating in some way the phonologies of the two inputs.[6] The syntactic representation will also presumably be composed via some algorithm, but once again this is not directly the issue for us here. The important thing is how the semantic parts of the triple compose. In the simple cases I begin with, the semantic parts of the triple will compose in the normal way by argument identification (simple conjunction of properties).

After the lexical symbolic part of the syntax is completed, I will assume that a functional item is merged with the result: namely, the head—which I will call *Evt*—that introduces the generalized deployment operator and is at the edge of this first phase of building. The Evt head deploys the lexical content built up so far and creates something that now denotes a property of events directly via the introduction of the demonstration event d. I take the use of d from the formalization in Henderson 2016, representing the performing act of communication. It is similar to the Kaplanian context c, but conceived as a Davidsonian situational variable corresponding to the utterance event.[7]

Henderson's (2016) denotation for the quotation meaning is shown in (12). $TH_\delta(d) = u$ says that the "theme" of d is the linguistic object u, and d "demonstrates" or has certain structural properties in common with e.

(12) QUOTE: $\lambda u \lambda d \lambda e[TH_\delta(d) = u \wedge \mathrm{DEMO}(d, e)]$

The central idea of my own adaptation is that the notion of demonstration is simply a special case of the more general idea that the speech event d is used to CONVEY an event in the world e. The deployment of a lexical item as the thematic content of d is also perfectly general. This very general schema underlies both acts of description and acts of depiction and indeed everything in between. Thus, more generally we want to say that symbolic content is deployed by the speaker to CONVEY an event. For concreteness, I define the Evt head at the edge of the first phase as introducing the utterance situation d, with linguistic content u, in order to CONVEY event e.

In the specific case of quotes, iconic items, and ideophones, the CONVEY relation becomes Henderson's (2016) DEMO relation. More generally, though, in the case of straightforward deployment of a linguistic item with no imitation or iconic elements in d, CONVEY simply reduces to the event e that d demonstrates possessing the very semantic property encoded by u. Thus, in the case of the EvtP built at the edge of the first phase in English, we get the denotation in (13).

(13) EvtP: $\lambda d \lambda e[\mathrm{Utterance}(d) \wedge \llcorner u \lrcorner(e)]$

Box 1.2
Deployment of the symbolic content at EvtP

---

1. EvtP: $\lambda d \lambda e[\text{Utterance}(d) \wedge \text{TH}_\delta(d) = u \wedge \text{CONVEY}(d, e)]$
   Property of an utterance event d and event e, which has u as its theme, and where d is deployed to convey e (where $u \in D_\mu$ is the denotation of the first-phase verbal description).
2. In the case of purely conventional (i.e., nondepictive) lexical items, uttered with sincerity and without metaphor or hyperbole:

   $\text{TH}_\delta(d) = u \wedge \text{CONVEY}(d, e) \longrightarrow \llcorner u \lrcorner (e)$

To return to the motivations and justification for this move, I note that it is a representational encoding of the intuition that reference involves a speaker and a context in addition to the symbol the speaker is deploying. But it is not just a matter of a speaker X using the symbol Y to refer to the object Z—we also need to leave room for the contextual circumstances and mode of deployment of the symbol in question. Once again, Chomsky (1995) puts it more accurately:

> More generally, person *X* uses expression *E* with its intrinsic semantic properties to talk about the world from certain intricate perspectives, focusing attention on specific aspects of it, under circumstances *C*, with the "locality of content" they induce (in Bilgrami's [(1992)] sense). (Chomsky 1995, 43)

Within the external clothing of speaker deployment, we can still maintain a quite conservative system of semantic composition, with verbal elements in the first phase simply denoting certain event properties. An important feature, however, is the stipulation that all event properties encoded in lexical items are *generalized abstractions and do not have any temporal, worldly, or locational properties*. They are thus partial descriptions that reflect the idea of "essential" properties or "event concepts." Technically speaking, in the lowest domain, the semantics just composes elements of type μ, in ways we will see more of in chapters 2 and 3. It is at the Evt level that I introduce the generalized equivalent of a quotation operator and crucially, in doing so, introduce the enclosing demonstration event, which I take to be the Davidsonian event corresponding to the utterance.

At this point, it is worth noting again the differences between this system and the ideas pursued in the related work of McNally and Gehrke (Gehrke 2015, Gehrke and McNally 2015, Grimm and McNally 2015). The problem with introducing event kinds as primitives lies in the work that needs to be done to state the conditions on composition at this level. For example, in Gehrke 2015, kinds and their subkinds are related by prototypicality relationships. There is an intuition here that seems essentially correct but is hard to pin down, especially since it seems to me that event kinds can be internally extremely complex and, indeed, novel. In the treatment I am proposing here, the illusion of lexical genericity in this sense is a by-product of the fact that symbolic members of D_μ are partial event properties that are *abstractions over space and time*. This means that the lexical item itself invokes only those properties that are independent of instantiation, by definition. The system then allows event properties to be added to and composed via a normal kind of Davidsonian conjunctivism.

Once the quotation operator has been introduced, we are in a position to define temporal and worldly operators. Recall that the central problem we face in capturing our typological generalizations is that certain types of information robustly occur outside others in the syntactic representation. We have constructed a domain of composition of lexical items that composes properties of events. What stops us from having temporal properties of those events in the lexical items' denotations? The answer I will give is that temporal and locational predications are not properties of events, but *relations* between events and deployment events d. This means that temporal information is simply not statable until Evt is merged at the edge of the first phase.

Further, I will follow Champollion (2015) in introducing the closure of the event variable low down, with the merger of what I will call the *Aspectual head*. I choose the label *Asp* here for the point of closure of the event variable in order to emphasize the convergence with work on the syntax-semantics of tense and aspect: namely, that this is the position where the switch from events to times takes place. In other words, empirically it seems as if the transitional point occurs precisely here, at the left edge of vP. I think the observation and intuition from previous work is essentially correct, but I will embed that intuition within a quotational semantics and incorporate Champollion's proposal about event closure and event properties.

Champollion's (2015) reason for introducing what he calls "quantificational event semantics" is that traditional event semantics sits rather uneasily beside certain other, welcome results and generalizations in formal compositional semantics. This has led some semanticists to reject formalisms using the event variable and to try to rework the system in other terms (see Beaver and Condoravdi 2007 for one proposal). The problem with events arises because the event variable, although treated like any other object variable for some purposes, has a curious relationship to other quantified variables within the sentence. Specifically, the event quantifier itself never interacts with any other quantifiers—it always takes narrow scope with respect to them. Champollion's innovation is to take verbs themselves to denote sets of sets of events. Essentially, verbs and their projections denote existential quantifiers over events, and the event variable is no longer considered to be bound at the sentence level as in standard accounts. Once this move is made, the rest of the semantics can be business as usual. Here is Champollion's (2015, 40) denotation for the verb phrase *see Mary*.

(14) $[\![\text{see Mary}]\!] = \lambda f \exists e[\text{see}(e) \wedge f(e) \wedge \text{th}(e) = \text{Mary}]$

The verb phrase now denotes a property of event properties, a move that is required to allow further properties of the event to be added after existential closure.

I will follow Champollion's insight here. The quotational approach is a species of quantificational event semantics in which the existential binding of the event variable is mediated by the introduction of the demonstration event at the edge of the first phase. As noted above, I will use the label *Asp* for the locus of existential binding for e. As in Champollion's system, the semantic type of AspP is a property of event properties (his f in (14)). In the quotational implementation, I will use f for my variable over event properties to indicate that these properties are essentially relations between an event and an anchoring utterance event d.[8]

In more standard theories, the origo is a fundamental part of the model that interprets semantic representations. The quotational theory reifies this as a part of the representation. Intuitively, f is the class of relations that locate an event with respect to an utterance situation, where location can be spatial, worldly, or temporal—the core indexical parameters of that situation.

We are now in a position to express the meaning of the Asp head that the EvtP combines with. Asp looks for a property of demonstration events for an event e, existentially binds that event variable and creates a property of spatiotemporal properties of e (rooted in d). The AspP built up by the quotational quantificational system will therefore look as in (15).

(15) $[\![\text{AspP}]\!] = \lambda f_{<v,<v,t>>} \lambda d \exists e[\text{Utterance}(d) \wedge \llcorner u \lrcorner(e) \wedge f(d)(e)]$

At the level of AspP, then, we have a property of relations that link the utterance context d with an existing event that is being demonstrated/described in d. That event has conceptual/perceptual properties as characterized by u. At this point, temporal information can be added to the event description that could not be added before.

In what follows, I will use the quotational semantics outlined above to implement the idea that there is a level of composition of concepts that is intuitively just about abstract properties, and that there is a level of composition where information about the instantiation of these properties is expressed. Words themselves do not have truth conditions: instead, they provide ingredients for truth conditions. Truth conditions only arise when words are deployed in a context d, with respect to which their particularity is established.

While the shift proposed here might seem drastic, I think it important to note that the distinction between the domain D_μ and the elements in it, on the one hand, and other primes of the syntactic computation that we will encounter when we reach the higher zones of the clause, on the other hand, closely parallels the distinction between lexical and functional items in classical generative grammar analyses. The "lexical," open-class items are members of D_μ, and they consist of a triple that has some representation of conceptual content as its third member. I have written this conceptual content in standard lambda notation (although this might not turn out to be the best way to think about it in the end) in order to keep as much as possible to standard expectations of what the meaning contribution of a lexical item is, and to allow for integration into representations that feed truth conditions. In addition to the third member of the triple, which I have elsewhere (Ramchand 2014b) called "conceptual content," I assume the presence of structural semantic content, which always exists whenever there is structure, but which is the *only* thing that exists for functional elements. Functional elements are not members of D_μ; in other words, they are not in the scope of the deployment operator. Speakers do not actively deploy functional elements in the same way that they actively deploy lexical concepts to build content. Once we are in the higher reaches of the clause, we will not be building complex symbols. Instead, we will be deploying them in world, location, and time, in an actual context, and the denotations of the representations formed by the computational system will look more like what we are used to. At that point, the formatives that are merged have a syntactic specification, a structural semantic denotation (and sometimes a phonology), but their content is not restricted to cognitive/perceptual association to the world. So in the proposed system, this is the way the lexical/functional distinction is captured. It is also similar in spirit to the idea of asyntactic roots that is an important part of Distributed Morphology (DM). Unlike DM's acategorial roots, however, members of D_μ have syntactic decompositional information (in order to account for selection and event structure generalizations), and more importantly, members of D_μ do not have to be atomic. Integrating the symbolic complex with contextual parameters to create an assertion bound in worlds and times is the job of the second phase of the clause, and it is with respect to this kind of instantiation-oriented syntax that members of D_μ are innocent.

The view of semantic layering I am building up here has much in common with the syntactic and semantic ideas being pursued by Wolfram Hinzen in recent work (Arsenijevic and Hinzen 2012, Sheehan and Hinzen 2011, Hinzen and Sheehan 2015, Hinzen 2017). I share with him the belief that meaning is grammatically grounded and that we need to build a new natural language ontology for semantics to match how language actually constructs meaning (see also Moltmann 2018). But more specifically, I share with Hinzen the idea that the lexical symbols of language are primitive "essences" and that the lower parts of the clause are then clothed with grammatical information to allow reference to specifics. As Sheehan and Hinzen (2011) put it:

In particular, while lexical items such as MAN or RUN reflect perceptually based conceptual classifications, and in this sense have a form of semantic reference, they are not used to refer to a particular man as opposed to another, or an event that happened yesterday over a certain period of time. ... Grammar based means of referring on the other hand, systematically establish relations of relative distance between the object of reference and the immediate features of the speech context. (Sheehan and Hinzen 2011, 406)

When it comes to the notion of instantiation, Hinzen and Sheehan also argue that "[g]enerally speaking, as we move from a given lexical root to the edge of the phase that it projects, reference becomes more specific. ... Reference is in this sense an 'edge phenomenon' " (2011, 406). They also emphasize the role of deixis in establishing actual reference.

The differences between my proposal and Hinzen's framework lie in the fact that Hinzen divides the grammar of language into three separate ontological domains corresponding to objects, events, and propositions, while I assume that events (situations in my terms) form an extended projection with the clause and "proposition"-denoting structures. Thus, the analogy with the nominal domain works out a little differently in matters of detail in my conception than in Hinzen's. In particular, the introduction of deictic information occurs quite low in my own structures, at the edge of vP (my EvtP). Hinzen's account also does not have an explicit domain of symbolic denotation, or a sharp ontological break at the little vP. Still, philosophically speaking, many of the substantive ideas behind the proposal I am arguing for are shared with Hinzen's approach.

1.3 The Grammar of Auxiliation

So far, I have laid out the intuitive ontological and formal background of the project, stated in schematic terms. I have also outlined the general motivation from typology for making such a move. In the rest of the monograph, I will flesh out the details of the proposal within a particular empirical domain to give it substance and plausibility. The main test bed for the proposal, from which I will draw the data used to ground many specific aspects of the theory, will be the English auxiliary system. I will attempt to account for the core semantic and ordering properties in this domain.

1.3.1   Ordering

As is well known, the ordering of English auxiliaries is rigid (see Chomsky 1957), as illustrated in (16).

(16) a. $\{T, Mod\} \prec Perf \prec Prog \prec Pass \prec V$
      b.   He could have been being interviewed.
      c.   *John is having returned.
      d.   *John is being hunting.
      e.   *John seems to have had already eaten.

Most modern syntactic representations of the phrase structure of the English verbal extended projection simply assume a templatic ordering of Perf(ect) over Prog(ressive) over Pass(ive) (Bjorkman 2011, Aelbrecht and Harwood 2012, Sailor 2012, Bošković 2014), when these elements need to be explicitly represented. Linguists differ with respect to whether they simply represent Perf, Prog, and Voice as functional heads (Bjorkman 2011, Sailor 2012) and handle the inflectional facts via "affix lowering" or Agree, or whether they in addition assume separate functional heads hosting -*en* and -*ing* (Harwood 2013, Bošković 2014).

Within Minimalism, the assumption seems to be that some kind of selection is at work and that this selection does not represent a universal functional sequence, and these projections are left out even for English when the literal perfect or progressive form is not expressed in the sentence. But the account as it stands barely rises above the level of description, since the labels for the functional projections Prog and Perf are tailor-made for just progressive and perfect, respectively, and no attempt is made to provide a higher-level analysis or generalization beyond the language-specific construction. Thus, the deep questions about what is responsible for this rigid ordering are never even asked in a meaningful way; they are essentially sidestepped by the stipulation of a deliberately locally descriptive template.

In fact, I think auxiliation is an interesting phenomenon in its own right. While many languages express tense, modal, and aspectual notions via inflectional morphology, the auxiliating languages take a more isolating strategy. If we were to tackle the typological generalizations about order of composition from a morphological perspective, we would face the additional theoretical/architectural question of the precise relationship between syntactic hierarchy and morphological order. While much is known in this area empirically (see specifically the Mirror Principle of Baker 1985 and subsequent work), it introduces an extra layer of theorizing into any discussion of the compositional semantic problem. Where isolating (and in particular auxiliating) languages are concerned, the semantic and hierarchical issues remain the same, but some of the issues about the internal structure of words and their relationship to the syntax can be sidestepped. It is for this reason that the English case is an interesting one to solve. It cannot be relegated to the padded cell of morphology (for those who think morphology *is* that kind of encapsulated world). It *must* be dealt with in the phrase structure and in the interpretation of phrase structures.

In Ramchand and Svenonius 2014, we argue that the observed cartographic orderings deserve an explanation in terms of the semantics that underwrites the building up of clausal semantics. Previous attempts to explain these orderings in semantic terms have been made (e.g., Schachter 1983), but not in a convincingly general way. One of the main goals of this monograph is to take the relatively concrete problem of auxiliation in English and show how a different kind of account can be crafted when combined with an explicit set of proposals about the semantics of verbal meaning. The idea is to make good on the promissory explorations of Ramchand and Svenonius 2014 and provide a detailed and explicit exposition of the auxiliary system of English in terms of structured situations that begins to make predictions for other languages. In other words, I will attempt to provide a compositional semantic theory that exploits the notion of distinct domains of composition from a semantic point of view.

1.3.2   Lexical Specification and Polysemy
As noted earlier, my methodology will be somewhat inverted from the standard procedure. One reason for the difference is that a guiding motivation for the system will be that individual lexical items should be as unified as possible. In other words, to the greatest degree possible I will try to assume polysemy by underspecification.

To give an example, suppose we have two meanings corresponding to English /bæŋk/: 'financial institution' and 'ground sloping up from a river'. In this case, we are all happy to assume that our lexicon includes $bank_1$ and $bank_2$, which accidentally happen to share a pronunciation. This is the standard case of ambiguity, or homonymy. Equally standardly, we are less inclined to see the uses of *game* in (17a) and (17b) as two separate lexical items.

(17) a. John is playing a game of solitaire.

b. I don't think Mary is serious—she's just playing games with me.

These are cases of lexical vagueness, or polysemy.

When it comes to verbal meaning, things become trickier. Are the two uses of *break* in (18) the same lexical entry, or two different but related ones?

(18) a. John broke the stick.

    b. The stick broke.

While the problems with nominal and verbal meaning have not been solved in all cases, they have been noticed and discussed extensively in the literature on lexical meaning.

    Lacking so far, however, is a serious discussion of the polysemy of certain functional morphemes and functional items like participial endings and auxiliaries. There are good reasons for this. In the theories of morphology that actively interact and engage with syntax, functional items are often assumed to be essentially devoid of interesting conceptual content, outside of the syntactically active features they possess.

    The functional polysemies I will address concern the interpretation of the *-ing* and *-en/ed* participles and the auxiliaries *have* and *be*. I will insist on meanings (however abstract) for all of these formatives and will consider it a virtue if any analysis can handle the data successfully using fairly unified denotations. I list the well-known English polysemies in this domain here for convenience.

(19) *The* -ing *participle*

a. John is running.	*Progressive* -ing*: Activities*
b. John is drawing a circle.	*Progressive* -ing*: Accomplishments*
c. The dancing children are happy.	*Attributive* -ing *participle*
d. Dancing is fun.	*Gerundive*[9]

(20) *The* -en/ed *participle*

a. I have rejected that idea.	*Perfect participle*
b. The offer was rejected.	*Passive participle*
c. the rejected offer	*Attributive* -en/ed *participle*

(21) *Auxiliary and main verb* have

a. John had a heart attack.	*Light verb* have
b. I have a brother.	*Possessive* have
c. I have seen that movie.	*Perfect* have*: Experiential*
d. I have broken my arm.	*Perfect* have*: Resultative*
e. I have lived in Paris a long time.	*Perfect* have*: Universal*

(22) *Auxiliary and main verb* be

a. John was in the garden.	*PP-predication* be
b. The computer was broken.	*AP-predication* be
c. The metal was hammered flat.	*Passive* be
d. The thief was running.	*Progressive* be

Since I will be concentrating on auxiliary constructions, I will not attempt to unify the *-ing* participle with its gerundive, more nominal-like distributions, although I will pave the way for a potential unification. In the case of the auxiliary *have*, I will not attempt to unify the lexical-domain *have* with the functional-domain *have* (see Myler 2017 for an attempt in this direction).

Many researchers think of *be* as an aspectual auxiliary and/or the mere spell-out of tense and so do not regard it as a desideratum to give a unified entry for such "functional" items. However, even functional items in this sense are elements of the lexical inventory. To the extent that all the verbs pronounced in the same way and sharing a morphological paradigm have the same entry, I consider that an advantage. Myler (2017) attempts to give a unified account of *have* across its main verb and causative uses. He does so by voiding *have* of any semantics whatsoever, while listing a set of insertion contexts. However, unless the insertion contexts themselves "have something in common" as opposed to just being a disjunctive list, this is also not a real unification. Throughout this monograph, I will focus on the reusable linguistic ingredients of the system and how they are efficiently deployed in the recursive combinatorics in building propositions. Reusability (and by extension polysemy) will be a seen as a design feature of the system rather than a bug. As a methodological principle, then, I will be guided by the fact of polysemous items and seek analytic unities to underlie them.

In addition to the aspectual auxiliaries, I will give denotations for the modals in English. Here, we are on more familiar ground when it comes to underspecification and polysemy. Kratzer's early position (Kratzer 1977) is to give a simple underspecified semantics for each modal and allow the richness of the meaning to emerge from the interaction of that meaning with contextual and pragmatic information. Going one step further, Hacquard (2006) allows the meaning of each modal to be affected by the syntactic height at which it is merged. My own account will continue the Hacquardian line of thought and attempt to fill in the underspecified semantics of a modal compositionally via the nature of the prejacent that the modal combines with.

(23) *Modal polysemies (e.g., circumstantial vs. epistemic)*
   a. John *must* be in his office now.   *Epistemic* must
   b. Mary *must* pass that exam.   *Deontic* must

Across the board, I will be seeking a unified, underspecified semantics for the ingredients of auxiliation. Such a semantics has the virtue of being simple, easy to acquire, and part of a modular system of interaction with other elements. Underspecified meanings will interact both with structure and with contextual information in order to achieve the correct effects for the ultimate truth conditions of those forms.

Polysemy is a pervasive feature of human language and affects lexical verbs as well as functional items. This is in fact the standard case. Moreover, it is

clear from the processing and psycholinguistic literature that greatly polysemous items are actually quicker to access and process than highly particular
items (what Baayen (2010) calls "contextual diversity"; see Adelman, Brown,
and Quesada 2006). While homonyms have an inhibitory effect on processing,
polysemes appear to facilitate each other. In practice, a speaker can deploy
any verbal item to describe a wide range of actual event particulars; since each
property encoded by the verbal item is *partial*, the item can be deployed by the
speaker in potentially many ways.

Consider again the core idea behind the quotational semantics approach,
repeated here.

(24) Evt: $\lambda u \lambda d \lambda e[\text{Utterance}(d) \wedge \text{TH}_\delta(d) = u \wedge \text{CONVEY}(d, e)]$

The deployment relation at the heart of the quotational semantics I will be
proposing could correspond in context to anything from full to partial imitation of certain properties of the event, invocation of a *particular subset* of the
conceptual properties of the linguistic item, or even invocation of event properties by deploying a saliently nondescriptive or oppositely descriptive linguistic
item. All we need minimally is the quite loose CONVEY relation, which in a
successful communicative context could even have the following content as a
special case: "e makes me think of this property even though it does not liter-
ally have it." I suggest that the contextual relation at the heart of the deployment
of the lexical item u in the utterance situation d to describe e is what makes
sense of ideophones, metaphorical uses, and sarcasm, and what makes itself
felt in the general pervasiveness of polysemy for lexical items.

As we have seen, however, in the standard literal case CONVEYing and
deployment $(\text{TH}_\delta(d))$ reduce to their most standard incarnation, which is that
the lexical item denotes a property of events that the described event has, as
shown in (25).

(25) EvtP: $\lambda d \lambda e[\text{Utterance}(d) \wedge \llcorner u \lrcorner (e) \wedge \text{DESCRIBE}(d, e)]$

This is what I will use in the representations in future, putting aside a detailed
exploration of metaphor, sarcasm, and other metalinguistic uses of those lexical items for future work.

1.4 Morphology and Spanning

On the morphosyntactic side, I will adopt a somewhat nonstandard, but I hope
fairly transparent view of the syntax-morphology interface and its relation to
lexicalization. Specifically, spell-out will allow reference to the notion of span,
defined in (26).

(26) *Span*

A span is a contiguous sequence of heads in a complementation relation.

As noted already in the discussion of auxiliation, English is a language with very little agglutinative morphology, and it is primarily analytic. This means that I will not have to take a strong stand on the relationship between syntactic dominance and morpheme order and how it is achieved. English is also a language that routinely orders specifiers before heads and heads before complements, transparently reflecting the mapping to linear order legislated by the Linear Correspondence Axiom (Kayne 1994). This means that with respect to linear order also, I will simply assume that precedence directly reflects syntactic height, and I will not have to engage with any word order movements or fancy linearization algorithms. Luckily, therefore, I will not have to take a strong stand on many of the syntactic issues that are at the forefront of current debate.

I will primarily be concerned here with cartography in the extended sense—that is, with the syntactic features that correspond to the functional sequence of the clause (regardless of whether this turns out to be spare and minimal, or somewhat richer than the labels used in the classical Goverment-Binding period). These are all "category" features, and they form complementation relationships. As discussed extensively in the literature, syntactic structure has well-known strong, typologically supported effects on morphology (Baker 1985, Julien 2000, Cinque 2005). The standard approach to such "mirror" effects is head movement, a device currently deprecated in Minimalist syntactic theorizing. Brody (2000) offers a different view based on direct linearization, whereby the heads in a complementation structure are linearized together as a word in reverse order (i.e., dominance in the complementation line corresponds to subsequence in terms of the linear order of the morphemes within the word). In this monograph, I will assume a version of the direct linearization view of the effects of head movement.

The importance of the functional sequence and the somewhat more fine-grained view of phrase structure that I will assume means that there are two core issues where my implementation will give rise to theoretical choices. First, although English is not well endowed with morphology, there will be clear cases where the syntactic properties of a lexical item in my analysis are related to the syntactic features on adjacent syntactic heads. These are the situations that would classically require either head movement or morphological "fusion" before vocabulary insertion, if I were to adopt more standard models. For example, DM requires lexical items to be inserted under a single terminal node (for an explication of the core properties of DM, see Halle and Marantz

1993, Marantz 1997, Harley and Noyer 1999, Embick and Noyer 2001). In cases where this is not sufficient, various devices such as "fusion" or "fission" are required to feed vocabulary insertion. Instead of either head movement or fusion, I will adopt the implementation known as *spanning* (after Williams 2003). In the spanning view of things, a morpheme may spell out any number of heads in a complement sequence (see Ramchand 2008, Adger, Harbour, and Watkins 2009, Caha 2009). Spanning is similar in some respects to Brody's (2000) system described above, in sharing a direct linearization solution to the problem of head movement. However, it differs in the sense that it is not confined to spelling out individual morphemes related to single heads; it operates on morphologically holistic forms that are specified for more than one category feature (see Adger 2010, Bye and Svenonius 2012, and Svenonius 2012, for a discussion of the system and how it differs from Brody's original conception).

Second, I will be working with something more similar to a projectionist model than a late insertion model. Since lexical items do possess syntactic information, I see no gain in building syntactic trees first and then implementing late insertion under a matching algorithm. In the system that assumes spans, this means that subtrees are merged together directly to build larger and larger structures. However, I leave it open that a different sort of implementation would be possible in principle.

Thus, in an abstract tree structure such as (27), vocabulary items can be specified, via their category features, to realize any contiguous span of heads in the complement sequence.

(27)

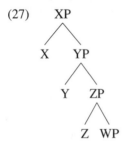

In this system, lexical items such as <X>, <Y>, and <Z> are possible in addition to the "spanning" lexical items <X, Y>, <Y, Z>, and <X, Y, Z>. Crucially, the lexical item <X, Z> cannot be used, since that would violate a requirement on the *contiguity* of lexical items (see (28a)). In addition, I will assume the spanning version of the Elsewhere principle here, which says that while a lexical item can realize a structure that contains its category features as a subset, it cannot be inserted in a tree where the lexical item does not possess one or more of the category features.[10] For example, if we tried to use $<X, Y>$ to span category heads X, Y, and Z, then a requirement on *specificity* would be violated (see (28b)).

(28) a. *Contiguity*
A lexical item can realize a phrase structure tree as the exponent of a span only if it spans a contiguous sequence of heads in the structure.
b. *Specificity*
A lexical item can realize a phrase structure tree as the exponent of a span only if its lexical entry contains all the features in the span.

In the current implementation, I move away from the late insertion model of expressing the separation between conceptual content and syntactic structure. Instead, the "separation" is enforced via the fact that lexical items consist of separate components. The individual lexical items are then combined directly in the first phase via Merge, in some cases contributing larger syntactic spines to the whole, as in the spanning intuition. Generalizations over phrase structure hierarchy must now be stated either as local generalizations about heads within lexical items or as macrogeneralizations derived from the universal compositional principles embodied in the quotational quantificational system. This immediately deconstructs the functional sequence in its templatic incarnation and gives us the challenge of recouping its effects from other sources, continuing on from the agenda in Ramchand and Svenonius 2014. In the direct Merge view, we no longer have competition for insertion or an Elsewhere principle. Elements of μ contribute the syntactic features they have and no more. However, unprojected features are possible under limited conditions.

Note that this system differs in certain ways from standard DM. As we have seen, lexical items are explicitly specified for category features, including lexical items that DM would consider to be acategorial roots as well as more "functional" items. This goes hand in hand with the abandonment of the late insertion model, which is no longer strictly necessary to express "separation." However, the system still has much in common with general constructional approaches to argument structure in that the Lexicon itself is not generative, and does not overtly express argument relationships. One single component located within the narrow language faculty is responsible for the productive generation of syntactic and semantic structures. All possible argument relationships are indirectly specified via the category features that build events of a particular type, but they are not directly represented as argument structure frames (see Ramchand 2008 for discussion). In many ways, given the introduction of the D_μ domain for the first phase, there is a sense in which the

first phase really is a kind of Lexical Syntax, to use the term favored by Hale
and Keyser in their groundbreaking work in this area (Hale and Keyser 1993,
2002).

For concreteness, I lay out the framework developed in Ramchand 2008 for
expressing verbal meanings, to illustrate the decomposition of event structure
that I will assume here. I argue in that work, and in Ramchand 2016, that
there are clear generalizations across languages with respect to aktionsart and
argument expression that converge on the following facts: verbal and argumental items that describe or undergo the result of an event are hierarchically
embedded under verbal and argumental items that describe or undergo change
simpliciter; the latter two in turn are hierarchically embedded under any verbal
and argumental items that express static or dynamic causes of those changes.
One could represent these relationships in a template as we do for in the rest
of the functional sequence, as in (29).[11] As in Hale and Keyser's work, the
causing or "leads-to" relation between subevents corresponds to hierarchical
embedding.

(29) *Achievements and accomplishments with result states*

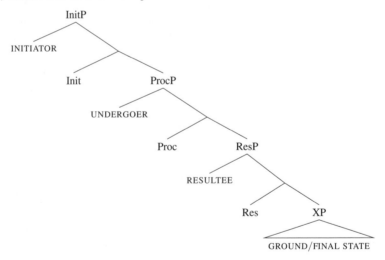

Tree (29) expresses the maximally expanded subevental structure for caused
changes leading to a result, with a stative predication embedding a dynamic
one, and the dynamic one in turn embedding a stative one. Thematic roles do
not need to be listed separately, nor do their properties need to be memorized
or known in advance. Interpreting phrasal embedding as causation will ensure
the relative prominence of the different argument positions, and the minimal

relationships of property-holding (both static and dynamic) will derive specific entailments for the different positions.

The highest specifier is the "holder" of a property that "leads to" the change occurring. This is just a fancy way of saying INITIATOR. The middle specifier is the "holder of a changing property." This is just an UNDERGOER. The lowest predication expresses a property that comes to hold, by virtue of being caused by the dynamic event. It is thus a "result," and the "holder" of that result property is the "holder of the result," or RESULTEE. The labels on the tree should therefore not be seen as labels in a template; they are simply there for ease of readability. The functional sequence here is actually quite spare, once the effects of hierarchy and predication are factored out.

In addition to the maximal subevental expression described above, activities and accomplishments can be built from structures that lack the Res projection. Bounded paths give rise to verb phrases that are classified as accomplishments in the literature, while unbounded paths give rise to activities.

(30) *Activities (path −bounded) and accomplishments (path +bounded)*

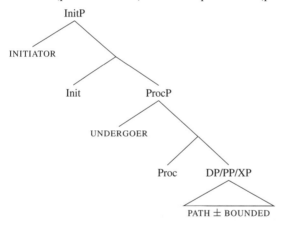

In this system, the event structure hierarchies and participant relation hierarchies track each other quite directly, and follow from a single decompositional structure.

But how does this structure relate to actual lexical items? The answer depends on one's assumptions about lexicalization, and there are many possibilities here. The traditional view, continued in DM, is that lexical items attach by insertion under *terminal nodes* of the syntactic representation. However, this view exists in tension with the increased elaboration of phrase structure (necessary to capture generalizations about hierarchical structure), where devices such as head movement, morphological fusion, and allomorphic selection have been employed to capture the fact that a single "word" seems to express a composite of syntactic information that is arranged hierarchically.

However, as previously discussed, I am assuming a model in which lexical verbs come listed with category features that express their insertion possibilities, in terms of spans. The English verb *destroy*, having all three features Init, Proc, and Res (or possibly just $V1_{state}$, $V2_{dyn}$, and $V3_{state}$), identifies the full structure "synthetically," as illustrated in (31).

(31) a. John destroyed the sandcastle.
  b.

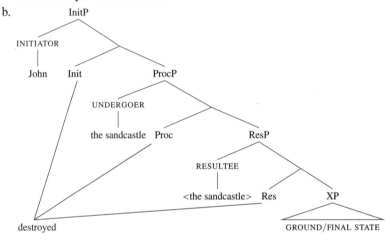

In the present system, we deal directly with elements of the D_μ domain. Syntactic structure is thus introduced by the merger of the elements of D_μ, whose syntactic specification consists of a single contiguous spine of categories (to account for the spanning intuition). Each lexical item contributes its conceptual content, which is unified with the structural semantic contribution of the node(s) in question.[12]

Allowing for spans in this way (see also Williams 2003), we are in a position to see that languages lexicalize decomposed verbal structures in a variety of different ways, depending on the inventory of building blocks at their disposal. In English, we also find a more analytic version of this decomposed structure, where a particle (e.g., *in* in (32)) explicitly identifies the result and combines with a verb that does not usually license a direct object (e.g., *hand* in (32)) to create a derived accomplishment structure with an "unselected object" (Simpson 1983, Carrier and Randall 1992).

(32) a. John handed in the money.

b.

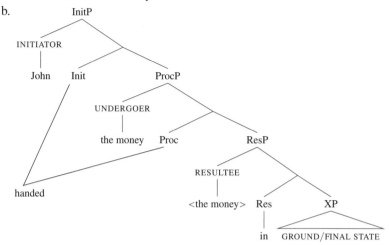

We can compare this with Bengali, which has a fully analytic construction: the perfective participle *lekh-e-*'written' identifies the Res head, while the "light" verb *phæla-* 'drop/throw' lexicalizes Init and Proc.

(33) Ruma cithi-ṭa   **lekh-e**   **phello**
      Ruma letter-DEF write-PERF.PART drop/throw-3PAST
      'Ruma wrote the letter completely.'

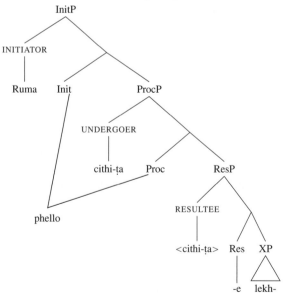

Bengali being a head-final language, aspect quite systematically appears out-side of the main verb stem, and tense in turn appears outside of that. They then line up sentence-finally as V-Asp-T. We can remain agnostic here about how that word order is derived, but note crucially that the "higher" functions of process and initiation in the verbal decomposition appear to the right of the "lower" description of the result state (the participle). This is exactly the order one would expect from a head-final language with this proposed hierarchical structure.

In previous treatments, complex predicates such as this, and even the English verb-particle construction, have posed paradoxes for lexicalist theo-ries of argument structure. On the one hand, they are clearly morphemically compositional, and it can be shown that the component parts are even indepen-dent syntactic units. On the other hand, the combination of lexemes changes the argument structure properties (something that lexicalists assume to be in the domain of the lexical module), and the constructions are monoclausal by all diagnostics. The constructivist view proposed here accounts for the predicational unity of the complex predicates as well as their resultative semantics. The complex predicate construction of the resultative type, the English verb-particle construction, and the synthetic English verb *destroy* have essentially the same hierarchically organized components—they are simply lexicalized/linearized differently.

In all of the above examples, it is still possible to conceive of lexical inser-tion in a more traditional manner under terminal nodes, with head-to-head movement in the syntax, or in the morphology as the need arises. I pre-sent the multiassociational/spanning view here because I believe it requires fewer ancillary "modules" (such as "fusion" in the morphology) and because it highlights the sharp difference between conceptual content and structural semantics.

In this event decomposition, what does it mean for a lexical item to have a particular syntactic feature label? It means simply that it is an element of μ that contributes a sensory/perceptual or cognitive property of that subevent. Thus, a composite verbal item like *destroy* potentially contributes conceptual content to all three subevents in its syntactic specification, although verbs may vary in how rich and specific those properties are. In the Bengali construc-tion, the conceptual content associated with the initiating event is extremely abstract but the specification of the result state is rather rich. The opposite is true in the particle construction in English, where the rich lexical content resides in the initiation and the process while the result is rather abstractly encoded. In general, I assume that all of these conceptual contributions to the specification of the event property are *unified*—added together to form the final composite description.

I will follow my own previous work (Ramchand 2008, 2014b) in assuming that it is in principle possible for syntactic information to remain unprojected. However, that possibility is highly constrained in the sense that any nonprojected category feature in an element of D_μ must in the normal case be licensed in an agreement relation with another D_μ that bears that feature. Any two elements of D_μ whose category features are in an Agree relation must moreover unify their semantic content. The principle is stated in (34).

(34) *Constraints on projection*
   a. Nonprojection of category features of an ordinary member of D_μ is in principle possible, constrained by Agree.
   b. Agreeing category features must unify their conceptual content.

Finally, and crucially for what will follow, I will assume one further principle on the regulation of lexical insertion that is familiar from the literature, but with a twist that relates to the other assumptions followed here. I will assume a pervasive system of blocking that adjudicates different possible lexicalizations of structure.

(35) *Poser blocking*[13] The lexicalization of a span by a single element of μ is always chosen over lexicalization of an identical span via separate elements of D_μ.

The reason I have had to be so clear about the principles of lexicalization is that auxiliation raises some of the very same issues that are raised by complex predicates. I will be thinking of auxiliation as the process by which structures that *could* in principle be lexicalized by single inflected verb forms can also be lexicalized piecemeal by individual forms. Only one of these forms will be finite, and only one will contribute the main event properties to the situational description. Auxiliary structures are a species of analytic spell out for the same abstract hierarchical structures that could in principle be spelled out synthetically. Auxiliary structures are therefore a crucial part of the puzzle concerning what these pieces/ingredients of verbal structure are.

Phrasal blocking will play a starring role in much of my analysis of *-en/ed* and *-ing* in English and their relationship to the corresponding simple verb expressions. It will turn out to be pervasive, and it will allow a simpler statement of the facts with fewer item-specific stipulations concerning selection.

1.5 Roadmap

The core idea is that the quotational semantics approach makes it possible to distinguish between a concept-building layer of the clause before the event variable is existentially bound, and the properties that arise in the context of instantiation in world and time. At this level, the proposal is that elements of type D_μ are restricted to nontemporal, nonmodal properties of events, learned by implicit generalization over experience. Following Champollion (2015), existential closure happens at the edge of the first phase. Thereafter, event-related aspectual temporal and worldly information can be added as properties of the relation between the utterance eventuality and the eventuality being described. These assumptions work together to derive ordering effects in the verbal domain.

In many ways, I see this monograph as an attempt to reconcile the important and robust results that have emerged from the syntactic tradition (particularly cartography) with the vocabulary of semanticists. More and more, it seems to me that semanticists and syntacticians are not part of the same conversation. More and more, the results of one subfield seem irrelevant to the results of the other. The ontologies are not commensurate, and the questions addressed are often not the same. Furthermore, it is even technically difficult to reconcile terminological assumptions and assumptions of what the "primes" of the representations are in order to get a conversation off the ground. In turn, we in formal linguistics are not in a position to present a usable set of hypotheses and predictions to psycho- and neurolinguists because of a lack of precision about the division of labor between conceptual content triggered by lexical open-class items and structural semantic content. Even if the implementations offered in this monograph turn out to have more elegant alternatives, I hope at least that they are concrete enough to be stimulating and that they will generate different and productive ways for semanticists and syntacticians to look at the central issues treated here.

In chapter 2, I look carefully at the English progressive, arguing for its position within the first syntactic phase of the clause and within the domain of event concept building. I claim that an explicitly intensional or "modal" account of the progressive in terms of possible worlds is both undesirable and inadequate empirically. Instead, I argue for a more primitive relationship between events and event parts as part of the denotation of the *-ing* morpheme.

In chapters 3 and 4, I look at the interpretation and distribution of the *-en/ed* participle in English, which appears in both the passive and the perfect constructions. I argue that while the participle is built within the first phase, the *have* auxiliary of the perfect is in the domain that is built *after* the existential closure of the event variable—the domain where temporal properties become possible to state. This sequence will account for the ordering between the prefect and the progressive. In turn, I will use the denotation proposed for *have* in analyzing the difference between the perfect and the passive constructions: I will build the latter using the auxiliary *be*, arguing that—like the progressive—*be* is generated low.

In chapters 5 and 6, I take up modals and modal ambiguities, proposing that modals are situational modifiers operating at different heights. This investigation will take us into the higher reaches of the clause, where situations will be anchored to the contextual utterance information. Chapter 6 also treats tense and anchoring to context.

In chapter 7, I return to the problem that started us off on this journey in the first place: the rigidity of auxiliary ordering in English. In this chapter, I take stock of the analyses proposed in the monograph and discuss how the proposed system actually forces the observed order and disallows the others. I assess the principles and assumptions that were used to achieve these effects. I also briefly discuss the implications of the proposed system (which is in fact quite general) for other languages and constructions, offering speculation and suggestions for further research.

Ideally, such a big change in proposed semantic primitives should be justified on the basis of many different languages, but in the context of a single volume I have to content myself with examining a spread of data from just one language. Even this is a mammoth task. Each English construction that I examine has had many books written about it alone. The advantage of this situation for the present work is that much is now known about the syntax and semantics of these constructions, and can be built on with confidence. I am in the enviable position of being able to build on this groundwork while spelling out my shift in perspective. Research such as this within a cumulative endeavor thus has two distinct aspects: to account for the insights and successful generalizations that are currently established in the literature, and to attempt to resolve some of the problems and paradoxes that have remained.

2 The Progressive in English

I start my analysis of the English auxiliary system with the progressive. There is a good syntactic reason to treat the progressive before the perfect or the modals: it occurs lower than they do in the structure. There is also a semantic reason: bolstering the arguments from chapter 1, the progressive will provide the clearest linguistic evidence for manipulations in the D_μ zone of the clause.

Considerable work has been done on the semantics of the progressive, specifically on the difficulty of stating truth conditions when the progressive is applied to accomplishment predicates. This problem, known as the *imperfective paradox* (Dowty 1979), is illustrated in (1).

(1) a. Mary was crossing the street.
    b. Mary crossed the street.

Essentially, the problem is that if we try to give truth conditions for the progressive in terms of truth conditions for the bare untensed version of the event description 'cross the street', then any extensional version of event semantics ends up committing us to the street getting crossed at some time in the real future. However, it is quite obvious to speakers of English that an utterance of *Mary is crossing the street* does not in fact commit them to the assertion that Mary will ever make it to the other side. The problem is a fairly deep one for the way the semantics is set up: in order to precisely express the truth conditions of 'cross the street', we are forced to be explicit about the telos; in order to precisely express the truth conditions of 'is crossing the street', we need to get rid of the telos *but still describe an event that would have that particular telos if it did culminate*.

It seems like a paradox; we do not want *is crossing the street* to be true of 'dancings' or 'walkings on the roadway'. We need to build in the semantics of street-crossing specifically, and that seems to require a description in terms of the telos being attained. The by-now-standard solution to the problem has been to describe the attainment of the telos in terms of nonactual worlds (Dowty's (1979) inertial worlds or Landman's (1992) continuation branches) in the semantics, while the assertion of the pre-telos portion of the event applies only to the world or situation that is actual. The accepted analysis of the progressive, then, is essentially a modalized semantics, requiring some kind of notion of possible worlds in its definition.

If this analysis is correct, it has immediate consequences for the compositional semantic system that I am proposing. This is because it essentially forces the progressive to be expressed at the level of situational particulars, where worlds can be quantified over. However, as I will show, there is good evidence from the syntax of the progressive that it lies quite deep in the clausal structure, *within* the very first phase of event building (section 2.1). If we take the converging evidence from syntax seriously, then we would be forced to say that quantification over possible worlds/situations is possible in the very lowest parts of the clause. But if this is true, then why does something like the progressive occur in the zone below tense anchoring and modal modification by auxiliaries? As we have seen, it is a robust crosslinguistic fact that the zone closest to the root appears to deal with event properties that are abstractions over temporal and worldly instantiations, and the English progressive falls squarely within this zone. In section 2.2, I will review the reasons for the modal analysis of the progressive in detail and conclude that it is neither adequate nor necessary for capturing the meaning of the progressive. I will instead propose an analysis that is most similar in spirit to Parsons's (1990) account, but avoids the notorious "part-of" objections to that view. In the account I will propose, the progressive creates a derived event property within the D_μ-denoting zone of the clause.

2.1 The Syntax of the Progressive: The Progressive is in the First Phase

I begin with the syntax of the progressive construction, demonstrating where its different components line up with respect to the more established elements of phrase structure such as V and v.

In what follows, I will show that there is an important syntactic and semantic boundary between progressive and perfect in English that should be represented explicitly by an abstract cutoff point in the phrase structure. Specifically, with respect to a number of different linguistic tests, the progressive, unlike the perfect, appears to pattern with the main verb and its arguments. (The following three syntactic arguments were also presented in Ramchand and Svenonius 2014 and Ramchand 2017, and the exposition is very similar to that found in the latter work.)

2.1.1 Expletive Associates

Harwood (2011, 2014) argues that the progressive must be inside what is usually thought of as the vP phase. Harwood's evidence includes an extended argument based on classical VP-ellipsis and the idea that ellipsis always targets a phasal spell-out domain. I am not convinced that traditional VP-ellipsis is *directly* sensitive to zones the way Harwood suggests. As it happens, though, his data regarding expletive associate placement are in some respects even clearer than his VP-ellipsis data (and don't require the notion of "flexible" phase that the full range of ellipsis data requires). Part of the discrepancy between our accounts is that I take the semantic characterization of the lowest zone as lexical "event description" to be primary and axiomatic.

However, the data that follow are relevant to both accounts. Harwood (2011) notes that the thematic subject of a verb in the expletive *there*-construction in English remains low in the clause and is confined to positions left-adjacent either to the main verb or to the passive or progressive participle. It can never surface to the left of the perfect participle.

The examples in (2), with the full complement of possible auxiliaries, show that there is only one position in the sequence for an expletive associate, between perfect *-en/ed* and progressive *-ing* (see Harwood 2011).

(2) a. *There could have been being *a truck* loaded.
    b. There could have been *a truck* being loaded.
    c. *There could have *a truck* been being loaded.
    d. *There could *a truck* have been being loaded.
    e. *There *a truck* could have been being loaded.
    f. *A truck* could have been being loaded.

Even when the progressive itself is not present, the position to the left of the perfect participle is unavailable, while the position to the left of the main verb and passive participle is fine.

(3) a. There could have been *a truck* loaded.
    b. *There could have *a truck* been loaded.
    c. *There could *a truck* have been loaded.
    d. *A truck* could have been loaded.

Similarly, sentences including just the progressive and the passive show exactly the same restriction: there is a "low" subject position to the left of the progressive participle.

(4) a. *There could be being *a truck* loaded.
    b. There could be *a truck* being loaded.

    c. *There could *a truck* be being loaded.

    d. *A truck* could be being loaded.

The low position of the subject is thus at the left edge of a domain that can include the *-ing* participle and the passive participle, but not the perfect participle.

2.1.2 VP-Fronting and Pseudoclefts

Examining a phenomenon concerning displacement, Sailor (2012) argues that VP-fronting and specificational pseudoclefts can target a constituent between perfect *-en/ed* and progressive *-ing*. In (5), we see the constituent headed by *-ing* undergoing fronting; and in (6), we see it forming a grammatical cleft. Crucially, neither the constituent selected by the perfect auxiliary nor the one selected by the modal can be targeted by movement in these constructions.

(5) a. * ...   [eaten], they will have been being.

    b.   ...   [being eaten], they will have been.

    c. * ...   [been being eaten], they will have.

    d. * ...[have been being eaten], they will.

(6) A: John should have been being praised. B: No, ...

    a. * ...   [criticized] is what he should have been being.

    b.   ...   [being criticized] is what he should have been.

    c. * ...   [been being criticized] is what he should have.

    d. * ...[have been being criticized] is what he should.

When the progressive is not present, as in (7), the constituent consisting of the passive participle can also be fronted, much like the progressive participle phrase. Nevertheless, the perfect participle phrase and the infinitival phrase selected by the modal are not legitimate targets.

(7) If Mary says that the cakes will have been eaten, then ...

    a.   ...   [eaten], they will have been.

    b. * ...   [been eaten], they will have.

    c. * ...[have been eaten], they will.

The examples in (8) show that when both the progressive and the passive are present and the perfect is absent, it is still the *-ing* phrase that fronts. The fact that the passive participle phrase does not front on its own seems to indicate that what is being targeted here is a maximal phrase of a certain type.

(8) If Mary says that the cakes will be being eaten, then ...

    a. * ...   [eaten], they will be being.

    b.   ...   [being eaten], they will be.

    c. * ...[be being eaten], they will.

These facts show that there is a privileged boundary at the point between per-fect -*en/ed* and progressive -*ing* that does not depend on the surface presence of any specific aspectual feature or morphological exponent.

The facts can be modeled by assuming that when they exist, the main verb, the passive participle, and the progressive participle all lie within a particular distinguished domain targeted by these fronting operations. In other words, there is a single privileged syntactic domain that is fronted in "VP-fronting" and clefted in the pseudocleft construction.

2.1.3   British Nonfinite *Do*-Substitution

Finally, I turn to an argument of my own from British nonfinite *do*-substitution, which exposes the same essential division. In British English, *do* is an abstract pro-form that substitutes not just for eventive verbs but for stative verbs as well, after an auxiliary.

(9) a. John might leave, and Mary might do also.
     b. John might really like oysters, and Mary might do also.

Although British nonfinite *do* can replace stative verbs, it is confined to replac-ing main verbs and never substitutes for an actual auxiliary. In other words, it is in complementary distribution with stranding by auxiliaries.[1]

(10) a. John might have seen the movie, and Mary might (*do) also.
      b. John might be singing a song, and Mary might (*do) also.

However, even within these constraints, not all nonfinite main verb forms may be replaced by *do*.

(11) a. John might leave, and Mary might do also.
      b. John has left, and Mary has done also.
      c. John is leaving, and Mary is (*doing) also.
      d. John was arrested, and Mary was (*done) also.

British nonfinite *do* can substitute for an infinitive modal complement or a per-fect participle, but not for a progressive or passive participle. This phenomenon too, motivates a cut between the perfect and the progressive. This diagnostic is in some sense the converse of the previous one: the very constituents that could participate in the fronting constructions are the ones that British nonfinite *do* cannot substitute for.[2]

There is thus robust evidence for two distinct domains, from three inde-pendent sets of grammatical facts. In each case, the facts point to a boundary between the progressive participial phrase and the perfect participial phrase when they exist (and I assume that the boundary exists even when the mor-phological evidence is not so articulated).

Convergent evidence for the lowest zone

- *-ing*-phrases, passive *-en/ed*-phrases, and main verb phrases all contain a base position for the external argument.
- *-ing*-phrases, passive *-en/ed*-phrases, and main verb phrases all form a unit with regard to independent mobility.
- *-ing*-phrases, passive *-en/ed*-phrases, and main verb phrases cannot be replaced by the pseudo-auxiliary verb *do* in British English.

Thus, with respect to a crude macrodivision of the clause into a VP domain and a TP domain, it seems the progressive and passive forms lie within the lower domain, while modals and the perfect lie within the higher. British English nonfinite *do*-substitution is a pro-form for the higher domain, but crucially not the lower one. This makes the difference between British English and more restrictive dialects, such as American English, quite simple to state: standard dummy *do*-support in American English has only finite instantiations, whereas British English possesses a nonfinite version of this pro-form as well. If we locate passive *-en/ed* in en$_{pass}$P and *-ing* in ing$_{prog}$P, then the phrase structural description for the above-noted purely syntactic evidence can be represented as in (12).

(12) *First phase*

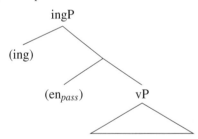

Facts regarding selection also support this division. We have already seen that aktionsart is one of the properties that are encoded by lexical items within the verbal domain. As is well known (see, e.g., Dowty 1979), the English progressive selects specifically for the aktionsart of its complement; that is, it combines with dynamic verbal projections and not stative ones.[3]

(13) a.   John is dancing the tango.
      b.   *John is knowing the answer.

Under the assumption that selectional restrictions are strictly local (Baltin 1989), the fact that the progressive places selectional restrictions on the aktionsart of the verb phrase it combines with is initial suggestive evidence that progressive is low enough in the extended projection to select for the nature of the event structure described by the verb.

However, the phrase structure in (12) is not yet either explanatory or satisfying, because it simply reuses the specific morphological forms as labels and as such is not generalizable to other languages. For example, we want to know whether the projection headed by -en$_{pass}$ is actually Voice, as described by Kratzer (1996). Similarly, what is the proper abstract label for the projection headed by -*ing*?

I will pursue the natural conjecture, given the proposal in chapter 1, that the lower domain diagnosed here is the domain of abstract eventive properties independent of specific instantiation. This lower domain denoting properties of D_μ contains the progressive and the passive *be*, while the higher domain is the domain of spatiotemporal properties of situations and contains the perfect auxiliary *have*.

Note that the perfect auxiliary *have* does not constrain the aktionsart of its complement. As (14) shows, the perfect can combine with *any* main verb in English. While it is true that the meaning of the perfect changes subtly depending on the type of main verb, one could argue that unlike the progressive, the perfect can technically be formed with any main verb regardless of aktionsart.

(14) a. John has destroyed the castle. *Telic verb*
b. John has driven on ice (before). *Atelic verb*
c. John has known Sue for three years. *Stative verb*

This goes along with the fact that the perfect's relationship to temporal anchoring differs from the progressive's: namely, it has a more indirect relationship to the VP event description. In chapter 4, I will discuss the details of this relationship further. But in brief, an adequate analysis of the perfect will require reference to an actual situational particular as a topic situation that mediates the relationship between the event and the utterance event d.

The progressive and the passive are the two lowest in the full possible expansion of auxiliaries in English, and while the passive has standardly been considered to reside within the first-phase zone because of its relationship to the traditional category of Voice, the same has not been systematically claimed for the progressive. Of course, the progressive shares with the passive the use of the auxiliary *be*, which Bjorkman (2011) argues is inserted as a default to spell out tense features. This makes it more similar to the passive, and less similar to the modals and perfect constructions, which introduce their own distinct tense-carrying auxiliaries.

Since the analysis I will end up proposing for the progressive will depart from previous approaches, I will begin by describing those approaches in the next section. The analysis I will propose should be able to do justice to the issues and subtleties already uncovered by the foundational work on this topic. However, as I set out to show, it will also avoid some of the bigger problems and paradoxes inherent in the previous approaches.

2.2   The Semantics of the Progressive

As stated earlier, the English progressive is most famous for introducing a puzzle for semanticists called the imperfective paradox. A rich literature has arisen seeking to solve the basic puzzle and account for the increasingly subtle judgments people have about the relationship between a completed event and its progressivized version. The current consensus seems to be that some sort of modalized semantics is necessary.

Here are a few examples of the denotations proposed in the literature. The first is the classic version proposed in Dowty 1979, whereby the progressivized version of a sentence is true if the nonprogressivized version *would have been true* in some inertial world that continues on from the current one in the most "normal" way. Crucially, the inertial world in question need not be the actual one.

(15)   *Dowty's (1979) semantics*
       [Prog ϕ] is true at $<I, w>$ iff for some interval I' s.t. $I \subset I'$ and I is not a final subinterval for I', and for all w' such that $w' \in \text{Inr}(I, w)$, ϕ is true at $<I', w'>$
       where $\text{Inr}(I, w)$ - set of inertial worlds for w and interval I.

       Inertia Worlds - are to be thought of as worlds which are exactly like the given world up to the time in question and in which the future course of events after this time develops in ways most compatible with the past course of events.
       (Dowty 1979, 148)

Landman's (1992) version is somewhat more sophisticated and is based on a wider range of tricky examples for which people have varying judgments. Landman's crucial, and correct, insight is that the inertia in question is more event internal than worldly. It turns out that one needs to zero in on the particular event situation and its ingredients when deciding what counts as most normal, since using the whole world in the calculation of normality, as in Dowty's semantics, leads to some counterintuitive predictions. For example, when a big truck is hurtling down the street and is about to run over Mary while she is crossing, we still allow ourselves to use the progressive even though in the most normal world continuing on from the present moment, she surely doesn't make it.

(16) *Landman's (1992) semantics*
   $[\![Prog(e, P)]\!]_{w,g} = 1$ iff $\exists f \exists v : <f, v> \in CON(g(e),w)$ and $[\![P]\!]_{v,g}(f) = 1$.
   where $CON(g(e), w)$ is the continuation branch of $g(e)$ in w.
   (Landman 1992, 27)

The crucial notion that does all the work here is that of "continuation branch" for an event in a world w. Once the event stops in the real world, we can "continue" the event by moving over to the next closest world as long as it is reasonable. If the event stops there as well, we can again move over to the next closest world and allow the event to continue. We can cobble together a continuation branch as long as the worlds we hop over to remain close and reasonable, *and* as long as we are still dealing with "stages of the same event." The progressive states that the event in question will indeed culminate if we build one of those continuation branches. (See also Varasdi to appear for a discussion of the formal and logical consequences of the move from worlds to events, which makes Landman's kind of system into one where the progressive involves the possibility operator, rather than a necessity one.)

Still, whether the intensionality is relativized to events or not, both of these systems involve an operator over possible outcomes. The machinery of possible worlds is invoked to make sense of and to formalize our intuitive grasp of possible event continuations. However, I would argue that the mystery is not dissolved by invoking the possible-worlds machinery. We still need to rely on an intuitive understanding of what it means for something to be the "stage" of an event, what counts as a reasonable world, and how close the world must be to be close enough. In subsequent work, Landman (2008) goes into more detail about what constitutes a "stage" of an event. In that paper, he examines the similarities and differences between the tense-aspect systems of Dutch and English, an agenda in many ways similar to my agenda here. But in Landman's system, expressing the progressive and the nonprogressive as being in some sense parasitic on the "same event," still relies on a notion of "cross-temporal identity" even if we put aside the modal component.

Thus, the notion of cross-temporal identity, as understood here, concerns *what we are willing to regard*, in a context, *as the same event* for the purpose of expressing how often something happened [my emphasis]. A full axiomatization of the intended notion of cross-temporal identity is beyond the scope of this paper. (Landman 2008, 7)

We might feel more comfortable if we follow Portner's (1998) proposal to use only the mechanisms and machinery standardly accepted in modal semantics as the primitive relations among worlds with which the intensional semantics of the progressive is defined. That is, Portner proposes to use the ideas of modal bases and ordering sources to get at the meaning of the progressive.

(17) *Portner's (1998) semantics*

The modal base: Circ(e) = "the set of circumstances relevant to whether e is completed."

The ordering source: NI(e) = "the set of propositions which assert that e does not get interrupted." (NI = No Interruptions)

"Prog(ϕ) is true at a pair of an interval and a world $<i, w>$ iff there is an event e in w such that T(e) = i and for all worlds $w' \in$ Best(Circ, NI, e), there is an interval i' which includes i as a non-final subinterval, such that ϕ is true at $<i', w'>$."

(Portner 1998, 774)

This way, we have some unexplained primitives, but they are the same primitives necessary for the understanding of modal meanings more generally, which we already assume we have. However, to make his proposal work, Portner does have to assume crucially that the construction of the modal base cannot strictly be that shown above; rather, it must be relativized to the *nature of the event description itself*. Otherwise, the truth conditions of (18a) and (18b) would be the same when describing the same event in the world.

(18) a. Mary was crossing the street.

b. Mary was walking into the path of an oncoming truck.

So in fact Portner argues that Circ(e) must be Circ(e,P) (where P is the event predicate itself) and Best(Circ,NI,e) must be Best(Circ,NI,e,P). The truth conditions of the progressive are therefore as follows:

(19) Prog(e,P) is true at a world w iff for all worlds $w' \in$ Best(Circ, NI, e, P), there is an event e' which includes e as a non-final subpart, such that $P(w')(e')$ is true.

(Portner 1998, 782)

While it does seem better to reuse mechanisms we already know to be active in the semantics of other expressions, there are aspects of Portner's solution that give us a clue that something different is going on here. The first is the relativization to the *actual event description*, the consequences of which are left at a completely intuitive level.

I think it can be shown in fact that the kinds of calculations that feed into modal judgments are *not* of the same nature as the ones that seem to be involved with the progressive. Specifically, the sensitivity to the nature of the description is quite special here, as is the extremely local nature of the worlds calculated over when licensing the progressive. In the street-crossing scenario, even though a bus is racing toward Mary, we are still inclined to say that (20a) is true; but if we avert our eyes at the last moment, we would probably say that (20b) is true, and not that (20c) is true.

(20) a. Mary was crossing the street.
     b. Mary must have been hit by that bus.
     c. Mary must have crossed the street.

The above argument is due to Klinedinst (2012), who sets aside the modal account of the progressive for this reason. Basically, the standards required for asserting the progressive are much lower than the ones we would require for making an epistemic prediction about future events. The calculation we are carrying out is based in quite detailed ways on the way in which the event itself is presented qua description, and the verbal result is invoked only as a means of ensuring that the right *kind* of event is being asserted as ongoing.

Another aspect of the progressive's semantics that is important to discuss here is that the progressive is "stative" from the point of view of its external semantic distributional behavior. As far as I know, the modern treatment that takes this fact most seriously is Hallman's (2009a), although he essentially builds on insights from Mittwoch (1988) and Vlach (1981). In Mittwoch's version, the output of progressivization is the construction of a homogenous activity that satisfies the subinterval property (if the progressive is true at an interval, it is true at every subinterval of that interval).

(21) *Mittwoch's (1988) semantics*
     PROG(A) is true in M relative to (w, i) iff i is a subinterval of an interval j and A is true in M relative to (w, j), where A is interpreted as an activity or state (i.e. homogenous situation).
     (Mittwoch 1988, 213)

Vlach (1981) is more specific about the stativity of the progressive and includes a processizing operator embedded within it.

(22) *Vlach's (1981) semantics*
     PROG[ϕ] if and only if STAT[PROC[ϕ] goes on]
     where PROC[ϕ] is that process P that leads to the truth of ϕ
     (Vlach 1981, 287–288)

It is important to note that when it comes to the behavior of *when*-clauses and other point adverbials, statives pattern one way in English and all the events go the other (including the activities). With regard to the progressive and *when*-adverbials, this point was originally made by Leech (1971).

(23) a. When we arrived she made some fresh coffee.
    b. When we arrived she was making some fresh coffee.
      (Leech 1971, via Hallman 2009a, 3)

Therefore, mere divisibility down to a certain grain size is not enough to capture the discourse effects. The progressive specifically patterns like a state; it does not have the restricted kind of homogeneity found in activities, which fail to be true at subintervals that are single moments.

In terms of narrative progression, the progressive patterns specifically with states and not with activities. In (24a) and (24b), the achievement and activity respectively advance the narrative time in the middle sentence, while in (24c) and (24d), the stative progressive in the middle sentence does not (see also Kamp and Reyle 1993).

(24) a. John arrived. He sat down. Then he left in a hurry.
    b. John arrived. He drank coffee. Then he left in a hurry.
    c. John arrived. He was sweating. Then he left in a hurry.
    d. John arrived. He looked hot and bothered. Then he left in a hurry.

Hallman (2009a) adds further diagnostics to the stativity claim. For example, complements of exceptional-case-marking *discover* and *reveal* in English must be specifically stative and are incompatible with events of all kinds, including activities. Once again, the progressive patterns with the statives.

(25) a. The inspector revealed/discovered Max to be a liar.
    b. The inspector revealed/discovered Max to be lying.
    c. *The inspector revealed/discovered Max to lie.
      (Hallman 2009a, 8)

In addition, as Hallman (2009a) points out, the progressive patterns with statives in being possible in the present tense in English with the same interpretation as the past tense (unlike eventives, which shift to a habitual interpretation or a narrative present). The reason is that (as Hallman also argues) statives and the progressives can be true at a "point" in time, while eventives, which have duration, cannot.

(26) a. Mary looked tired when I saw her yesterday, and she looks tired now too.
    b. Mary was writing a novel when I saw her yesterday, and she is writing a novel now too.
    c. Mary ate a mango when I saw her yesterday, and ??she eats a mango now too.

Portner (2003) points out yet another stativity diagnostic in English: namely, that the universal reading of the perfect is triggered in English for states, but is impossible for events of all stripes including activities. In (27), I use the phrase *since 5 o'clock* to trigger and force the universal reading of the perfect. Only statives and progressives are licit.

(27) a. John has been in the park since 5 o'clock.
   b. John has been jogging since 5 o'clock.
   c. *John has driven a truck since 5 o'clock.
   d. *John has broken the vase since 5 o'clock.

Hallman (2009a) gives an interpretation for the progressive that abstracts away from the possible-worlds problem and concentrates only on making sure that the denotation properly expresses that the output of the progressive operator is a state that is only true of points in time (essentially following Taylor 1977).

(28) *Hallman's (2009a) semantics*
   $[\![PROG(\Phi_{EVENT})]\!] = \lambda t \in T \lambda e \in E\ [\tau(e) = t \wedge \exists e' \in E\ \exists i \in {}^*T$
   $[\Phi(i, e') \wedge Cul(e, e')]]$
   where Cul is "intended to be understood as a metavariable for whatever set of circumstances relates the present goings on to the possible culmination, which will inevitably involve reference to possible worlds." (Hallman 2009a, 22)

Finally, in separate work, Hallman (2009b) adds to the complex problem of how to identify an event from its processual subpart, by examining data from the interaction of the progressive with quantification. Hallman notices that the intuitive truth of a progressivized VP depends in an interesting way on the quantificational properties of the direct object. Hallman invites us to imagine a machine that is checking 300 manufactured transistors for flaws. If a transistor is OK, it accepts it; if not, it rejects it. In scenario 1, the machine systematically rejects one out of every three transistors it examines in the pattern YES-YES-NO-YES-YES-NO, and so on. Once the machine has done its job on all 300 transistors, the sentence in (29) would be judged true.

(29) The machine rejected one-third of the transistors.

In scenario 2, the machine accepts the first 200 transistors and rejects the last 100. Here, too, the sentence in (29) would be judged true after all 300 trials. However, now consider the progressivized sentence in (30) uttered after the first 120 trials.

(30) The machine is rejecting one-third of the transistors.

This can only be true in scenario 1, not in scenario 2, *even if* we are watching the process on film and know what the outcome will be.

Hallman's response to this problem is to devise a semantics that utilizes situations and requires that the situation of which the progressive is true be divisible (i.e., for the progressive must be true of all its subsituations).[4] His proposed solution predicts that VPs with quantifiers in the scope of the progressive that are not proportional will not be licit. This seems to be true.

(31) a. ??John was eating exactly three apples.
      b. ??John was drawing less than ten circles.

Hallman's (2009b) denotation for the progressive is given in (32). Note that in this work, he does not directly build in the stative properties of the progressive that he argues for in Hallman 2009a.

(32) *Hallman's (2009b) semantics*
      $\forall \phi \subseteq [\![PROG(\phi)]\!]^w = \lambda s \leq w \ \forall s' \leq s \ R(s', s) \rightsquigarrow \phi(s')$
      where R "essentially represents the 'is a relevant subpart of' relation"
      (Hallman 2009b, 36)

Hallman's analysis of the progressive directly utilizes situations instead of possible worlds (as, for example, in Cipria and Landman's (2000) work on Spanish perfective and imperfective tenses). This kind of analysis is helpful in that it can, like Landman's account, build in the sensitivity to events via the exemplification relation, avoiding the unwanted detail found in complete worlds. Nevertheless, Hallman's account has the property common to the other accounts discussed above: it builds some kind of intensionality into the semantics of the progressive.

Finally, it is worth highlighting a fact that is implicit in much of the discussion around progressive meanings so far: namely, that native speakers' judgments of the truth of a progressivized sentence are highly dependent not only on the specifics of the description, but also on details of the context of utterance and what kind of information is in the common ground. These kinds of considerations are famously used by Landman (1992) to argue for the notion of event continuation branch. For example, I am willing to assent to the truth of (33a) in a particular scenario if I know that Mary is a robot with superhuman skills in a science fiction movie where she is sent back in time, but not if she is the girl from the farm next door. If I know that Mary has been training hard on her swimming and that she just jumped into the water at Dover, I might well agree to (33b), but not if she is my 6-year-old daughter. Also, my answer to whether I think (33c) is true when Mary sets off will differ depending on whether I know that she intends to cross the street or know that she intends to simply stand in the middle of the road and block the traffic.

(33) a. Mary is wiping out the Roman army.
     b. Mary is swimming the English Channel.
     c. Mary is crossing the street.

In a slightly different vein, if I know that digging a deep hole for foundations is the first stage of building a house, I could look at a bunch of workers digging a hole and truly assert, "They are building a house." But people can also disagree in their judgments depending on how well they think a certain activity represents the corresponding named nonprogressivized event. For example, I can point to Mary sitting in the library with a huge mound of books on sixteenth-century maps and tell you knowingly, "Mary is writing an article on maps." You might disagree with my description of the facts and say, "No, she isn't. I'll count those publication points when I see them. Let's hope she eventually does get around to writing, but knowing her I doubt it."

But one thing remains curiously robust in all of this contextual sensitivity and variability: people will all agree that the sentence in (34) is good.

(34) Mary was crossing the bridge when the earthquake hit, so she never
     made it to the other side.

So ways in which the world might be or necessarily must be are irrelevant to our willingness to agree to that statement. Internal facts about Mary and about her own intentions *are* relevant, but external circumstances are not. This highlights the fact that the judgments here are not equivalent to modal possibility in a general sense, but have to do with our judgment of whether certain "essential" properties of an eventuality are being evidenced or not.

Other well-known problems arise with purely modal accounts if the specificity of the event description is not taken into account. For example, in the following scenario (attributed by Dowty (1979) to Richmond Thomason), even though the possible continuations of an event where a coin has just been tossed into the air involve equal numbers of worlds where it comes up heads and where it comes up tails, *neither* (35a) nor (35b) seems to be intuitively true.

(35) a. The coin is coming up heads.
     b. The coin is coming up tails.

A modal possibility account seems to predict falsely that both should be true.[5] On the other hand, a modal necessity account runs into trouble with Abusch's (1985) sentences in (36), where the two apparently incompatible outcomes can *both* be judged true in the progressive in the same situation.

(36) a. John was crossing the street.
     b. John was walking to his death.

The point is that neither (35a) nor (35b) is a good way of "describing" or identifying a "coin toss resolution" event, given what we know about tossing a fair coin. On the other hand, both (36a) and (36b) are legitimate ways of "describing" a "walking in front of an oncoming truck" event, depending on which aspect one wants to emphasize.

In short, we as linguists know a lot more about the difficulties of expressing the meaning of the progressive than we knew before we started on this journey. As a way of summarizing the discussion and paving the way for what is to come, I will list here the core semantic properties/paradoxes having to do with progressive meaning that any successful analysis needs to be able to account for.

(37) *Core semantic features of the progressive*
   a. The progressivized eventuality is related in an organic way to its non-progressivized counterpart, but does not actually entail it (in the actual world) at a future time. Judgments of event sameness are due to some judgment of "essential identity," rather than to prediction of outcome.
   b. The relationship between a progressivized event and the event simpliciter is not qualitatively the same as epistemic uncertainty (Klinedinst's (2012) observation).
   c. The perceived relationship between a progressivized event and the event simpliciter is affected by contextual properties of the discourse and gives rise to variable judgments across speakers. In this regard, *internal properties of the participants and their intentions* and the *nature of the observed process* seem to be more important than external circumstances (Landman's (1992) Observation).
   d. The progressive functions like a state in its temporal semantics (Vlach 1981, Parsons 1990, Hallman 2009a).

I think it is fair to say that all of the possible-worlds accounts we have looked at fall short of complete objective explicitness when it comes to point (37a). In all cases, the appeal to possible worlds leaves an unexplained residue completely independent of the possible-worlds mechanisms themselves. In Landman's version, it is his appeal to the "stage-of" relation; in Portner's it is the relativization to event descriptions; in Hallman's, it is the relation R (the "relevant-subpart-of" relation). The essential question—"What does it mean to be an in-progress version of an event?"—remains a primitive, and essentially a mystery.

The possible-worlds framework of Lewis and most subsequent formal semanticists has appealed to the field because of its formal explicitness. Possible worlds allow us to extend the ordinary notations for extensional reality and express hypotheticals and uncertainties by means of regularities over multiplicities of worlds. The core of the semantics remains extensional; it is just the worlds that are hypothetical/possible/likely, and so on. Possible worlds are a convenient fiction that seems on the face of it to make the formalization of many aspects of natural language more tractable, elegant, and well suited to compositional treatment. But in the case of the progressive, the possible-worlds accounts are much less compelling. A basic mystery remains at the heart of all of these accounts, which I would argue is the judgment we humans make instinctively regarding essential event identity.

2.3 The Proposal: Progressive as Identifying State

In my own proposal regrading the progressive, I will assume the equivalent of the above-mentioned unexplained part as a basic cognitive primitive. To anticipate, the ability to identify a snapshot state of an event as being a *part* of that event is a sensory/cognitive judgment that forms the basis of our ability to classify the world in terms of symbolic labels. In an important way, the proposal I will make is a close sister of the position taken by Parsons (1990), although I will define my equivalent of Parsons's "in-progress state" somewhat differently, avoiding the mereological part-of relation.

Taking a particular cognitive judgment to underlie a primitive property does not necessarily make the analysis any more objectively verifiable or accurate, although I do think it makes predictions as well as other accounts. This choice of primitive will have a number of positive payoffs with respect to polysemy and the interaction between the *-ing* participle and the rest of the grammatical system. It will also be the starting point for testable predictions within cognitive psychology and acquisition.

2.3.1 Parsons's Account

Before giving my own account, I will present Parsons's (1990) account, which is, intuitively speaking, the closest intellectual precursor to mine. I will discuss the criticisms of that account and use them to define my own version, which avoids what I see as the major problems.

Parsons (1990) avoids modality in his account of the progressive by assuming the notion of "incomplete event" as a primitive. Technically speaking, he assumes the predicates Hold and Cul as primitives and asserts that "incomplete" events and objects still count as those very events and objects as far as speakers are concerned. The representations Parsons proposes for progressive sentences and ordinary past tense accomplishment sentences are given in (38a) and (38b), respectively.

(38) *Parsons 1990*

    a. Mary was crossing the street.
   $\exists e \exists I \exists t[I < now \wedge cross(e) \wedge Agent(e) = Mary \wedge Theme(e) = the\text{-}street \wedge$
   $Hold(e, t)]$

    b. Mary crossed the street.
   $\exists e \exists I \exists t[I < now \wedge cross(e) \wedge Agent(e) = Mary \wedge Theme(e) =$
   $the\text{-}street \wedge Cul(e, t)]$

This account avoids the imperfective paradox because (38a) does not entail (38b). In the semantics of Hold, there is no entailment that Cul ever becomes true.

It has been objected that this account simply has nothing to say about the actual judgments people have about (38a)—namely, *when* it is they would agree to its being true. I submit that this charge is unfair. Parsons would say that people judge (38a) to be true precisely in the circumstances in which they would agree that (38a) is a *part* of an event that could be described by (38b). We have seen that all the modalized accounts reduce to the equivalent of this mysterious statement as well.

Another objection to this account concerns our intuitions about incomplete objects. The idea is that from the denotations given, it seems that Parsons is committed to the idea that if one says, "John was drawing a circle," then there was "a circle" that he was drawing, even if he had just begun to draw. Parsons bites the bullet here and says that in some sense this is true, there *is* a circle, albeit an incomplete one, just as there is an incomplete event of drawing a circle. Many English speakers feel uncomfortable with this judgment.

Another version of the objection also zeroes in on the problematic aspects of the notion of partiality, but with respect to the event denotation. The objection is due to Zucchi (1999), who points out that Parsons's account makes a prediction about the underlying denotation of the bare verb phrase: namely, that it should be able to denote partial events, at least optionally. This is because Parsons assumes an underspecified semantics for the VP and then allows the predicates Hold and Cul to build unambiguously atelic and telic events, respectively. On the other hand, the modal accounts assume a completed-event denotation and use the progressive operator to remove the entailment to completion in the real world. To the extent that bare untensed verb forms can be found in English, the data seem to favor the modalized account. In other words, the bare VPs in (39) seem to be interpreted as complete events.

(39) a. John saw Mary cross the street. #He saw the bus hitting her when she
   was halfway across.

    b. John saw Mary crossing the street. He saw the bus hitting her when
   she was halfway across.

So is this objection the final nail in the coffin of Parsons's account? I think it speaks against the particular implementation that Parsons offers in terms of partiality, but it will not apply to the version I will describe next in terms of linguistic event concepts and Identifying States.

2.3.2 Identifying States

The Identifying States account will share with Parsons's (1990) account the idea that the relationship between the progressivized version of an event description and the underlying event description is not to be described in terms of possible worlds.

First of all, as I argued in chapter 1, we use the lowest phase of the syntactic representation—the first phase—as the level at which linguistic items are combined to create a symbolic, constraining description of the event being conveyed. The information expressed by the verbal linguistic items at this level is devoid of temporal or locational content; it simply represents a classification at the level of basic sensory/perceptual commonalities. However, I think the empirical evidence shows that the domain of linguistic symbols D_μ is complex, hierarchically structured, and part of a generative, compositional system. The question is, what sorts of compositional relationships exist at this level?

We need to be explicit, therefore, about the relationship between the -*ing* form of a verb and its tensed form. The -*ing* form is the crucial linguistic ingredient in the formation of what is known as the English progressive. The relationship between the progressivized event description and the bare event description cannot be expressed in terms of Hold and Cul as in Parsons's treatment, because these are notions that apply to instantiated, temporal entities and not between atemporal event descriptions.

The task, therefore, is to express the denotation of the -*ing* participle as an *ingredient* of the progressive. I will assume first of all that -*ing* is a productive suffix that applies to and takes scope over the whole VP constructed so far with all of its required arguments, as illustrated in (40).

(40)

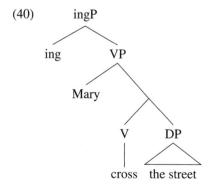

Taking seriously the evidence for the stative nature of the progressive in English, I propose that the semantic part of the *-ing* morpheme is a function from event descriptions to event descriptions such that the derived eventuality is an Identifying State for that event.

In the quotational semantics in chapter 1, linguistic items are elements of the ontology and can be composed to give complex linguistic items with a derived conceptual contribution. By default, I have assumed that the standard way of combining the semantic content of the individual pieces is by simple argument identification (of the event argument variable). In the case of *-ing*, I will assume a special rule for its composition with a complex phrase within the D_μ domain, shown in box 2.1. Identifying state (ID-state) is then defined as in box 2.2.

Box 2.1
The formation of the *-ing* participle

> If A is formed from the merger of ing and B where $B \in D_\mu$, then A is also in D_μ, and
> $\llcorner A \lrcorner = \lambda e[\text{State}(e) \wedge e \text{ is an ID-State for property } \llcorner B \lrcorner]$

Box 2.2
Identifying State: Definition

> For every event description P, an *Identifying State* for P is a stative eventuality that manifests sufficient cognitive/perceptual identifiers of the event property P.

Thus, the denotation of an *-ing* participle is as shown in (41).

(41) $\llcorner u_V\text{-ing} \lrcorner = \lambda e[\text{State}(e) \wedge \text{ID-State}(e, \llcorner u_V \lrcorner)]$

Intuitively, the Identifying State relation is one in which speakers can infer the existence of a (possibly complex) event E by means of a state that provides sufficient evidence (given everything else they know about the world) for that type of event. These states are conceptual snapshots, which, if rich enough or with rich enough insider knowledge, license inferences to the existence of a more complex extended eventuality in practice, given the right conditions. I assume that Identifying State is a primitive relation, intuitively accessible to the youngest of children and at work every time we make claims about durational eventualities based on immediate perceptual contact.

In addition to shifting to states, we need to shift the argument structure so that there is a designated "holder" of the derived state. This, empirically

speaking, is always the "highest" argument in the already built-up event description. I assume that the merger of -*ing* triggers the movement of an argument to
its specifier, which is then interpreted as the HOLDER of the Identifying State.[6]

(42) $\llcorner u_V\text{-}ing \lrcorner = \lambda x \lambda e [\text{State}(e) \wedge \text{ID-State}(e, \llcorner u_V \lrcorner) \wedge \text{HOLDER}(e) = x]$

(43)

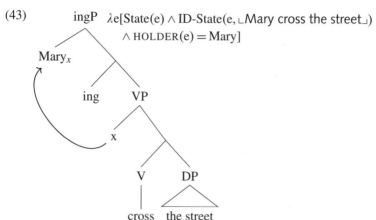

It is easy to see that this kind of analysis does not give rise to the imperfective
paradox: the -*ing* event bears a stative identifying relationship to the non-*ing*
event property, but so far neither of them is asserted to exist in any particular
world or time, so no entailments automatically exist between the instantiated
versions.

The notion of "Identifying State" as defined above also makes explicit that
what gives rise to the variability of the judgments we have seen so far is the
flexible and slippery nature of "evidence," which is affected by our knowledge
of the intentions, proclivities, and abilities of the participants as well as basic
common-ground facts about how event types proceed in the world normally
or prototypically. Because the judgment is about the relationship between an
event property P and its identifying state, facts about the world that would
affect full temporal instantiation of the event property are irrelevant.

Thus, the account satisfies all four desired properties outlined in (37). Moreover, it gives us a handle on Hallman's quantification problem. This is because
of the problem of evidence. If Mary is eating two apples, the evidence that
two apples are involved is entirely lacking in a completely serialized eating
scenario, but visible and present in a situation where she bites into them both
simultaneously, or where we see them together on her plate, or where we know
her intentions. These facts, I think, conform to our intuitive judgments. The
divisibility of the enclosing situational description (up to a certain granularity)
is a kind of guarantee of the persistence of evidence.

2.3.3 Relating Event Properties to Situational Particulars

Once we sever event descriptions from temporal and worldly instantiation, we are in an entailment vacuum. Judgments of entailments from one propositional form of English to another are simply not predicted. We have exploited this fact and used it as a virtue in eliminating the unwanted entailments from the progressivized version of the sentence to the simple past version, but we are in danger of predicting no relationship at all between *-ing* forms and tensed forms unless we spell out the relationship between the existentially bound and anchored *-ing* forms and the corresponding existentially bound and anchored non-*ing* forms. What we know is that this relationship is sensitive to the aktionsart of the base non-*ing* form. Sometimes the two forms are related by entailment and sometimes they aren't. How do we make sense of this?

The first core fact is that a past tense utterance of any eventive verb in English entails the past tense version of its progressivized counterpart. Thus, (44a) entails (44b) for any (nonstative) verb of English.

(44) a. John built a house.
    b. John was building a house.

I will assume the following natural relationship between events that fully instantiate a particular property and Identifying States for that property:

(45) *Event existence entails existence of Identifying State*
    The existence of an event entails the existence of at least one Identifying State. The state in question is always a mereological subpart of that event.

Importantly, the converse does not hold. The existence of an Identifying State for an event property does not guarantee the existence of an event that fully exemplifies the property. This means in particular that (44b) will not in general entail (44a), although (44a) entails (44b).

On the other hand, it is usually assumed to be the case that (46a) does entail (46b).

(46) a. John was running.
    b. John ran.

We also need to be able to explain the judgments for activities here, and why they differ from the judgments for achievements and accomplishments. In fact, I would like to propose that (46a) does not actually entail (46b) at all. It is just that the fact that the progressive version does not entail the simple past version is much more obvious in the case of accomplishments than in the case of activities. We can explain this effect because of *inferences* based on real-world information combined with the homogenous properties of activities—the fact that if they are true at any interval at all, they are true at *every* subinterval of that interval larger than a moment, including extremely short intervals indeed. The meaning postulates for different primitive aktionsart categories of events, adapted from Taylor 1977, are given in box 2.3. They constrain the possibilities for temporal instantiation for the different eventuality types.

Box 2.3
Temporal properties of different primitive event types

1. *Temporal properties of simple dynamic events*
   A process event must have a temporal parameter longer than a moment. If a simple process is true at an interval I, then it is true at every subinterval of that interval larger than a moment.
2. *Temporal properties of states*
   A state can have a moment as its temporal parameter. If a state is true at an interval I, then it is true at every subinterval of that interval, including at each moment.
3. *Temporal properties of complex events*
   An event with complex subevental structure must have temporal run-times corresponding to *each* of the subevents in that structure. If a complex event is true at an interval I, then we cannot guarantee that there is any subinterval of I at which the complex event is true.

Now, consider how the property of activities interacts with the definition of Identifying State assumed above. If (46a) is true, then an Identifying State exists. Minimally, then, it could hold for exactly one asserted time moment. The existential closure of this event variable does not mean that the event is unique. In fact, if there is even one other temporally abutting Identifying State for the event property, then we could form the join of those two situations to create something that *would* be an instance of the event itself. Thus, the nonprogressivized version would be true. In context, the inference is that the real-world situation that would support an utterance of (46a) would also support an utterance of (46a) one second later. Because of the homogeneity of activities, that inference is enough to guarantee the move to (46b) in the case of activities that are true at every subinterval larger than a moment; and depending on the context, it may even be enough to guarantee such inferences for activities with larger minimal subparts such as *dance a waltz*. In this story, then, there is no actual *entailment* from (46a) to (46b)—just a strong inference, which in certain cases can be denied, which we can detect when the activity is

more complex. If the music started up in waltz time and John went out inten-
tionally on the dance floor with Mary and took the first step, then I could see
that and utter truthfully *Look, John is waltzing!* But if he crumpled to the floor
with a cramp after that first step, then we would be unlikely to agree after the
fact that he actually "waltzed." This is what the proposed account predicts.

Finally, I need to say a few words about the status of the object domain
in this kind of account, which treats the lowest part of the verbal extended
projection as compositions of linguistic items. In the semantic part of the linguistic item, we find by hypothesis the specification of participant relations
that relate entities from the regular object domain D_e to events. We need to ask
how nominal projections compose with verbal projections to build descriptions
of full events. In fact, the rethink I am proposing requires a parallel rethink
in the domain of object entities. At the lowest part of the nominal extended
projection, we need to be trafficking in nominal linguistic items introducing
conceptual content as abstractions over actual instances of referents. It is plausible that in the first phase of the verbal extended projection, we are dealing
only with entities of type D_μ instead of instantiated objects as participants (in
domain D). Movement to the second, inflectional domain of the clause will
then be required to anchor this content to actual claims about particular referents. This assumption will avoid the "incomplete object" problem faced by
Parsons's (1990) account, because no "actual" object will be asserted to exist,
once we make this move. Just as event concepts get "instantiated" as particulars only in the inflectional domain of the clause, so too do nominal extended
projections only get actualized at the higher levels of the functional structure.
They then get related to the situational domain by abstract Case licensing.[7]

Much recent work on the syntax-semantics interface of nominal projections
has indeed proposed a zoning of the nominal extended projection much like the
proposal I will make here for the verbal extended projection, an idea already
present in Grimshaw 1990. In particular, see Zamparelli 2000, Borer 2005, and
Pfaff 2015 for arguments that the functional sequence of the nominal projection
contains zones for kind-level meanings or substances, followed by packag-
ing and counting mechanisms. As with verbal genericity, there has been a
debate about whether nominal genericity should be handled quantificationally
or whether there is a notion corresponding to the primitive "kind." Following Fine (2005, chap. 9), I am taking the position that, consistently, there is
a level of "deep genericity" within (both the verbal and) the nominal domain
that involves a type of essential noninstantiated description, and that this type
of deep generic interpretation—or "kind" interpretation, if you will—is distinct from the higher, more complex forms of "quantificational genericity." It
is captured by the fact that at the lowest level, we are trafficking in partial
nominal properties of actual referents.

2.3.4 The *-ing* Participle and Blocking

In what follows, I show how the denotation given above for *-ing* can carry over plausibly to the attributive uses of the *-ing* forms in English. This represents a simplification of the grammar that previous accounts do not attempt. It is a unification made possible by associating the *-ing* morpheme with the idea of Identifying States.

So far, the proposal is that the morpheme *-ing* in English is a function from D_μ to D_μ that has the denotation in (47), where the value for x is filled in by the movement of the highest argument to the specifer of the ingP.

(47) $\llcorner u_V\text{-}ing\lrcorner = \lambda x\lambda e[\text{State}(e) \wedge \text{ID-State}(e, \llcorner u_V\lrcorner) \wedge \text{HOLDER}(e) = x]$

Notice that there are some well-known things about the progressive that I have not built into this denotation. One is the restriction to dynamic events that the English progressive is famous for. An obvious way to build in this selectional requirement would be to make it a brute force presupposition on the nature of the P that *-ing* combines with. However, there is compelling evidence that the restriction to dynamic eventualities is a property of the progressive construction as a whole, not of the *-ing* participle per se. Even the most closely related form, the reduced relative or attributive participle in *-ing*, faces no ban on stative verb phrases as the input to *-ing*.

(48) a. A man is dancing in the corner.
　　　b. A man is eating an apple.
　　　c. *The wall is surrounding the castle.
　　　d. *The boy is fearing the dark.

(49) a. The man dancing in the corner is tall.
　　　b. The man eating an apple is tall.
　　　c. The wall surrounding the castle is high.
　　　d. The boy fearing the dark was the only one who could not get to sleep.

For this reason, I will not build a presupposition into the denotation of *-ing* itself. Instead, I will assume that the ban on (48c) and (48d) is due to competition for lexical insertion with the simple tensed forms in the case of stative verbs.[8]

The progressive is composed of the participle in *-ing* and the progressive auxiliary *be*. I will essentially follow Bjorkman's (2011) analysis in proposing that the *be* auxiliary is inserted as a dummy verb in order to host inflectional features whose exponence is required. Forming a participle in *-ing* does more than create a derived state-description; it also has syntactic effects. Specifically, I will assume that the output of the merger of *-ing* with a verbal root has no unvalued features for tense or aspect.[9] On the assumption that tense information needs to be expressed in English for sentential well-formedness, a dummy verb must be inserted.[10]

Recall that in the proposed system, an Evt head occupies the edge of the D_μ domain as shown in (50), introducing the utterance situation d and expressing the relation of deployment of u in conveying e.

(50)

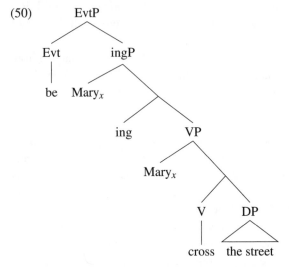

We can now account for the distribution of auxiliary *be* by saying that it spells out Evt in the absence of any other overt exponent. *Be* contains unvalued features and can host both aspectual and tense information. *Be* otherwise has no semantics.

To build the same phrase structure for a stative verb, we would build (51a) with the semantics in (51b).[11]

(51) a.

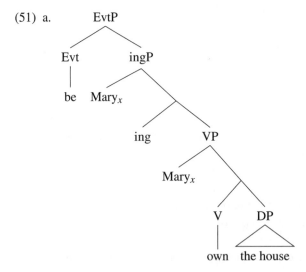

b. $\lambda e[\text{State}(e) \wedge \text{ID-State}(e, \llcorner \text{Mary own the house} \lrcorner) \wedge \text{HOLDER}(e) = \text{Mary}]$

Since we have assumed that a definitional property of states is that they are true at a moment, the existence of the Identifying State for a property entails the existence of the state, and vice versa. Thus, for states and states alone the two notions are mutually entailing. We can state this explicitly as an axiom of the proposed system, as in (52), although I suspect it can be derived by the fact that the lexical stative property is adduced by the very same sort of evidence that the Identifying-State requires, so that there could be no difference between the two.

(52) If $u_V \in D_\mu$ is a state semantically, then

$\llcorner u_V \lrcorner = \llcorner u_V\text{-ing} \lrcorner$

(i.e., The ID-State of s is just s)

It is only in the case of states that there is no difference between the state itself and the Identifying State. For more complex events, the identifying and inferential properties of the Identifying State are distinct from the conceptual properties of the whole extended eventuality it is related to (the latter expresses unfolding properties in time, while the former is static). This means that the semantics of the tree in (51) is strictly identical to the semantics that would be derived by (53b).

(53) a. Mary owns the house.

b. $\lambda e[\text{own-the-house}(e) \wedge \text{HOLDER}(e) = \text{Mary}]$

I will assume that this means that by some reasonable statement of semantic economy, the attachment of *-ing* is prohibited in precisely this case.

When we look at passive formation in chapter 3, we will see that the passive auxiliary *be* is the very same lexical item *be* that is inserted because of participle formation in the progressive. Thus, apparently it is the form that is inserted not just here, but in any head within the first phase that fails to have its own overt exponent. Insertion of the dummy verb *be* is therefore sensitive to the semantic zone of the clause. In particular, *be* is inserted in the first phase, and *do* is inserted for unfilled heads in the situational domain proper.

The simple denotation for *-ing* given in box 2.1 as an ingredient of the progressive can then be seen as the same input to attributive participle formation, provided that we allow it to be embedded under an abstraction operator, which I will call A* (to evoke the idea of adjectivalization). A* will abstract over the highest argument position in the event description it combines with to create a derived property of individuals. A core fact about the *-ing* participle is that it always modifies the argument that would end up as the subject of the corresponding active verb.[12] I capture this fact with two properties of the *-ing* lexical item. The first is that *-ing* combines with an already complete event description (i.e., one whose arguments are all already present). This is simply a matter of height of attachment. The second is that *-ing* can be selected by the property abstraction operator. I assume that nothing need be stipulated about A* except for the semantics of predicate abstraction and the restriction to states. In the denotation in (54), P stands in for the event description contributed by the nonprogessivized VP. The crucial point is that it is always the HOLDER of the progressivized event description that gets abstracted over in attributive participle formation in *-ing*—the position abstracted over is thus always the one most local to the A* head.

(54)   A*P $\lambda x \lambda e$[State(e) $\wedge$ ID-State(e, ⌊cross the street⌋)
                         $\wedge$ HOLDER(e) = x]

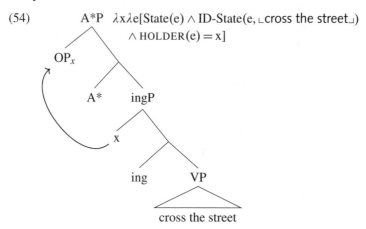

Finally, the participle in *-ing* is also found in nominalized uses. Here again, as expected, the ban against stative inputs is lifted, and the form is found in gerundive phrases with the external distribution of nominalized clauses. As in the attributive use, the external argument position is often missing, but not always (see (55a)). (I assume this will fall out from independent facts concerning Case/DP licensing in nontensed and nominalized environments; I will not make any proposals about the choice here.)

(55) a. John eating all the chocolates was a good thing.
     b. John's eating all the chocolates was a good thing.
     c. Eating chocolate is good for you.
     d. Eating chocolate all the way, I eventually reached the top of the mountain.
     e. The eating of chocolates is considered to be good for the health.
     f. John's eating of the chocolates was quick and messy.

This is not the place to discuss the syntax and semantics of nominalization. It would take us too far afield, and I do not have anything to add about the combinatorics that goes beyond the basic intuition in Abney 1987. (However, see Borer 2013 for a more recent discussion of the properties of nominalizing *-ing*.)

I do wish to point out, though, that the above proposal regarding the denotation of *-ing* is suitable for a range of nominalized uses because of its identity semantics. Moreover, the underspecified denotation I have given does not require any possible worlds or event partiality; rather, it is defined in terms of the notion of Identifying State. This means that the *-ing* participle bears an *identifying* relationship to the corresponding event and can therefore be used to name it. The *-en/ed* participle does not have nominalizing uses in English, although it does have adjectival, attributive ones. In addition, as we will see in chapter 3, the semantics for the *-en/ed* participle is more variable and does not involve any "identity" semantics. I therefore conclude tentatively that the notion of identification is at the heart of the meaning for *-ing* and that this makes it suitable for both nominalizing and progressive participial functions. Since the *-en/ed* participle does not have nominalized uses, I will not derive the nominalized versions of *-ing* by general mechanisms from participles. But I remain cautiously optimistic that the semantics of the Identifying State can be further input to a generalized nominalizing operation in English.

2.4   Conclusion

In summary, in this chapter I have argued that we get a better account of the *-ing* participle if we abandon explicitly intensional accounts and instead couch the analysis in terms of event concepts contributed by the deployment of lexical items that express partial event descriptions independent of time and place and by the construction of derived Identifying States.

An important point directly favoring this kind of account is that it has long been known that the progressive participle in *-ing* is one of the earliest pieces of morphology acquired by English-speaking children. It is acquired between the ages of 19 and 28 months, as early as the two-word stage, and appears *before* both irregular past tense (which in turn often appears before regular past inflection) and the copula (Brown 1973, Owens 2001). The *-ing* participle thus appears before any actual tense inflection or modal expression, and is immediately used correctly.[13] A fully modal and intensionalized analysis of the progressive would require us to believe that English-speaking children acquire a modalized meaning accurately before they are two years old, and always do so before they even have the ability to express tense or use modal auxiliaries. The pragmatic complexity of inferences connected to the setting up of modal bases and ordering sources is supposed to be something that children need some social and interactional maturity to develop. But standard accounts force us to assume that they master this pragmatic complexity even before they pass theory-of mind tests! The role of *-ing* in identifying and naming complex generalizations over events seems like a good candidate for the type of meanings necessary at the very earliest stages of language learning.

Another advantage of the present proposal is that it provides a unified denotation for the *-ing* participle as it is used in the progressive, the attributive participle, and a range of gerundive constructions. In each case, the participle is embedded within syntactic structure that adds to the distributional properties of the construction. In the case of the progressive, what is added is a dummy verb that is inserted to carry tense information, and the structure is built into a full proposition. In the case of the attributive participle, the *-ing* phrase is embedded under the abstraction operator A*. In the case of the various gerundive forms, I assume that the very same *-ing* phrase is built here as well, but embedded under an independent nominalizing head N* (also assumed to be null). The hope is that the different kinds of nominalizations and gerundives formed with *-ing* will fall out from the height at which the nominalization is attached. Given that the nominal functional sequence is intended to interleave with the verbal one, and given that nominal structure can extend into the second phase, a number of different possibilities arise. Pursuing this topic is clearly beyond the scope of the present monograph. However, the point about the denotation of *-ing* is that, as an Identifying State for the corresponding event property, it can be seen as an ingredient for these forms in addition to the verbal ones explicitly treated here.

As we have seen, the syntactic evidence from substitution, movement, and clefting shows that the *-ing* participle lies deep within the clause, before the first phase is complete. An account of the semantics of the progressive in terms of possible worlds does not dissolve the mystery of the imperfective paradox; at the same time, it forces us to build in modal meanings at the very lowest domain of the sentence. However, typological evidence from verbal morphology and inflection shows that modal and tense morphology reside high in the clause. The English progressive is low, and it is the first morpheme acquired by children, as early as the two-word stage, and before any other tense or modal inflection.

All the evidence converges on a simple primitive relationship between a verbal root and its productive *-ing* derivative. I have argued that the best way to think about this relationship is in terms of the notion of Identifying States.

3 The Passive and Its Participle

This chapter and the next deal with the auxiliary constructions in English that employ the participle in -*en*/*ed*, called either the "passive participle" or the "perfect participle" depending on whether it appears in the passive (1a,c) or the perfect (1b) construction. The participle in question is the same lexical item in that it is formally identical in both uses (and indeed in the attributive use as well (1d)), with no allomorphic variation.

(1) a. The cat was chased by the dog.
     b. The dog has chased the cat.
     c. The cat has been chased by the dog.
     d. The recently chased cat ...

   Much work on the passive participle has focused on the difference between the "adjectival" passive and the "verbal" passive (see Wasow 1977), and more recently on the difference between stative target state passives and stative resultant state passives (Kratzer 2000, Embick 2004). While early work explored the idea that adjectival passives are formed in the lexicon while verbal passives are built up constructionally in the syntax, more recent research has cast doubt on this idea as a way of explaining the different semantic and distributional properties of this form (Bruening 2014). Instead, in constructivist approaches such as Distributed Morphology (DM), it has become standard to analyze the difference in terms of different heights of attachment of the participial morphology in the syntactic tree (Anagnostopoulou 2003, Embick 2004). Whether one attempts to express them syntactically or lexically, there are a number of acknowledged differences of usage that need to be accounted for. The challenge lies in accounting for the differences while maintaining a common abstract core representation. To my knowledge, the assumption that there is an underlying unity to this participle has not so far extended to the use of the participle in the perfect.[1] However, the formal identity of the two participles is at least suggestive, and in this chapter I will propose an analysis that strives for a unified denotation, locating the differences in behavior in the structural size of the participle. I acknowledge here previous unpublished ideas by Michal Starke (CASTL seminars), who early on championed the idea that the *-en/ed* participle, up to and including the past tense form, is actually the same item spelling out successively different sizes of structure. This indeed is the view that I will build up to over the course of this chapter and the next. However, since I have been unable to discover any concrete proposal for the syntactic labels or denotations of all the heads involved in such spans, I have been unable to compare my implementation of this view with Starke's specfic proposal.[2] The chapter is organized as follows. In section 3.1, I will examine the stative predicative uses of the *-en/ed* participle. In section 3.2, I will analyze the eventive passive construction within the first phase, giving an interpretation of the participle that is unified with the stative version. I will also analyze the role of ingredients such as the *be* auxiliary and the Evt head, which are the same as in chapter 2. In section 3.3, I will treat the use of the passive participle as input to adjectivalization.

In chapter 4, I will attempt to analyze the English perfect, with the same participle as an ingredient. In general, I will seek a unified representation of the *-en/ed* participle, which is why I treat the passive and perfect constructions one after the other. My strategy will be to keep the meaning of the participle constant and use different heights of attachment and the different semantic properties of the zones to ground the known semantic differences. Later, I will argue that *have* is merged in the situational domain, which in turn will have important consequences for temporal modification and interpretation.

But before we get to the domain of situations, we need to look closely at the passive participle, which lies, as I will argue, in the lowest domain of D_μ, event concepts.

3.1   The Stative Participle in *-en/ed*

One crucial semantic distinction that has been noted between different uses of the passive participle[3] in predicative position is whether the resulting predication is stative or dynamic. I will start in this section by examining the stative participle that can be formed with *-en/ed* in English, then turn to the eventive passive in section 3.2.

An immediate complication is that a number of different types of stative participle have been claimed to exist. Embick (2004) calls these "resultative" vs. "stative" participles (although they are both actually stative, as he acknowledges). Kratzer (2000) distinguishes a "resultant state" vs. a "target state" passive participle. In fact, these two authors do not make precisely the same distinction with these labels, so we cannot simply choose our terminology here. In Embick's system, what is important in distinguishing the two classes is the presence or absence of "event implications": resultative stative participles have event implications, pure stative participles do not. In Kratzer's system, what is important is the relationship of the stative meaning to the meaning of the verb as a whole: target state participles denote a state that is already an internal component of the verbal denotation; resultant state participles denote a state that holds forever by virtue of the event in question having occurred, as in the distinction originally proposed by Parsons (1990) for the perfect. Each of these distinctions comes with its own set of diagnostics. In fact, as we will see, it is not the case that target state participles are the non-event-implicating participles and resultant state participles are the event-implicating participles. Rather, target state participles can be both event implicating and non–event implicating in the relevant sense, while resultant state participles are only event implicating.[4]

Since my focus here is on understanding the English system first and foremost, I will only secondarily make reference to other languages. The classification that I will propose for English will look slightly different from what would arise from an inspection of either Greek or German. I think this is inevitable because, as I will argue, the diagnostics will play out differently in different languages. This is because of the meanings of the individual morphemes in question and because of the properties of the English verb *be*. In addition, the notion of blocking will play out differently in different languages depending on the other forms available in the system.

3.1.1   Event Implications

Another reason why the present discussion will inevitably differ somewhat from the discussions in the literature so far is that I have proposed a rather different semantic ontology, one that has a profound effect on how we interpret the notion "event implications." Recall that I have argued that the lowest phase in the syntactic hierarchy consists of a domain where elements of D_μ, actual linguistic items, are concatenated—items that contribute to the conceptual content of the situation being asserted by the speaker. These meaning contributions are event properties that are abstractions/generalizations over space and time, and therefore are partial descriptions based purely on immediate sensory and cognitive classification/judgment. These are still in some sense "properties of events" and contain qualitatively different information from properties of objects or static relations, but the structures built up at this level do not yet entail the *instantiation* of any particular situation. In this context, then, we must rethink what we mean when we say that a form has "event implications" or not. First, let us consider the following diagnostic, proposed by Embick (2004).

(2) a.   The door was built open.
    b. *The door was built opened.

According to Embick 2004 and much subsequent work, the problem with (2b) is that the state of being "opened" simply cannot be true in the world unless there has been a prior event of "opening"; that is, being opened can't be one of the door's properties before anything has happened to it. In the case of English, the fact that -ed is often used for both event-implicating and non-event-implicating forms is potentially confusing, which is why the few cases where there is an underived adjective such as *open* to use as a clear, unambiguous point of comparison are useful for separating the readings. When there is no corresponding underived adjective to "block" the use of the participle, it does appear that a participle in -en/ed can be used to give the non-event-implicating reading.

(3) The door was built closed.

What is important to note, however, is that event implications are defined in the literature as "entailing the previous instantiation of an event particular," not as having conceptually eventive properties.

  But the diagnostics for "actual event implications" are actually not so clear. It has been claimed that temporal modifiers like *recently* diagnose the existence of a previous event because they explicitly locate the event in an immediately previous time interval. However, the test needs to be applied carefully because even adjectival statives like *open* can sometimes cooccur with such adverbials; in such a case, *recently* only asserts that the state held at some time in the recent past.

(4) a.   The recently opened door ...
    b.   The recently open door ...
         (Embick 2004, 357)

The existence of nontemporal modifiers that refer to other parts of an event description are even murkier in the context of this monograph. *By*-phrases, instrumentals, and manner adverbials could be thought of as diagnosing conceptual subparts of an eventive description, but do not in and of themselves require instantiation in space and time. It turns out that some of these are judged much better than others when they occur with stative participles. Regardless, Embick systematically argues for a distinction between stative participles with event implications (his resultative participles) and stative participles without event implications (the misleadingly named pure stative participles).

Embick's (2004) examples in (4) show the participle in attributive position. Embick assumes that the attributive position is a "pure stative" position, but in fact the situation is much more complicated since attributive participles seem to show a wider range of modificational possibilities in some languages than the "pure stative" assumption would suggest (see Lundqvist 2008 for some discussion).

Setting aside the attributive position since it is not our central concern here, we face the problem that it is quite difficult to test Embick's resultative participle because it is quite systematically degraded across the board in predicative position. In other words, once we put the participle in a stative context—say, following the present tense of the verb *be*—and add an event-implication-forcing adverb such as *recently* or *carelessly* (keeping the relevant reading in mind), the results are marginal at best. To my ear the examples in (5) are ungrammatical, and ten years of reading these examples in the literature hasn't improved them for me. In (5a), the stative context is triggered by the present tense of the verb *be*; in (5b), the stative context is the complement position of *turn out* (after Hallman 2009a); and (5c) illustrates the universal reading of the perfect. (5d) shows that the universal reading of the perfect is of course felicitous with the non-event-implicating version of *closed*.

(5) a. ?The door is recently/carelessly closed.
    b. ?The door turned out to be recently/carelessly closed.
    c. ?The door has been carelessly closed since Monday night.
    d. The door has been closed since Monday night.

It has been acknowledged in the literature that these examples are degraded in many cases, but the explanation given is that the resultative participle is degraded only because of the necessity of coercing activity verbs into having a salient result state in context—a kind of 'job done' reading. This indeed seems to be the case for German, as Kratzer (2000) reports. However, it is only plausible for English if we restrict ourselves to sentences with verbs like *hammer*. The examples in (5) with *closed* demonstrate that a verb with a perfectly respectable result state is still degraded in the stative resultative in English.

Kratzer (2000) distinguishes between resultant state participles and target state participles, but as Embick (2004) points out, the phrasal target state reading that she analyzes and gives a denotation for necessarily has event implications, since it requires existentially binding the Davidsonian event variable corresponding to the verb. It is only a pure adjectival reading that would correspond to the pure stative reading in Embick's terms. Kratzer's denotations for the adjective *cool* vs. the target state *cooled*, cited by Embick (2004, 361) are given in (6).

(6) a. *cool*: $\lambda x \lambda s[\text{cool}(x)(s)]$
    b. *cooled*: $\lambda x \lambda s \exists e[\text{cool}(x)(s) \wedge s = f_{target}(e)]$

Kratzer's (2000) resultant state passives, on the other hand, are the ones for which there is no readily available state within the verb's own denotation. Instead, the state that the participle denotes is the state that Parsons (1990) calls the "resultant state." Parson's definition is given in (7).

(7) *Resultant states*
    For every event e that culminates, there is a corresponding state that holds forever after. This is "the state of e's having culminated," which I call the "Resultant state of e," or "e's Rstate." If Mary eats lunch, then there is a state that holds forever after: The state of Mary's having eaten lunch. (Parsons 1990, 234)

Kratzer's diagnostic for distinguishing resultant states in this sense from target states and pure adjectives comes from German: namely, incompatibility with the adverb *immer noch* 'still'. Since the definition of resultant state means that the state persists forever after the event is over, trivially the adverb 'still' cannot meaningfully be applied to it.[5] The resultant state passives given by Kratzer (2000, 386) are shown in (8)–(11).

(8) Das Theorem ist (*immer noch) bewiesen.
     the theorem is (*still)   proven
     ? 'The theorem is (*still) proven.'

(9) Der Briefkasten ist (*immer noch) geleert.
     the mailbox   is (*still)   emptied
     ? 'The mailbox is (*still) emptied.'

(10) Die Gäste sind (*immer noch) begrüsst.
     the guests are (*still)   greeted
     ? 'The guests are (*still) greeted.'

(11) Die Töpfe sind (*immer noch) abgespült.
     the pots   are (*still)   washed.up
     ? 'The pots are (*still) washed up.'

Kratzer's semantics for the resultant state does not produce a property of events; rather, it produces a property of times directly. However, it is important to note that her semantics for both the target state and the resultant state requires actualization and has real event implications, since for her events are instantiated particulars. With respect to event implications, then, target state passives and resultant state passives are on a par. The only difference lies in the way in which the state is constructed.

Note that the semantics of the resultant state is claimed to be the same as the semantics we would find with the perfect in English (and German), and indeed it is inspired by Parsons's (1990) analysis of the English perfect. But the English "resultant state" construction cannot be built so easily along these lines, as shown by the fact that direct translations of the German sentences in (8)–(11) into English are ungrammatical/degraded, while they are completely natural using the perfect of the passive (*The mailbox has been emptied, The pots have been washed up*), as Parsons's system would predict.

In German, the resultant state passive in (12) and the perfect passive in (13) are strikingly similar in meaning.

(12) Das Theorem ist bewiesen.
   the theorem is proven
   'The theorem has been proven.'
   (Kratzer 2000, 387)

(13) Das Theorem ist bewiesen worden.
   the theorem is proven gotten
   'The theorem has been proven.'
   (Kratzer 2000, 387)

However, Kratzer (2000) claims there is a subtle difference between (12) and (13) in that the resultant state passive is compatible with a reflexive interpretation in principle (as can be seen by comparing a verb such as *waschen* 'wash' in the two constructions), while the perfect passive is not.

In German, the resultant state passive exhibits another surprising feature: namely, its complete incompatibility with statives and the requirement of coercion with activities.

(14) *Dieses Haus ist besessen.
   this house is owned
   'This house has been owned.'
   (Kratzer 2000, 389)

(15) ??Die Katze ist schon gestreichelt.
   the cat is already petted
   'The cat has already been petted.'
   (Kratzer 2000, 388)

In English, the perfect of the passive is entirely good with stative verbs, so the semantic constraints on building the perfect of the passive must be different for states in English. But we know already that the English and German perfect differ in the presence vs. absence of the universal perfect reading that arises in the case of states. On the other hand, a "resultant state" reading is also possible for states in English; there is nothing logically wrong with building that kind of reading from stative verbs as far as the semantics is concerned in the perfect, and no coercion seems to be required. So it is *still* surprising that the "resultant state" passive is degraded in German for states. Further, according to Kratzer (2000), (15) is quite bizarre when uttered out of the blue, even with activities, and needs to have a "job done" kind of context explicitly imposed on it to be acceptable. Once again, the perfect of the passive in English is entirely good and there is no problem with building a resultant state semantics from an activity verb in principle (this in fact was the motivation behind Parsons's (1998) analysis in the first place since English activity verbs in the perfect give classic resultant state readings, with activity verbs, with no coercion required).[6]

I conclude that the semantics that Kratzer (2000) gives for the resultant state passive in German (exemplified in (12)) is actually too weak.

(16) *Kratzer's (2000) semantics for resultant state participles*
    Stem + object: $\lambda e[\text{prove(the theorem)}(e)]$
    Stativizer: $\lambda P \lambda t \exists e[P(e) \wedge \tau(e) < t]$
    Output: $\lambda t \exists e[\text{prove(the theorem)}(e) \wedge \tau(e) < t]$

This denotation is too weak by itself because it generates a well-formed output as long as the run-time of the event, given by $\tau(e)$, has some final moment. It is precisely what we need for resultant state readings of the perfect in English, but it predicts that *all* eventualities should be input to it without any problem or coercion, just as long as the activity has terminated or the state in question has ceased to hold, contrary to fact.

By contrast, the target state passive, the one that is compatible with *immer noch* 'still', really does have a strong constraint imposed on it. For such passives to be formed, the verb in question must contain a result state in its denotation. Kratzer's (2000) diagnostic for this is that a 'for-'phrase is felicitous as a measure of the duration of that caused state. Kratzer argues that it is precisely the verbs that consist of an activity portion and a final state that form good target state passives with *immer noch*. It is this final state that ends up being the denotation of the formed-up participle.

Kratzer herself argues against expressing this decomposition in the syntax, because she perceives a mismatch between morphological constituency and the results of the tests diagnosing the existence of a target state. I will depart from her conclusion (instead taking a line more similar to the DM approach) and assume syntactic decomposition of these verbs into ProcP (activity portion) and ResP (caused final state), on the basis of the linguistic tests, regardless of morphological makeup.[7]

If we consider the denotation Kratzer assumes for the target state verb *auf-pumpen* 'pump up', we see that it contains the representation of a caused final state.

(17) *das Boot aufpumpen* 'pump up the boat'
     λsλe[pump(e) ∧ event(e) ∧ inflated(the-boat)(s) ∧ cause(s)(e)]

Following the general theory of decompositions proposed in Ramchand 2008, I will represent the existence of a caused internal state as a ResP embedded under Proc. Thus, the tree structure licensed by a verb that gives rise to a target state participle looks like (18).

(18)

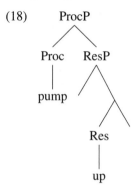

According to Kratzer's semantics, the output of the stativizer *-en/ed* is a predicate of states, exactly the one that is inside the verb's complex event semantics. The external event variable (the process variable in my terms) is existentially bound.

(19) Stativizer: λRλs∃e R(s)(e)
     Output: λs∃e[pump(e) ∧ event(e) ∧ inflated(the-boat)(s) ∧ cause(s)(e)]

So the participle morphology in Kratzer's system does not do very much work except to existentially bind the Davidsonian event and to license the absence of verbal inflection. My own analysis will be very similar to this idea, but without any actual existential binding of event variables. I implement my version by associating the participial form with a *subportion* of the phrase structure potentially determined by the verb. When the participle is syntactically truncated in this way, the element of D_μ so formed has a reduced conceptual contribution.

3.1.2   An Implementation in Terms of Reduced Spans
Since the implementation of spell-out in terms of spanning is somewhat non-standard, I begin by emphasizing the intuition behind it. As I proposed in Ramchand 2008, the lexical entry of a particular verb contains specific

information about the subevents it denotes. In fact, in the implementation proposed here, a lexical item has a syntactic span as one component of its identity, and complex elements of D_μ are built up by merging those syntactic contributions.[8]

For concreteness, let us look at the verb *destroy*. This verb has the syntactic representation <Init, Proc, Res> and the semantic contribution shown in (20).

(20) $[\![\text{destroy}]\!] = <\text{destroy}, <\textbf{Init, Proc, Res}>, \lambda e[\text{destroy}(e)]>$

Further, if we subscribe to the decompositional approach proposed in chapter 1, needed here to account for the constraints on target state formation, then we must also decompose the semantic part of representation (20) into the relevant subevents, as in (21).

(21) $[\![\text{destroy}]\!] = <\text{destroy}, <\textbf{Init, Proc, Res}>, \lambda e\lambda e_1\lambda e_2\lambda e_3[e = e_1 \rightarrow$
       $[e_2 \rightarrow e_3 \wedge \text{destroy}_{init}(e_1) \wedge \text{destroy}_{proc}(e_2) \wedge \text{destroy}_{res}(e_3)]]>$

In other words, if we have an element in D_μ that is syntactically specified with these three subeventual category heads, then the item in question provides conceptual content to each of the subevents in the decomposition. Recall that the central proposal for the event concept domain is that these conceptual properties are sensory and cognitive generalizations over experience. The natural hypothesis is that these particular event properties are those that can be ascribed on the basis of immediate and direct observation. So, I can look at the Lego installation my son has been working on and characterize it as a "destroyed city" on the basis of its visual aspect and my background knowledge of the world. And I can do this even if I haven't seen it being destroyed. It also may be the case that my son built it that way—that is, he built it "destroyed", as it were. That is the joy of Lego and the joy of participle use. It is crucially relevant that I call it a "destroyed city" and not a "flattened city" or a "bombed city" because *flatten* and *bomb* present subtly different aspects. Basically, the verb *destroy* contains information about what the result subeventual state should look like, and I exploit that when deploying it to characterize an object in my visual field. Verbs that have Res in their lexical specification have decomposed conceptual content, one crucial component of which characterizes the final state arising from the event.

We do not require a previous destroying to deploy the target participle *destroyed*, but it is still eventive in the sense that it makes reference to our conceptual knowledge of destruction events in characterizing that final state. It does not help either to try to express this intuition in terms of some kind of intensional calculation over inertial or prototypical worlds. The fact that human beings use result participles without needing a preceding event particular to support them is evidence that this use is fed by a complex, learned, but essentially primitive judgment. Sensory/Cognitive generalization as an abstraction over the space-time reality of experience is the whole basis for the reusability and efficiency of language.

So, the idea is simply that the participle in *-en/ed* is the realization of a *subpart* of the structure listed in a verb's specification. Instead of invoking existential binding of event variables, we simply drop the nonexpressed elements of the syntactic-semantic representation. Thus, in the case of *destroy*, the formation of the target state participle *destroyed* would give rise to a derived element of D_μ, which denotes just a simple state.

(22) $[\![\text{destroyed}]\!] = \; <\text{destroyed}, <\mathbf{Res}>, \lambda e[\text{destroy}_{res}(e)]>$

The subpart notion corresponds to the Kratzerian intuition that *-en/ed* existentially binds off event variables and licenses the absence of verbal inflection. In spell-out terms, this certainly requires the participial form to realize a structure that lacks whatever syntactic head it is that hosts the agreement information for tense and subject phi-features in the normal case. But in addition, the claim throughout this chapter will be that the participial form is defined negatively, as the form that is any proper subpart of the verbal root within the first phase. It will therefore be able to spell out chunks of various sizes, as long as the subset property is met.

Recall that the decompositional system for the D_μ domain also includes an Evt head within the first phase, as discussed in chapters 1 and 2. The Evt head is the locus of the introduction of the utterance event and the deployment operator; otherwise, it is most similar to the Voice head assumed by many other researchers on argument structure, since it is also the locus of the external argument. I will assume following original proposals in Pylkkänen 1999 (and against the assumptions made in Ramchand 2008) that the Init head introduces the causation subevent but not an external argument, while Evt introduces the external argument when it exists.

In her work on Hiaki, Harley (2013) shows convincingly that whatever morpheme expresses causation in the verbal stem must be hierarchically lower than the head that introduces the external argument. Within her framework, she concludes that Voice and Cause/little v must be distinct, and that Voice embeds little v. Here, I conclude essentially the same thing, with the difference that Evt, the projection that hosts the external argument, should have a label more abstract than Voice, since the progressive is embedded within it (as argued in chapter 2).

As in Ramchand 2008, I will assume that the Evt category feature of a particular lexical item can be specified as being either raising or not (i.e., specified for internal or external Merge). This will have different effects corresponding to the different "flavors" of Voice proposed in the literature.

This system of event decomposition, as it applies to the first phase, is shown schematically in tree (23).

(23)   EvtP ⇐ Locus of external argument

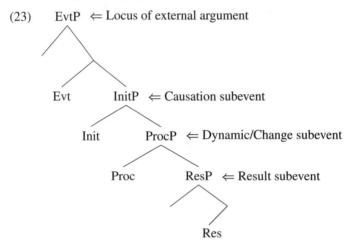

Evt   InitP ⇐ Causation subevent

Init   ProcP ⇐ Dynamic/Change subevent

Proc   ResP ⇐ Result subevent

Res

The Ramchand 2008 classification of verb types in terms of event structure then predicts the entries for the different verb types shown in (24). Raising heads—that is, those stipulated to be filled by internal Merge—are subscripted with i. The argument introduced in the specifier of Init in Ramchand 2008 is now introduced in the specifier of Evt. Transitive verbs are a heterogenous class from an event structure point of view, depending on whether Res is present or not.

(24) a. *Unaccusative*
        <Evt_i, $Proc_i$, Res>
     b. *Unergative*
        <Evt_i, Init, Proc>
     c. *Transitive*
        <Evt, Init, Proc>
     d. *Transitive(result)*
        <Evt, Init, $Proc_i$, Res>

Under the spanning view of lexical Merge within the lowest zone, the verbal lexical entry is specified for a span of category features that it provides the lexical content for, and it can be merged in the first phase to create complex symbolic forms. We first need to be specific about the entry for the tensed verbal form, which I will assume has a different category bundle than the participle in *-en/ed*. Specifically, even though the tensed main verb in English stays low by all the usual diagnostics, it does in fact inflect for both tense and agreement, properties of the higher situational domain. I will assume therefore that the verbal entries for tensed roots contain Asp and T features.[9] At any rate, the tensed verb in English must be allowed to span all the way up to Asp (via the phase edge Evt). I will use *Asp* as a general category label for all syntactic heads within the situational domain, and it will be my name for the domain in which temporal and locational information is added to the event-conceptual description. Thus, the entries for the tensed verbs in English look as shown in (25). Each of (25a–c) actually represents a linked cluster of entries corresponding to the different values of the tense and agreement information, unified under the following categorial specifications.

(25) a. *Unaccusative (tensed)*
    $<$Asp, Evt$_i$, Proc$_i$, Res$>$
   b. *Unergative (tensed)*
    $<$Asp, Evt$_i$, Init, Proc$>$
   c. *Transitive (tensed)*
    $<$Asp, Evt, Init, Proc$>$

Now the idea is that the participial form for a particular root will be the form that spells out any verbal span that does not contain the Asp feature. In other words, the participial form is any non-tense-information-carrying contiguous *subset* of the root's features.

(26) a. *Unaccusative (-en/ed participle)*
    $<$((Evt$_i$), Proc$_i$), Res$>$
   b. *Unergative (-en/ed participle)*
    $<$((Evt$_i$), Init), Proc$>$
   c. *Transitive (-en/ed participle)*
    $<$((Evt), Init), Proc$>$

Further, since in this system category features correspond to the existence of particular subevents and arguments in the semantic denotation, we can state an interpretation rule for the case where a subset of syntactic event structure is deployed. Namely, in such cases, the corresponding conceptual characterization is radically absent from the denotation. This means that when existential closure kicks in at the edge of the first phase, no subevents that have been "reduced" in this way are entailed to exist.

Thus, for *The stick is broken*, the proposed implementation of the generation of the stative passive participle in *-en/ed* gives the interpreted tree in (27).

(27)

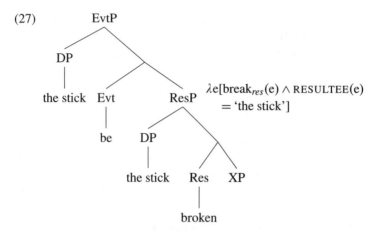

λe[break$_{res}$(e) $\wedge$ RESULTEE(e)
= 'the stick']

Unlike Kratzer's (2000) analysis of the target state, the implementation in terms of reduced elements of D_μ does not have event implications in the sense of requiring an actual situational instantiation of the relevant event. This is in fact the derivation of pure states using -*en/ed*, without event implications (in Embick's (2004) sense). While such forms do not require a previous actual event instantiation, they do allow some modification by low adverbs, *if* those adverbs can felicitously modify the result state in question.[10]

(28) a. The door was built closed.
    b. Her hair is still sloppily combed.
    c. She is still well dressed.

Even though these forms do not have event implications in Embick's (2004) sense, they *are* crucially derived from verbal meanings and their truth conditions depend on the interpretation of the internally complex event that is named by the verb. To this extent, the denotation of the pure stative participle *closed* is different in my analysis from the denotation of a simple adjective such as *open* or *empty*, which does not have an event-dependent meaning. This is because the system I have been building incorporates two different versions of the notion of event implications. The first requires an actual event particular (what I have been calling a "situation") to be instantiated in the world. The second only requires the existence of event concepts as encoded by particular elements of D_μ. Note that the verbal item and its participle in -*en/ed* are part of the same paradigm of forms. My analysis of these -*en/ed* forms differs crucially from my analysis of -*ing*. The suffix -*ing* is a lexical item on its own, and a member of D_μ. By contrast, in the -*en/ed* participle the ending itself does not have an independent status as a member of D_μ; rather, it is a morphological part of, and systematically and productively related to, a bare verb member of D_μ. This difference correlates with the fact that the actual form of *-en/ed* participles can be idiosyncratic and potentially subject to allomorphy, while the *-ing* forms of verbs are completely regular.

Because the participle *closed* and the verb *close* are linked to the same lexical item, the meaning relationship between them is in fact not arbitrary, but systematic and productive. They are connected because they both form part of an event description that has a particular label for the English language user. The recognition of a state as being "closed" is closely tied to the speaker's understanding of what a "closing event" looks like and what kind of state the relevant object must end up in. In elucidating the truth conditions of the derived adjective *closed*, we need to make reference to the idea of closing events: the closing event is primary, and the idea of a "closed" final state is parasitic on it. It simply would not do for *closed* to somehow come to mean 'flat', or for *closed* to be used of objects that do not in principle have some way of being opened and closed.[11] Moreover, since stative participles of this kind are formed productively all the time, their meanings must be productively derivable from the meaning of the caused-state verbs they are based on, and we must be able to derive them constructionally since particles and certain final-state-modifying adverbs can help to license and identify result states in English. We need to be able to express the relationship between the event description and the result state—*even though we do not require that an actual situation have occurred* in order to assert the existence of the result state. So the derivation here is both constructional and productive, but also in some sense lexical since it creates derived members of D_μ.

With regard to intensionality, we are in precisely the same situation that we were in with regard to the progressive, where we needed to be able to assert the existence of an in-progress state without necessarily committing ourselves to the instantiation of the event essence that it was identifying. This kind of "pseudointensionality" is the hallmark of the conceptual domain, which traffics in abstractions of event properties and where these are manipulated before the existential closure of the event variable that is being built up. We need to be able to relate meanings systematically at the level of event concepts and primitive partial descriptions, without committing ourselves to the actual existence of those events (whether in this world or in possible worlds).

Crucially, a conceptual representation dependent on a verbal root is *not* appropriate for underived adjectives such as *open* and *empty*, which I assume have their own truth conditions independent of verbal meanings, just like other lexical adjectives. However, it may be that adjectives like *open* and *empty* are the source of the corresponding verbs (here, of course, *open* and *empty*) and that *their* semantics is at the core of the verbal meaning, with only underspecified process and initiation components. Furthermore, their existence could be seen to directly block the use of the *-en/ed* participle to express the result state meaning.

The other type of participial adjective that has been cited as not having event implications is exemplified by *obstructed* in (29).

(29) The blood vessel was obstructed.

In Kratzer's (2000) system, this is because the participle ending attaches to a verb that has a stative interpretation in the first place, making dynamic event implications go away. This seems correct. But the same reasoning does not extend to the pure state participles formed from potentially dynamic verbs like *close*. These do not have necessary situational implications.

(30) The box is still closed. It was made that way, and no one has tried to open it yet.

In my proposal, all of the pure state participles that are formed with *-en/ed* in English and that are compatible with *still* are formed by spelling out the ResP portion of the verbal meaning. They do not have any event implications in the sense of requiring an actualized situational instantiation, but they are consistent with such actualization. Unlike the denotation of the *-ing* suffix (see chapter 2), the denotation of the *-en/ed* suffix does not take the root meaning as its argument. The denotation of the *-en/ed* participle is just a property of states, when it projects only the stative part of the verbal root's denotation. Verbs with Res in their lexical meaning give rise to *-en/ed* forms that are *just* a result stative projection. Verbs without Res in their lexical meaning cannot form such "target state" participles.

Such participle uses are tricky for speakers to judge, because the state is being described on its own, but the use of the participle means that it is the kind of state that typically arises from a certain kind of event. I assume that this imposes certain pragmatic constraints on the use of the stative participial construction. It seems that low adverbials often improve the use of these constructions, for some verbs, especially when the result in question is not visible and evident. Discussion of these factors is beyond the scope of this monograph, however.

What then of Kratzer's (2000) resultant state readings, or the resultative passive stative pointed out by Embick (2004)? First of all, as should be clear from the previous discussion, I think that the resultant state passive as described by Kratzer simply does not exist in English. Consider the German sentence in (31).

(31) Das Gebäude ist geräumt.
      the building is evacuated
      'The building is evacuated./The building has been evacuated.'

Kratzer carefully describes the two different readings that exist in German. As a target state passive, (31) means that there is currently no one in the building. As a resultant state passive, it just means that someone has evacuated the tenants from the building, but they might now have moved in again. As far as I can tell, the latter meaning is absent from the English sentence *The building is evacuated*. The resultant state reading that Kratzer refers to is simply not one that emerges in a stative construction with *be* and an *-en/ed* participle for any verb in English.[12] In English, this meaning is expressed by means of the perfect of the passive.

On the other hand, it is true that activity verbs with *be* do get some sort of stative interpretation in sentences like (32b–c), although the sentences are judged marginal.

(32) a. ?The doors are all opened now.
      b. ?The metal is hammered.
      c. ?The dogs are chased.

These forms are bad precisely because only a target state derivation is possible for this construction. If a resultant state reading were possible as input to the *be* auxiliary, then (32b–c) should be *as grammatical as the corresponding perfects*, with the same meaning for the participle. But they are not as good as perfects, and they do require coercion. The reason is that in order to get a stative interpretation, the participle must express a stative subcomponent of the verb's entry. If the verb does not have a stative subcomponent, as is the case by hypothesis with activity predicates, then the stative participle construction will be bad. The construction can be saved by coercion, but what is coerced is the existence of a *contextually available result*, where getting the object acted on in this way is an explicit goal of the situation. Specifically, the object must be interpreted as achieving a special new status by virtue of having been "hammered" or "chased." This is a much more special kind of situation than the resultant state semantics of the perfect, which is very neutral and requires no special effect on the object. The event simply must be *over* for the perfect to be good (as far as the object is concerned, at least). I therefore contend that what is going on with (32b–c), to the extent that they are good, is that their verbs are being coerced into the structure in (27) with a contextually available ResP within the event description. In many cases, in order to build this contextual result we rely on contingent facts about the actual instantiated situation (whose existence is compatible with the derivation in (27) although not required by it). Thus, in many cases the contextual requirements of the coercion give rise to true actualized situation implications. But the structure is the very same as in the pure state participle derivation. The existence of the extra implications that arise from the process of the contextual coercion, and the fact that true resultant state passives are probably good in some Germanic languages, is what is responsible for the illusion that we have two different constructions in English. In fact, Alexiadou and Anagnostopoulou (2008) reach a similar conclusion for Greek at the end of their paper, finding it no longer possible to structurally distinguish between target states and resultant states (in Kratzer's sense). This is because the nature of the state that must be inferred is actually independent of the structure in their analysis. Rather, the way in which the ResP must be construed is sensitive to the nature of the verb that is being participialized. The same is true of my analysis here. So instead of resultant state passive statives *and* target state passive statives, we have *just* target state passive statives, but depending on the verb, coercion is either required or not. The situation is summarized in (33).

(33) *Participles in* -en/ed
   Stative participles are always the expression of ResP in a phrase structure.
   i. 'Target' state: Verb has Res in its lexical specification.
   ii. 'Resultant' state: Verb has no Res. ResP is coerced and added constructionally.

Neither of these two versions of the target state stative has genuine situational entailments in terms of actual event particulars, but contextual coercion gives rise to situational implications in the case of activity verbs.

Now, the standard way of implementing the presence or absence of event implications in DM is to include a little v categorizing head in the former case and leave it out in the latter. (In Embick's (2004) system, the participial morphology is merged as the category Asp.) However, as we have seen and as (34) summarizes, at least two different notions are conflated in the idea of having or not having event implications, and the diagnostics originally laid out by Embick do not all diagnose the same thing.

(34) a. *Event actuality implications*
      An event of the type named by the verb *must have actually occurred* for the state ascription to be true.
   b. *Conceptual event implications*
      An event of the type named by the verb *is the type that has such a state type as its result.*

Pure stative participial passives have conceptual event implications and can be modified by low adverbials that can be construed as result state modification; in some cases, they even make the result phrase more salient and improve the stative passive interpretations. Pure underived adjectives cannot be modified by eventive adverbials in the same way, and they are not parasitic on event concepts for their truth conditions. On the other hand, event actuality implications arise in a straightforward way for the English perfect (as we will see in chapter 4) and possibly for some statives in German using *sein* 'be'. They also arise from the coercive effects of putting non-ResP verbs in certain kinds of contexts, but this is a contingent fact related to those particular coercions and does not arise from the structure itself.

3.2   The Eventive Passive

3.2.1   Core Properties

We now move to the eventive passive, one of the most common auxiliary constructions in English, which utilizes the same participial form as the stative constructions discussed above. In constructing an adequate analysis of the passive in the framework I am proposing, a number of known facts and properties should be accounted for.

First of all, and most obviously, when a verb is passivized, the agent is no longer expressed as an argument and the object is promoted to the eventual subject position. However, the external argument is semantically present in some way and can control into purpose clauses.

(35)   a. John ate the apple.
       b. The apple was eaten (by John).
       c. The apple was eaten to make a point.

Because of these basic facts, the passive voice has been treated as involving existential closure over the external argument position. In some cases, the *-en/ed* ending has been considered to be the existentially bound external argument (Baker, Johnson, and Roberts 1989).

Second, when the eventive passive applies to a verb, it does not change the eventive vs. stative character of that verb: dynamic eventualities remain dynamic (36), and stative eventualities remain stative (37).

(36)   a.   John ate the apple in 30 seconds flat.
       b.   The apple was eaten by John in 30 seconds flat.
       c.   *John turned out to eat the apple in 30 seconds flat.
       d.   *The apple turned out to be eaten in 30 seconds flat.

(37) a. John owns that house.
    b. That house is owned by John.
    c. John turned out to own that house.
    d. That house turned out to be owned by John.

In English, passivization is restricted to transitive verbs, which has led to the Government-Binding characterization of its function as the removal of the ability of a verb to assign accusative Case (Chomsky 1981).

(38) a. The apple was eaten.
    b. *The leaves were fallen./*There was fallen some leaves.
    c. *The train was arrived./*There was arrived a train.
    d. *The man was danced./*There was danced a man.

However, in other Germanic languages, notably Norwegian, unergatives can also be passivized (Åfarli 1989, 1992), giving rise to the so-called impersonal passive construction seen in (39)–(41) (from Åfarli 1989, 101). This indicates that the agent-suppressing function is probably more definitional of the passive construction than accusative case suppression. In fact, accusative Case seems to be preserved optionally in the impersonal passive construction in Norwegian, as (41) illustrates.

(39) Det vart sunge.
    it   was sing.PPL
    'There was singing.'

(40) Det vart gestikulert.
    it   was gesticulate.PPL
    'There was gesticulating.'

(41) Det vart sett   ein mann.
    it   was see.PPL a   man
    '*There was seen a man.'

Even in Norwegian, though, unaccusatives do not passivize.

(42) *Det vart falle   eit blad.
    it   was fall.PPL a   leaf
    '*A leaf was fallen.'

In all the Germanic languages, the passive participle, when used in attributive position, modifies the *internal* argument of the verb (see (43)). This is in stark opposition to the *-ing* participle analyzed in chapter 2, which modifies the thing that would have been the subject of the simple verb.

(43) a. John ate the apple.
    b. The half-eaten apple ...

   c. John ate.
   d. *The half-eaten man …(meaning 'John had half-finished eating')
   e. John danced.
   f. *The well-danced man …

Finally, the data from existential constructions and clefting discussed in chapter 2, are relevant here. By those diagnostics, the participle in the eventive passive sits squarely inside the lowest event concept domain, before event closure: (i) it is lower than the base-generated subject position (44a); (ii) it can be clefted (44b); (iii) the eventive participle phrase cannot be replaced by British English *do*.

(44) a. There were two men arrested at the party.
     b. I thought Mary should have been scolded, and indeed scolded she was.
     c. *Mary was arrested, and John was done too.

To summarize, the properties we must account for are listed in (45).

(45) *Central properties of the passive*
     a. Semantically, the external argument is present but existentially bound.
     b. Verbal aktionsart is preserved.
     c. The participle modifies only the internal argument.
     d. The passive VP lies within the lowest event domain of the clause.
     e. Passive does not occur with unaccusatives in Germanic, or with intransitives more generally in English.

To this list, we can add two more desiderata. The first is that the analysis of the -*en/ed* participle in section 3.1 should be unified with the one that builds the eventive passive. The second is that the *be* auxiliary found with the eventive passive should be unified with the one found in the progressive construction— namely, as a noncontentful element that is inserted in the first phase purely to host inflectional features.

I propose that the analysis of the eventive passive that fulfills these requirements involves the expression of a slightly larger subtree than the one expressed in the stative participle by the -*en/ed* form. In this case, however, the only "leftover" feature is the one corresponding to the generation of the external argument, namely, Evt. I will assume that the existence of the Init (causing) projection implicates the existence of some sort of "agent" for the passive event, but because the verb does not actually project the Evt head that will allow external Merge of a DP fulfilling that role, the external argument gets bound by default existential closure. Instead, an independent Evt head hosting *be* must be merged, its specifier being filled by internal Merge from the direct object position. This is shown in tree (46) for *The man was chased* (for simplicity, the denotation given for EvtP abstracts away from the introduction of the utterance situation).

(46) *Building the eventive passive*

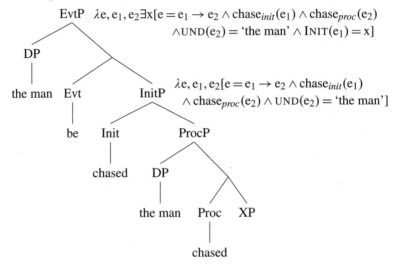

EvtP $\lambda e, e_1, e_2 \exists x [e = e_1 \to e_2 \wedge \text{chase}_{init}(e_1) \wedge \text{chase}_{proc}(e_2)$
$\wedge \text{UND}(e_2) = \text{'the man'} \wedge \text{INIT}(e_1) = x]$

DP

the man   Evt   InitP $\lambda e, e_1, e_2 [e = e_1 \to e_2 \wedge \text{chase}_{init}(e_1)$
$\wedge \text{chase}_{proc}(e_2) \wedge \text{UND}(e_2) = \text{'the man'}]$

be   Init   ProcP

chased   DP

the man   Proc   XP

chased

This derivation immediately accounts for properties (45a–d). The denotation for the *-en/ed* morpheme carried over from section 3.1 is the equivalent, in my system, of the existential binding of content corresponding to unmatched features in the participle's denotation. Since the *-en/ed* participle is just an expression of the verbal span up to InitP, it does not affect the aktionsart properties of the verb it is built from. The fact that the only argument that is actually merged at this point is the internal argument means that whatever adjectivalization head is subsequently merged, the argument abstracted over will be the internal one.

Next, I will show how to account for (45e), the restriction against intransitives and particularly unaccusatives.

3.2.2 Blocking

Because Norwegian allows passivization of unergatives but not unaccusatives, there must be two different reasons for the prohibition in English against passivization of these two types of intransitive verbs.

First, consider unergative verbs such as *dance* in English. In principle, nothing should prevent *danced* from spelling out InitP here too, as proposed above. However, under the assumption that the lone argument of *dance* is base-generated as a specifier of EvtP, this argument will be existentially bound off at the event domain and effectively removed from the further syntax, leaving no argument at all to raise to subject position. As is well known, English sentences require an overt subject (47a). However, expletive insertion also fails in these cases (47b).

(47) a. *Was danced.
      b. *It was danced./*There was danced.

While I have no deep explanation for this fact, any explanation needs to be English-specific, since the facts differ in Norwegian. I will assume that in addition to the overt subject requirement, English has an EPP requirement (in the descriptive sense) at the level of the first phase. In the present system, this means essentially that there must be an overt DP in Spec,EvtP. In other words, EvtP requires an overt topic argument in English. By hypothesis, expletives are not available in the event domain, so the requirement amounts to the constraint that in English, at least one event structure argument must be available to construct a grammatical proposition.

On the other hand, the failure of unaccusatives to passivize must have a different sort of explanation. Consider what would happen if the *-en/ed* participle expressed the ProcP determined by an unaccusative verb such as *arrive*.

(48) *Eventive passive of an unaccusative*

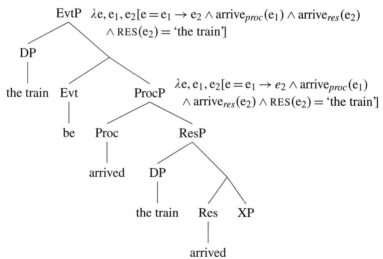

Given the discussion so far, this should in principle be a fine contribution for the participle; moreover, an argument would be available in Spec,EvtP. There would simply be no extra external argument that would undergo existential binding. Why, then, is the resulting passive construction ungrammatical (49a), although the corresponding stative passive is marginally acceptable (49b)?

(49) a. *The train was arrived.
     b. ?The train is newly arrived at the station.

One might naturally think that the problem is a kind of prohibition against vacuous quantification. However, I think we must reject this possibility. I say this because structure (48) is perfectly legitimate as the input to adjectivalization. In that case, the effect of participle formation is not vacuous, presumably because it suspends the continuation of the verb to tense inflection and anchoring, and makes adjectivalization possible.

(50) The recently arrived train ...

Indeed, we have already seen something similar in the internal distribution of the -*ing* participle, which was different in predicative and attributive positions. Having said that, the data are tricky to interpret in English because many verbs that qualify as unaccusative actually undergo the labile causative alternation. There are not many unaccusative verbs that do not, and this makes it hard to be sure that there isn't something independently going wrong with eventive passivization for these verbs. In the case of unaccusative *melt*, the grammaticality of (51a) is presumably built on the transitive alternant of the verb,[13] as is the successful attributive modification in (51b) (likewise for *break*).

(51) a. The chocolate was melted over the fire.
     b. The melted chocolate dripped over the car seat.

But does (51b) also have an unaccusative source? The eventive passive in (51a) certainly seems to force the existence of an (existentially quantified) agent, but what about the attributive modification in (51b)? My intuition here and the judgments of other English speakers I have consulted indicate that the attributive participle can indeed have an unaccusative/inchoative interpretation.

We can look to another, closely related language to complete the argument about where the source of the ungrammaticality should be located. Like English and Norwegian, Swedish does not form eventive passives from unaccusative verbs. However, Lundqvist (2008) shows that in Swedish, the passive participle of an unaccusative is perfectly good in attributive position (where no labile alternation occurs to create ambiguity); witness the grammatical passive formed from the transitive version of 'sink', in (52) and the ungrammatical passive based on the unaccusative in (53). Finally, the unaccusative passive participle is perfectly good in attributive position (54), and has an eventive interpretation, as diagnosed here by the fact that it is ungrammatical with *fortfarande* 'still'.

(52) Skeppen blev sänkta.
   ship.DEF was sink*tr*.PPL
   'The ship was sunk.'

(53) *Skeppen blev sjunkna.
   ship.DEF was sink*intr*.PPL
   'The ship was sunk.'

(54) Den (*fortfarande) sjunkna ubåten ...
   the (*still)   sink.PPL submarine.DEF
   'The (*still) sunken submarine ...'

This means that there is nothing in principle wrong with a reduction from <Evt, Proc, Res> to <Proc, Res>. In other words, well-formedness does not require that there be an external argument to be existentially bound off; the passive is not somehow contributing an existential quantifier that will give rise to ill-formedness if its binding effects are vacuous. Instead, the existential binding of the external argument found in eventive passives must be some sort of default rule that kicks in when appropriate.

A more interesting account for the unavailability of eventive passives of unaccusative verbs emerges if we compare the final passive verb phrase in (48) with the simple tensed unaccusative in (55).

(55) *Simple unaccusative*

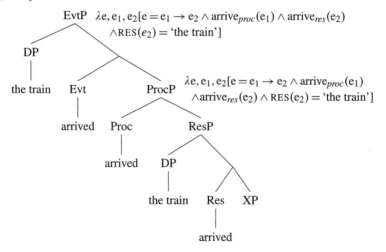

94

Chapter 3

This is identical to the tree proposed for the participial structure in terms of both phrase structure and semantic interpretation. The only difference is that in (55) the structure is spelled out with one lexical item, whereas in (48) it is spelled out by the unaccusative participle plus *be*.

Lundquist (2008) gives a phrasal blocking account for the same phenomenon in Swedish, adding evidence from Hindi presented by Bhatt (2008). Hindi has a productive construction by which a simple underived adjective combines with the light verb *ho* 'become' or the light verb *kar* 'do' to give an intransitive or transitive dynamic predication, respectively. (56) and (57) (cited from Bhatt 2008 in Lundquist 2008, 189–190) illustrate with the adjective *gillaa* 'wet', (showing *-e* in the masculine plural).

(56) kapṛe   giile   ho   gaye
     clothes.M wet.MPL become go.PERFECTIVE.MPL
     'The clothes became wet.'

(57) Atif-ne   kapṛe   giile   kiye
     Atif-ERG clothes.M wet.MPL do.PERFECTIVE.MPL
     'Atif wet the clothes.'

Interestingly, Hindi has another class of adjectives, which are participial forms derived from verbs. These have the same *-aa* ending as the underived adjectives and decline for agreement in the same way, *but they are systematically ungrammatical in the very same constructions*!

(58) *kapṛe   suukhe ho   gaye
      clothes.M dry.MPL become go.PERFECTIVE.MPL
      'The clothes became dry.'

(59) *Atif-ne   kapṛe   suukhe kiye
      Atif-ERG clothes.M dry.MPL do.PERFECTIVE.MPL
      'Atif dried the clothes.'

Bhatt notes the following generalization: forms like the ones in (58) and (59) are blocked precisely when a simple unaccusative verb, or a transitive verb exists, respectively, as in (60) and (61).

(60) kapṛe   sukh   gaye
     clothes.M dry$_{intrans}$ go.PERFECTIVE.MPL
     'The clothes dried.'

(61) Atif-ne   kapṛe   sukhaaye
     Atif-ERG clothes.M dry$_{trans}$.PERFECTIVE.MPL
     'Atif dried the clothes.'

I therefore take the phenomenon of phrasal blocking to be well attested: lexicalization via deverbal morphology plus an auxiliary verb is systematically blocked by the existence of underived lexicalization via the simple verb (see box 3.1). In the context of this monograph, this is an important enough phenomenon to deserve its own label: *phrasal blocking*.

Box 3.1
Phrasal blocking in auxiliary constructions

> For any two identical phrase structure representations, lexicalization via a deverbal form plus an auxiliary verb is systematically blocked by the possibility of lexicalization by the corresponding simple (underived) verbal form.

We used this fact to account for the absence of stative verbs in *-ing* in chapter 2, and we have used it now to account for the absence of unaccusatives in passive constructions with the *-en/ed* participle (the latter being attested not just in English, but also in Swedish and Hindi).

3.2.3   Interaction of Passive and Progressive within EvtP

I have now made a proposal for analyzing of the verbal passive, which, like the progressive, lies firmly within the event concept domain. Immediately, a question arises about how the two interact and combine, and what their relative ordering derives from. Recall that in English the two constructions combine grammatically in only one order.

(62) a.   Vidar is being photographed.
      b.   *Vidar was been photographing (the cat).

We know that the passive can combine with both stative and dynamic projections, so the fact that the output of the progressive is a state cannot be the impediment to passivization per se. In fact, the way I just posed the question isn't correct—we should be asking about the combinatoric properties of our building blocks and trying to derive the fact that (62b) cannot be generated. So far, I have made a proposal about the height of attachment of *-ing* and the possible expressive structures for the *-en/ed* participle: *-ing* is an independent member of D_μ that attaches to the expression of an EvtP, a complete event description as expressed by a verbal root: the *-en/ed* participle is a building block that corresponds to truncated versions of the verbal root.

The phrase structure I have assumed so far for the lowest domain of verbal concepts contains three force-dynamical heads—*Init*, *Proc*, and *Res*—and an

Evt head where the highest argument is merged.[14] (I have also assumed that the Evt head is the locus of introduction of the utterance situation and the deployment operator, but I will be abstracting away from that for the time being, at least until I start discussing the situational domain and the interpretation of the perfect in chapter 4.) I have also assumed lexical entries containing spans for both inflectable roots and participles. I have assumed that inflected stems contain the full specification of category features of the root plus a feature that allows them to inflect for tense and agreement, the Asp feature. The bare uninflected root, on the other hand, contains everything *except* the Asp feature since it does not inflect for tense. Finally, the participial forms are subsets of the root form that are contiguous. Comparing the forms, we have the following specifications:

(63) a. *Inflectable transitive verb*
         <Asp, Evt, Init, Proc, Res>
      b. *Bare root form*
         <Evt, Init, Proc, Res>
      c. *Participle in -en/ed*
         <(((Evt), Init), Proc), Res>

(64)   EvtP ← Scope of bare root span

       Evt   (InitP) ← Scope of participle span for eventive passive

               Init   ProcP ← Scope of participle span for eventive passive

                      Proc   (ResP) ← Scope of participle span for stative passive

                             Res   XP

In chapter 2, I argued that *-ing* is a head in the lowest event domain as well, and that it creates a derived state from the event description that it attaches to. The span up to EvtP can be spelled out by the bare root form, and this step can be followed by Merge of *-ing*. Once *-ing* has been merged and a new event description built, a new Evt head will have to be merged to provide the edge of the event concept domain and the event concept domain topic for further syntactic action. This will essentially force insertion of the dummy verb *be* in Evt. In what follows, I will assume *Evt* as a general label for a head in the first phase of the clause, and reserve *Evt_{edge}* for the highest such head in the domain. It is the Evt_{edge} head that has the quotational semantics motivated in chapter 1, and that closes off the D_μ denotational domain. The successful *-ing* derivation in (65) therefore involves EvtP recursion, the hallmark of which is dummy *be*-insertion.

(65)

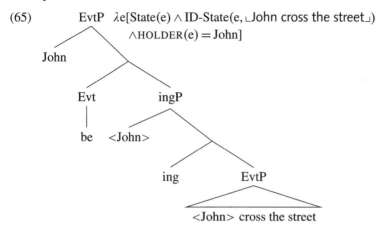

EvtP $\lambda e[State(e) \wedge ID\text{-}State(e, \llcorner John\ cross\ the\ street \lrcorner)$
$\wedge HOLDER(e) = John]$

John

Evt   ingP

be   <John>

ing   EvtP

<John> cross the street

The merger of the higher EvtP is forced by the requirement of having a verbal form with an Asp feature that will allow tense inflection. I will assume that the lexical item *be* in English has the specification in (66).

(66) *be*: <T, Asp, Evt>

Under these assumptions, it is clear that a passive structure should be able to feed progressivization because it builds an EvtP (albeit with its own dummy *be*, which should be irrelevant), which is what *-ing* attaches to. Sentence (62a), *Vidar is being photographed*, is thus straightforwardly derived. Note that **Vidar is photographeding*, is not possible in English, for the simple morphological reason that the *-en/ed* participle cannot host suffixation.

Consider again the ungrammatical (62b), repeated here.

(67) *Vidar was been photographing (the cat).

Can this be ruled out in the system we have been constructing so far? To build this sentence, we would first need to attach *-ing* to the EvtP formed by *Vidar photograph (the cat)*. So far so good. Now we would need to insert the *-en/ed* form of *be*. By assumption, this should be the form of *be* that has no Asp feature in its lexical entry, just <Evt>, something clearly allowed by the rules we have given for participles in *-en/ed*. However, because this form does not bear any tense or agreement features, Evt head recursion would be forced, once again by assumption, as well as Merge of a new *be*, creating (67). Insertion of the participial version of *be* is entirely vacuous here, since the thing it removes, when compared to the nonparticipial form, is simply re-added as another token of *be*, this time as a root. I will assume that this sort of derivation with superfluous lexical items is prohibited by some version of lexical economy.

However, there is one case where something like (67) can in fact be built: namely, the case where the truncated form that is the *participle* is actually the expression of everything in the root up to and including Asp (but missing the uninterpretable tense and agreement features). In this case, the derivation can only be saved by adding an appropriate auxiliary verb in the higher domain. This will be the story of the perfect.

But before we turn to that, I close this chapter with a brief discussion of adjectivalization of the passive participle.

3.2.4 Adjectivalization

I have given a very simple and abstract denotation for the *-en/ed* participle in its usage as a passive participle in English in both stative and eventive passives. Any span of event concept domain heads lacking an Asp specification, regardless of size, can be expressed by the *-en/ed* participial form of the corresponding verb. The conceptual content associated with syntactic information truncated in this way is radically absent. When Init is present but Evt is absent, the causing subevent is conceptually present but no actual causer is projected. I have proposed that this is precisely the situation that gives rise to the notional existential binding of a "causer" argument (the presupposition of existence of such a participant) and licenses *by*-phrases and other agent-oriented modifiers. Modulo truncation, the denotation of the participle in *-en/ed* is claimed to be simply identical to that of the corresponding verb. Depending on the size of the span expressed by the *-en/ed* participle, it is either stative or dynamic, but it has so far lacked an external argument because of the truncation of Evt.

So far, the selectional properties of the progressive and the passive have been derived by combinatorics, and by the existence of blocking with simple verbal forms when in the verbal domain. But what about the adjectival uses of these participles more generally? How are these built, and how are the restrictions on their usage captured in this system? In chapter 2 on the progressive, we saw that the ingP built up by attachment of *-ing* in the Event domain feeds adjectivalization. There, I assumed a null adjectivalization head, which I called A*, that induces lambda abstraction over the highest argument in the ingP, giving a property of individuals. This derived the fact that the *-ing* participle in English always modifies the argument that would have been the grammatical subject if the construction had been input to a verbal progressive. The resulting representation, (54) in chapter 2, is repeated here.

(68)   A*P $\lambda x \lambda e$[State(e) $\wedge$ ID-State(e, ⌞cross the street⌟)
                      $\wedge$ HOLDER(e) = x]

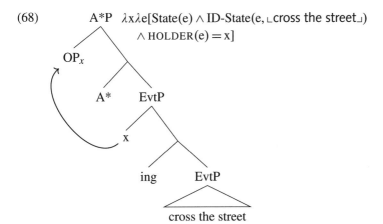

Now, we know that the -en/ed participle only ever modifies the argument that would have been an *internal* argument of the related verbal event. Importantly, this is true regardless of whether the argument in question will end up in subject position of the corresponding simple verb or not.

(69) a. John photographed a bear. → The much-photographed bear ...
     b. John loved a pop band → The much-loved pop band ...
     c. John danced a jig. → *The much-danced man ...
     d. The leaves fell to the ground. → The fallen leaves ...

We can now invoke the very same A* head in the case of the -en/ed participle and create an abstraction over the highest argument. This gives exactly the right results for both the stative and the eventive passive participles, with A* attaching to ResP and InitP/ProcP, respectively.

Note that the prohibition against "subject" modification by bare -en/ed participles carries over to the attributive use.

(70) a. John is photographing a bear. → The man photographing a bear was tall.
     b. John photographed a bear. → *The man photographed a bear was tall.

This fact was noted already by Bresnan (1982), who stated that the "passive participle" can be input to the adjectivalization rule, while the perfect participle cannot. In the present case, we might ask why a hypothetical EvtP participle could not be input to adjectivalization in this way, on the same model as the participle in -ing. (We have blocked its construction in predicative positions on grounds of economy, but as we saw with the -ing participle, such reasoning does not carry over to attributive positions.)

(71)

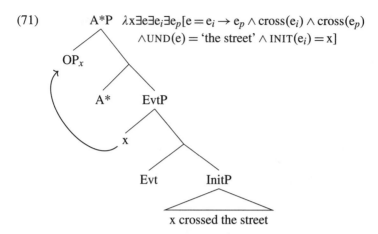

A*P $\lambda x \exists e \exists e_i \exists e_p [e = e_i \rightarrow e_p \land \text{cross}(e_i) \land \text{cross}(e_p)$
$\land \text{UND}(e) = \text{'the street'} \land \text{INIT}(e_i) = x]$

x crossed the street

To account for this gap, I will note the stative nature of the A category
more generally, and stipulate that adjectivalization via A* in the first phase
is restricted to *stative* projections with one designated "subject of predication"
position. It can be fed by *ing*-participle formation, which is a derived state
constructed over the highest position (the other event description and its participant roles are rendered opaque by the derivation of a higher, derived stative
event), but only by the participle in *en/ed* if it is based on ResP. In that case,
too, we have a state and there is a unique argument in the specifier position.

In discussing the stative participle in *-en/ed* in section 3.1, I assumed that
purely stative participles can be built from ResP verbs, and also from activity
verbs via coercion if a contextually relevant ResP can be inferred. These stative
predications have no event entailments in the sense of requiring actual eventive
instantiations, but they have event implications in many cases of coercion. We
also saw that adding adverbials describing the result state is often felicitous,
sometimes even facilitating the construction of a result state. I speculate that
all instances of derived adjective formation with *-en/ed* are based on the latter
attaching to ResP, either with or without coercion. This predicts that the argument that is abstracted over will always be internal, but it also predicts that
there may be contextual and pragmatic restrictions on whether the adjectivalizations will be felicitous or not. For example, I think that the adverbial *well* in
(72b) modifies the coerced result state of hammering. This licenses the structure whereby the participle (plus modifier) identifies Res, thus feeding stative
participle formation.

(72) a. The window is broken. → The broken window ...
     b. The metal is well hammered. → The well-hammered metal ...

I am able to claim that only extremely low attachment of *-en/ed* can feed adjectivalization because of my assumption about the nature of event-conceptual meaning and its (re)usability. This means that we can allow event "dependence" and felicity of adverbials without assuming full situational entailments.

The claim in this section about A* is essentially the claim that the null adjectivalizing head has no power to construct a derived state from what it attaches to (adjectives themselves being externally stative). The constituent that feeds adjectivalization must itself already have a stative denotation, and have a unique argument available for abstraction.[15] This means that if the *-en/ed* participle spells out either ProcP or InitP (or indeed EvtP) as we will see in chapter 4, it may feed further verbalization but never adjective formation. For dynamic verbs, only ResP *-en/ed* participle adjectivalizations are possible, and these will therefore always involve an internal argument. In the case of stative verbs, *-en/ed* must attach low enough so that there is only one unique argument position in order to feed adjectivalization.

Note that my proposal involving A* is not the same as DM's categorizing little-a head. A* is a head that converts something whose category is already otherwise specified into something that behaves externally like an underived adjective. It is not a lexicon-internal device, either, since it can attach to phrases and can have quite a lot of internal structure (see also Bruening 2014). I assume that the constraints on adjectivalization are related to the amount of structure that is present inside the A* head. I assume further that stronger constraints on phrasally derived adjectives come either from their lack of scalar properties or from the coercions independently required to construct salient result states in different contexts.

Certainly, I do not take external adjectival distribution to be a hallmark of lexicon-internal derivation. In addition, the system I am elaborating here is one in which forms in attributive position and forms in predicative position can in principle have different selectional constraints. This is because although both predicative and attributive uses of the participle have the same participial ingredient, blocking operates differently in the two cases depending on the nature of the embedding structure.

The purpose of this section has been to show how the proposal made here for the participles in the English auxiliary system can be deployed in nonverbal constructions as well. However, it is beyond the scope of this monograph to discuss in detail how the pragmatic restrictions are to be stated in each case. That question must be left for further research.

4 The Participle, the Perfect, and the Spatiotemporal Domain

In this chapter, I take a close look at the perfect auxiliary construction in English. Like the passive, this construction deploys the participle in *-en/ed*. But in other ways we are in new territory, because the perfect construction implicates the second phase of the clause. We will leave the domain of linguistic lexical items, D_μ, and enter a zone where spatiotemporal and anchoring properties of eventualities are introduced and modified.

To summarize the proposals so far, I have argued that the *-en/ed* participle in English expresses any contiguous subchunk of the verbal root's span, via the nonprojection of higher features and the concomitant suppression of conceptual content. Other than that, the participle simply denotes the property of events that has been built up to that point, as conceptually elaborated by that particular verb. Unlike the *-ing* morpheme, which actively builds an Identifying State for the event description it attaches to, *-en/ed* leaves the nature of the event description intact. This has the effect that target state participles will be stative, while verbal passives will have the same aktionsart as their active counterparts. On the other hand, *-ing* never interferes with the argument structure of the projection it attaches to: it attaches to a full EvtP as expressed by the bare root, and always raises the highest argument in that event description to its HOLDER position. The participle in *-en/ed* does however potentially affect argument structure because it aborts the expression of higher subevents, changing the options for the choice of externalized argument.

The participle in *-en/ed* is important in the construction of derived adjectives, since a stative form with a single privileged subject of predication seems to be systematically able to feed lambda abstraction. So far, I have assumed that this is achieved by the addition of the A* functional head. However, this use of *-en/ed* in the construction of passive and attributive adjectives seems quite distinct from the use of the *-en/ed* participle in perfect constructions, illustrated in (1).

(1) Vidar has written the letter *V*.

Perfect participles do not involve any diminishment of the verb's argument structure, and they also do not seem to feed adjectivalization, as discussed earlier.

(2) a.   The nicely written letter V ...
    b.   *The boy nicely written the letter V ...
    c.   The boy writing the letter V ...

So even though (2a) is grammatical, there is no evidence that anything other than the passive participle is at work here. Any attempt to build participial modification over the highest argument of the perfect construction fails. This contrasts with the behavior of the progressive participle in *-ing*, which does privilege the highest argument of a transitive predication, and which can subsequently feed adjectivalization, as seen in (2c). If we now translate (2a) directly into Swedish, where the form used in the perfect (the supine) is morphologically distinct from the one found in the passive, it is clear that modification of the internal argument is always achieved via the *passive* participle (3a) and not the supine (3b). Once again, modification of the subject of the verb 'write' is impossible even with the supine participle, as in (3c) (Björn Lundqvist, pers. comm.).

(3) a.   Den   vel   skrivna   bokstaven V ...
         the.M well write.PASSPPL letter V
         'The well-written letter V ...'
    b.   *Den   vel   skrivit   bokstaven V ...
         the.M well write.SUPINE letter V
    c.   *Den   vel   skrivit V pojken ...
         the.M well write.SUPINE V boy
         Intended: 'the boy who has written well'

Finally, while formation of the participles in *-en/ed* and *-ing* systematically interacts with simple lexical forms with respect to blocking, there are no such restrictions on formation of the perfect. *Every* verb in English can form a perfect.

Thus, there are differences between the perfect and passive participles that might suggest treating them differently. The fact that Swedish makes a morphological difference between the two means at least that there is no *necessity* for languages to use the same form for both functions.

(4) *Differences between perfect and passive participles*
    a.   Perfect participles never feed adjectivalization.
    b.   Perfect participles never reduce argument structure.
    c.   Perfect participles are always possible—never "blocked."

However, the facts of English strongly suggest that the participle found in the perfect is paradigmatically the same form found in the passive. Allomorphic quirks of the latter carry over without exception to the former. Ideally, we would like an analysis for the perfect participle that shares a substantial part of its denotation and function with the passive participle, so that the same vocabulary item can do duty for both.

We have already embarked on a methodology that derives the differences between *-en/ed* forms from the scope of the span they express. Let us see whether this can also be the source of the differences between passive and perfect versions of the *-en/ed* participle.

By the tests of height and zone introduced in chapter 2, the perfect and passive participles are not in the same position. Specifically, the perfect participle comes *before* the expression of the low subject in expletive constructions ((5a) vs. (5b)); the passive participle must come *after* the expression of the low subject ((5c) vs. (5d)).

(5) a. There might have *arrived* many trains at this station.
    b. *There might have many trains *arrived* at this station.
    c. There might be many people *arrested* at the demonstration.
    d. *There might be *arrested* many people at the demonstration.

When it comes to VP-fronting, the perfect participle does not seem to front very easily (6a), but the passive one does (6b).

(6) a. ??If Mary says that the children will have eaten already, then [eaten], they will have.
    b. If Mary says that the cakes will be eaten, then [eaten] they will be.

Finally, while British *do*-substitution is crashingly bad for the passive participle (7a), it is OK for the perfect (7b).

(7) a. *Mary was arrested and John was done as well.
    b. Mary has written to her local councillor and John has done as well.

To my ear, the VP-fronting of the perfect (6a) is not completely out, and British *do*-substitution (7b) is not completely perfect. In expletive constructions, however, the choice of position with respect to the subject is very clear.

It is also true that the *-en/ed* participle of a main verb can be embedded under the *-en/ed* participle corresponding to *be*, as in (8).

(8) The boys have been chased.

When they cooccur, then, the passive participle is clearly lower in the spell-out order than the perfect participle.

What I would like to propose, therefore, is that in the case of the perfect participle, *-en/ed* spans all the way up to Asp in the proposed functional sequence, just as inflected verbal forms do, lacking only the uninterpretable syntactic features for tense and agreement found with the latter.

If the suffix *-en/ed* is allowed to express a span all the way up to Asp, then the result is the very same property of events as that determined by the verb, including the addition of the external argument, and the position of the participle is higher than the low position of the external argument as diagnosed by the expletive construction test. But now the verb cannot express tense anchoring directly itself; it must combine with an auxiliary to receive anchoring information.

I have assumed in chapters 2 and 3 that the dummy verb *be* is an element of D_μ and can only be inserted in the first phase.[1] What we need here, instead, is to insert a functional auxiliary directly in the inflectional domain: the auxiliary *have*, which is not a member of D_μ.[2]

But before I can make an explicit proposal, I need to lay out what is known about the semantics of the perfect, to ensure that the proposal captures its core properties, while maintaining the desideratum of unifying the *-en/ed* participial vocabulary item.

4.1 Semantic Background of the English Perfect

4.1.1 The Intermediate Topic/Reference Situation

The Asp head that I have introduced for transition into the situational domain is named Asp for a reason. The location of this head just outside the first-phase verbal domain makes it equivalent to the functional position that has been the locus for viewpoint aspect in the literature, and that has been crucial for explicating the semantics of the perfect, starting with Reichenbach 1947.

That tradition sees the Asp head as introducing a topic time, or reference time, which is a crucial intermediary between the utterance time and the event time in expressing the meanings of the perfect (see Klein 1994, Demirdache and Uribe-Etxebarria 2008). In Reichenbach 1947, the perfect tense is characterized by the fact that the reference time is the same as the utterance time, while the event time precedes (see figure 4.1).

The Reichenbachian view has been generalized by Klein (1994) and others to conceive of the Asp node as something that can be used to impose viewpoint on the event time by selecting portions of it as the reference/topic time. Examples of the use of the Asp node to characterize perfective vs. imperfective more generally are given by Giorgi and Pianesi (1997) and Demirdache and Uribe-Etxebarria (2008), among others. For example, Giorgi and Pianesi

Simple past: ——E,R——————————U——————

Present perfect: ——————E————————R,U————————

Past perfect: ——————E————————R———U————

Figure 4.1
The Reichenbachian view (1947)

(1997) hypothesize that various tenses are the result of the composition of a relation between E and R (their Relation 2) and a relation between U and R (Relation 1).

(9) Relation 1:   U_R   future   Relation 2:   E_R   perfect
                R_U   past   R_E   prospective
                (U,R) present   (E,R) neutral

In much of the later work building on Reichenbach 1947, Relation 2 has been associated with an aspectual phrase structure node, specifying the relation between the event variable e and the reference time variable t. The Tense node specifies Relation 1, which anchors the reference time to the utterance time (see Klein 1994). (10) shows Demirdache and Uribe-Etxebarria's (2000) proposal for the different aspectual values in Romance and English (where AST-T = assertion time).

(10) a. [+central coincidence]: (FIGURE within GROUND)
          Present tense: UT-T within AST-T
          Progressive aspect: AST-T within EV-T
    b. [−central, +centripetal coincidence]:
          (FIGURE before/toward GROUND)
          Future tense: UT-T before AST-T
          Prospective aspect: AST-T before EV-T
    c. [−central, +centrifugal coincidence]: (FIGURE after/from GROUND)
          Past tense: UT-T after AST-T
          Perfective aspect: AST-T after EV-T

The Asp node in the system I am building up here is in some senses in line with this general pedigree of analysis, but differs from it in others. In the present proposal, in binding the eventuality argument of EvtP, the Asp node introduces a variable of spatiotemporal properties of events anchored in d. In this sense, the Asp node must always be present in any phrase structure building a proposition, and it *is* the locus where temporal viewpoint or orientation properties for the event can be expressed for the first time.

(11) $[\![\text{AspP}]\!] = \lambda f_{<v<v,t>>} \lambda d \exists e[\text{Utterance}(d) \wedge f(d)(e) \wedge \llcorner u \lrcorner(e)]$

To anticipate, however, I will depart from the Kleinian intuition in arguing that an intermediate reference situation, or topic situation (with a distinct situational variable), is *only* actually introduced in the context of auxiliary constructions. This will make a clearer distinction between constructions involving modals and perfect auxiliaries (which involve intermediate reference situations) and constructions like perfective and imperfective aspectual constructions (which do not).

For the perfect tense, the consensus indeed seems to be that an intermediate reference or topic situation is necessary. The central problem of the present perfect is that it seems to say two things at once:[3] on the one hand, the tense morphology indicates that a present state is being asserted; on the other, there is an undeniable entailment that a certain event occurred prior to that. The twofold nature of the perfect is what Reichenbach (1947) intended to capture with his notion of reference time and event time. But there are questions about exactly how to implement this intuition within a formal theory of the perfect. How are the two eventualities related to each other? Accounts differ regarding their position with respect to this relationship between the topic situation and the event-related situation in this sense. I summarize the major views in (12).

(12) a. *The resultant state analysis*
        The (present) perfect is a present tense assertion of a situation that
        carries with it an entailment of a past event (Parsons 1990, Smith 1991,
        Kamp and Reyle 1993).
      b. *The indefinite past analysis*
        The (present) perfect is an assertion of a past event, with a pragmatic
        component/presupposition requiring present relevance (Reichenbach
        1947, Inoue 1979, Klein 1992).
      c. *The extended-now analysis*
        In the (present) perfect, a temporally complex situation is being
        asserted, starting from the past and extending to overlap with the
        utterance time (McCoard 1978, Pancheva and von Stechow 2004).

Thus, the crux of the matter lies in understanding the relationship between the present state and the event in question. Is that relationship purely temporal, or is it causational? How do the participants in the two situations overlap? To answer these questions, we need to take a closer look at the semantic peculiarities that researchers have uncovered to date about the perfect. In what follows, I am indebted to the discussion in Portner 2003.

4.1.2 Aktionsart Sensitivity

Even though what I said about the event preceding the present state is generally true for dynamic eventualities, it is now understood that the English perfect gives rise to a number of different readings with different temporal relations between the "state" and the "event" in question. The interesting fact is that these readings are not just available across the board, but are dependent on the aktionsart of the event that has been participialized.

In the *target state perfect*, there is a target state for the verb that still holds at the utterance time. In this case, the present state is clearly *caused* by the event's having occurred. Obviously, this reading is possible only for verbs that have a target state to begin with.[4]

(13) *Target state perfect*
   a. Mary has thrown the ball on the roof. (and it's still there)
   b. Mary has pushed over the chair. (and it's still there)
   c. Mary has broken her glasses. (and they're still broken)

In the *resultant state perfect*, on the other hand, there is a state that holds forever afterward simply by virtue of the fact that a particular event came to pass. This state holds now. The semantics of this state is so weak that the only thing we can conclude from it is that the event occurred at some time in the past (making the state's existence truth-conditionally equivalent to an indefinite past tense analysis). The resultant state perfect is sometimes called the *experiential perfect*, with which it shares temporal properties. The experiential perfect gets its name from the fact that the current relevance of the state in question gives rise to an implication that the subject has "gained the experience" of having participated in the past event. It seems that this implication arises very easily in the resultant state perfect. I will discuss the "relevance" facts in section 4.1.4; here, I will just classify the event structure relationships. Resultant state perfects seem possible across the board; for activities (14a), achievements (14b), accomplishments (14c), and even states (14d). However, for some aktionsart types—namely, activities and events without a reversible final state—the resultant state reading is the only one possible.

(14) *Resultant state perfect*
   a. Mary has driven a truck (before).
   b. Mary has reached the top of that mountain (before).
   c. Mary has broken her glasses (before).
   d. Mary has lived in Paris (before).

Finally, the other major temporal type of perfect is the *universal perfect*. In this reading, the state that is asserted to exist in the present is extended backward to a particular past moment in time and is assumed to hold continuously from that point. This reading is only possible for stative verbs in English, and is always available for them. The universal perfect usually requires a framing interval or *since*-adverbial to trigger the continuous interpretation (otherwise, states get a resultant state interpretation).

(15) *Universal perfect*
    a. Mary has lived in Paris for three years. (i.e., from three years ago up until now)
    b. Mary has lived in Paris since 2012.

The "resultant state" analysis found in the literature is designed to deliver the resultant state reading easily. It needs some pragmatic boosting to give the target state reading, and has problems with the universal perfect reading. The same is true of the "indefinite past" analyses, which have very similar truth conditions. By contrast, the "extended-now" theories are good at accounting for the temporal properties of the universal perfect, but need to put in some extra work to explain how the situational complexity of the dynamic readings fits in with standard theories of tense interpretation. Finally, all of the current analytic options face the problem of how to get aktionsart sensitivity to fall out from a unified definition of the perfect.

4.1.3 Temporal Modification and the Present Perfect Puzzle

The schizophrenia of the perfect can be probed by testing the felicity of temporal adverbials. The present perfect is morphologically marked for "present tense," even though the strongest truth-conditional contribution is that of a past occurrence of the event named by the participle. Given an analysis that makes reference to both a reference time and an event time, one might expect to be able to modify either or both with temporal adverbials. The *present perfect puzzle* is that in the present perfect (both target state and resultant state readings), the event time resists modification by such adverbials and only the "now" seems to be accessible (16a–b). For the universal perfect, the entire time span from a particular past moment to the present one can be provided via a temporal adverbial (16c), although interestingly the universal perfect reading is not easily available without it and the edges of the the time span cannot be separately specified (16d).

(16) a. *Mary has done her homework yesterday.
    b. *Mary has driven a truck yesterday.
    c. Mary has lived in Paris for three years/since 2012.
    d. *Mary has lived in Paris now/three years ago.

The puzzle becomes even deeper once we notice that in the pluperfect, both the event time and the reference time do seem to be separately accessible; see (17a) and (17b), respectively. So, in (17a) the doing of the homework can have taken place 'on Thursday', and (17b) favors the reading where the topic interval is included in 'Thursday'.

(17) a. Mary had done her homework on Thursday.
      b. On Thursday, Mary had already done her homework.

The event time is also accessible for modification when the perfect is embedded under a modal (18a) or is part of a nonfinite clause (18b).

(18) a. Mary must have done her homework on Thursday.
      b. Having done her homework on Thursday, Mary was able to go to the party.

An account for these puzzling facts should ideally emerge from the analysis of the perfect and how the different subparts are linguistically represented. For now, I note only that the fact that the English present tense only combines felicitously with states, either simple or derived, should be a factor in the analysis. I return to this puzzle in section 4.2.2.

4.1.4 Lifetime Effects and Current Relevance

Finally, the relationship between the present state and the past event is not as free as the pure resultant state semantics would suggest. The present state has to have some sort of "current relevance" for the perfect to be felicitous. In (19a) and (19b), the perfect is appropriate if it is relevant to know whether John eats raw fish when planning a joint restaurant visit or whether John is familiar with Paris, respectively.

(19) a. John has eaten sushi.
      b. John has visited Paris.

In the following dialogues, although the English past tense and the English perfect are often both possible, to my ear (20B) is odd in the perfect as an out-of-the-blue description of my day, and I would prefer the simple past. But the dialogue in (21) is fine if I am telling my partner that I have done some exercise and am now ready for a hearty dinner.

(20) A. How was your day?
      B. ??I have swum a whole kilometer today in the pool./I swam a whole kilometer today in the pool.

(21) A. Are you hungry?
      B. I have swum a whole kilometer today, so yes.

Crucially in these cases, the relevant state seems to be one of newly gained "experience" on the part of the subject. Current relevance is therefore not the whole story here, although it is pertinent in the extremely general Gricean sense of speaking relevantly to one's interlocutor. In addition, it seems that some pragmatic work needs to be done to create a post-state for a verb that does not naturally have one. In this case, the experiential effects of the event on the subject seem to come to the fore.

In the case of verbs that have target states built into their meaning, the state in question can always be the target state. But here, we seem to get a kind of evidential constraint on felicity (see also Pancheva 2003). In (22), the perfect is infelicitous if A is interrogating B back at the cabin, even though the tracks are still in the snow and even though that state is clearly "relevant."

(22) *Context:*
Back at the cabin
A. How did you find the wounded deer?
B. The poor animal left bloody tracks in the snow.
C. ??The poor animal has left bloody tracks in the snow.

On the other hand, (23) is perfect if A and B are together in the woods and contemplating the tracks as they speak.

(23) *Context*:
Out in the woods
A. How will we find the deer?
B. No problem. Fortunately, it has left tracks in the snow.

The perfect is also sensitive to the nature of the subject or HOLDER of the present state; this may or may not be the same as the idea of "current relevance." It has been noticed that if the subject of the perfect is a historical person, then the perfect is very odd. As Chomsky (1970) points out, (24a) is rather odd out of the blue, while (24b) is perfectly fine. (24c) is a classic example given by McCoard (1978) (cited along with (24a,b) in Portner 2003, 464).

(24) a. ??Einstein has visited Princeton.
b.   Princeton has been visited by Einstein.
c. ??Gutenberg has discovered the printing press.

However, as Portner notes, if the discourse topic is understood to be "famous people who have visited Princeton," (24a) improves considerably. Portner's own account develops Inoue's (1979) intuition that "a proposition expressed by the perfect sentence is 'relevant' in that it is in a logical relation to another which is 'at issue' in the conversation" (Portner, 2003, 469). In Inoue's account, which is a version of the "indefinite past" theory, this pragmatic requirement of relevance sits over and above the temporal contribution of the perfect form itself.

According to Moens and Steedman (1988), on the other hand, the perfect is only acceptable if one can identify a sufficiently relevant result, given real-world knowledge. Smith (1991) identifies the result state with the *subject*'s having some relevant property. This involvement of the subject argument goes some way toward helping to account for the lifetime effects noted above—a person who is no longer alive cannot possess any properties.

These facts are all relevant to establishing what the asserted state actually is in the case of the perfect and how it relates to the event description contributed by the participle.

To summarize, there appears to be a condition of discourse relevance on the use of the perfect that is often connected to some property of the subject. In addition, in many circumstances there is an evidential flavor to that stative property.

4.2   The Proposal: Perfect as Intermediate Evidential State

4.2.1   The Perfect as Derived Evidential State

My own version of the perfect will follow the syntax and morphology of the perfect directly and will be built around the present tense assertion of a situation s' that is necessarily a consequence of the situation denoted by the participle, s_0. Thus, the analysis involves two distinct situations: an embedded one; and another one related to it, which will be the essential equivalent of what has been called the reference (or topic) situation. Respectively:

(25) a. *The dependent situation s_0*
         The situation existentially closed at Asp
      b. *The asserted situational state s'*
         The situation introduced by *have* that is truth-conditionally connected to the dependent situation

The crucial question now is what the HAVE predicate that relates s' to s_0 actually means. The meaning of the perfect needs to include the idea that s' *entails* s_0, that the existence of s' necessarily entails the existence of s_0.

In Portner's (2003) system, the relationship between s_0 and s' (in his terms, the prejacent event and the reference state, respectively) involves a necessity operator utilizing an epistemic conversational background. Moreover, in Portner's system the perfect presupposes that the reference state (here, s'; q in Portner's formula in (26)) is a partial or complete answer to the discourse topic. Portner's version of the presupposition is as follows:

(26) A sentence S of the form PERFECT(ϕ) presupposes:

$\exists q[\text{ANS}(q) \wedge \mathbf{P}(p, q)]$, where

p is the proposition expressed by S,

$\mathbf{P}$ is a necessity operator utilizing an epistemic conversational background, and

ANS is true of any proposition which is a partial or complete answer to the discourse topic at the time S is uttered.

(Portner 2003, 481)

In addition, as we have seen, the relationship between p and q (i.e., s_0 and s') famously depends on aktionsart. This is expressed in Reichenbachian terms in (27) (from Portner 2003, 484).

(27) a. Mary has read *Middlemarch.*
   Reference time r = speech time (contribution of present tense)
   Event time e < r.
   b. Mary has been upset (since noon).
   Reference time r = speech time (contribution of present tense)
   Event time e ⊙ r or e < r.

Portner's crucial innovation is the use of a temporal sequencing principle (TSP; see (28)) that acts as a default and allows the semantic contribution of the perfect itself to be unified instead of disjunctive.

(28) (TSP) For any tenseless clause ϕ, reference time r, and event e,
   i. if ϕ is not stative: $[\![\phi]\!]_{r,e}$ implies that e precedes r; and
   ii. if ϕ is stative: $[\![\phi]\!]_{r,e}$ implies that e either precedes or overlaps r.
   (Portner 2003, 484)

Portner points out that the TSP, or something like it, seems to be operative not just in the perfect but also in embedded clauses and in discourse sequencing. These are contexts where states and events systematically behave differently when related to other eventualities. For example, consider the sequence-of-tense sentences in (29), where a past tense attitude predicate embeds another past tense. In (29a) with an embedded state, the "believed" eventuality can either precede or overlap with the "believing"; in (29b) with an embedded dynamic event, the "believed" eventuality must precede the "believing."

(29) a. John believed that Mary was ill.
   b. John believed that Mary won the race.

I think that Portner's insight here is important, and I will use a version of it in my own analysis. The insight boils down to the idea that the difference between the perfect of dynamic events and the perfect of states cannot and should not be built into the denotation of the perfect itself; rather, it should be made to fall out from the way that eventualities relate to each other *independently of the perfect*.

In fact, a version of the core difference between dynamic and stative eventualities was already built into our constraints on temporal instantiation in chapter 2. Ideally, this very principle should be enough in our case as well to account for the aktionsart sensitivity of the perfect.

I should point out here that Portner (2003) does not in fact attempt a decomposition of the different morphological/lexical components of the perfect, although he does try to separate the semantic from the pragmatic effects. To accomplish my agenda here, which is somewhat different, I need to give a denotation for the participle, as well as a denotation for the auxiliary *have* that will compose to give the required effects.

I have assumed, as I think is natural, that the *-en/ed* participle is the component that directly contributes the embedded situation s_0, and that the auxiliary *have* introduces the secondary stative situation s'. Syntactic evidence points consistently to the perfect participle's being placed higher than the base position of existential arguments and therefore I have proposed that it must result from the *-en/ed* participle's spelling out AspP.

Have must now attach to this constituent to build the perfect, raising the highest argument to its own specifier position. Recall again the proposal for AspP given in (11).

(30) $[\![\text{AspP}]\!] = \lambda f_{<v<v,t>>} \lambda d \exists e[\text{Utterance}(d) \wedge f(d)(e) \wedge \llcorner u \lrcorner(e)]$

At the level of AspP, then, we have a property of relations that link the utterance situation d with an existing event that is being demonstrated/described in d. That event has conceptual/perceptual properties as characterized by u. At this point, we must allow *have* to combine with this constituent to build a derived state that will have a particular relationship to e, but will itself be the actual eventuality that is explicitly anchored to the utterance by means of tense.

As the final ingredient, we need a denotation for the interpretation of *have* and how it combines with the default AspPs so generated. The denotation I propose is given in box 4.1.

Box 4.1
Denotation for perfect *have*

$[\![\text{have}]\!] = \lambda Q \lambda x \lambda f' \lambda d \exists s' \exists f[Q(f)(d) \wedge \text{State}(s') \wedge \text{HOLDER}(s') = x \wedge f = \lambda s \lambda d[s'$ gives evidence for the spatiotemporal relation between s and d in the same world as $s'] \wedge f'(s')(d)]$

The key to the semantics is the definition of the notion of inference-licensing state, or Evidential State (EVID-State).

(31) For all s′, s, s′ is an Evidential State for s iff s′ is a state that gives evidence for s in the same world as s′.

By asserting that the f relation between s_0 (earlier, e) and d is facilitated by the existence of s′, I am saying essentially that s′ is an evidential state that allows us to infer the existence and spatiotemporal location of s_0, the event built up by the AspP that *have* combines with. Putting *have* together with the denotation of the AspP (and renaming the eventuality variable s_0 to make the connection with the previous discussions clear) gives the following denotation:

(32) $[\![haveP]\!] = \lambda x \lambda f' \lambda d \exists s' \exists f \exists s_0 [\text{Utterance}(d) \wedge f(s_0)(d) \llcorner u \lrcorner (s_0)$
      $\wedge \text{HOLDER}(s') = x \wedge \text{EVID-State}(s_0) = s' \wedge f(s')(d)]$

The Evidential State s′ will have a HOLDER in the domain of real instantiated individuals, and its position will be filled by internal Merge from the AspP, raising the highest argument there to that role.

In simple terms (abstracting away from the quantificational event semantics formulas), this composition results in the tree in (33), (for the sentence *Vidar has eaten the chocolate*), with the simplified denotation given. At this point, it is the Evidential State situational variable s′ that will be input to modification and tense modulation (anchoring to the utterance), and the embedded situation s_0 will accrue anchoring entailments from those relations indirectly because of its relationship with s′.

(33)   HAVEP $\lambda s' \exists s_0$ ['vidar-eaten-the-chocolate'(s_0)
                        $\wedge$ EVID-State$(s_0) = s' \wedge$ HOLDER$(s') =$ Vidar]

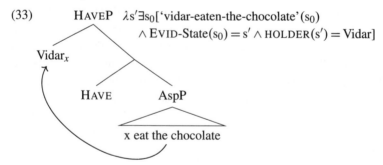

The denotation in (33) says that *have* combines with a situational description and creates a *derived stative* situational description, such that the derived stative situation is an Evidential State for that situational description. As we saw in chapter 2, *-ing* builds an Identifying State, which is a relationship between event properties, where the Identifying State property does not entail the existence of the whole event. Now we have entered the situational domain after the existential closure of the event variable. Here, if one situation is inferrable from another, then the existence of the one entails the actual existence of the other.

It is here that the temporal relationship between s' and s_0 becomes crucial. As in Portner's (2003) system, this is the independent factor that is sensitive to aktionsart. Unlike Portner, however, I will not invoke an explicit temporal sequencing principle. Rather, all that are needed are the principles of temporal instantiation already proposed in chapter 2, inspired by Taylor (1977).[5]

Here's how the aktionsart conditions work. Inferring the existence of a situational particular s_0 from s' requires that whole situation to exist *at or prior to* the onset of s'. This is because, according to Werner (2006) and others, only the present and the past are "determined" in this sense. As I have already assumed, a situation instantiating a dynamic eventuality has a temporal parameter that must be an interval larger than a moment, while a situation instantiating a state only requires that the state have the temporal parameter of a moment. A stative situation can therefore overlap with the stative s' and still be consistent with s' giving evidence for s_0 (because all that is required is a moment). Precisely in the case of dependent states, then, s' can in fact perfectly overlap with the dependent stative situation (and potentially continue on from there), as in the case of the universal perfect. In the case of dependent dynamic situations, the evidential situation can at best overlap with its final moment or result state, and so the dependent dynamic subsituation must end up *preceding* it.

Thus, for the assertion of s', an Evidential State based on the dependent situation s_0, we have the corollaries shown in box 4.2.

The proposed denotation of *have*—namely, as introducing an Evidential State based on the dependent situation contributed by the *-en/ed* participle plus

Box 4.2
Aktionsart sensitivity for Evidential States

> If f (relating s_0 and d) is inferrable from s', then s' is an Evidential State for s_0, and then s_0 must be *determined* by the onset of s'.
>
> If s_0 is a state, then $s_0 \odot s'$, or $s_0 < s'$.
> If s_0 is dynamic, then $s_0 < s'$.

default Asp—has the immediate consequence of making the perfect entail the actual existence of an event as described by the main verb. It also automatically makes the specifics of the interpretation depend on the state vs. dynamic event distinction for the dependent situation.

I assume that the Swedish supine (the spell-out of the participle in the perfect as distinct from the passive) is the undergrown version of the corresponding tensed formative just like the English participle is, but that Swedish also possesses a distinct lexical item, which is the truncated version of the Asp-less (nontensed) form of the verb. In a spanning model, in contexts of competition, the item with the least extra categorial material is chosen. This means that it is only in the case of the perfect, which spells out all the way to Asp, that the supine will be selected.

Next, I consider how the current proposal can account for the other important properties of the perfect—namely, the pragmatic effects and the distribution of temporal modifiers.

4.2.2 Accounting for the Pragmatic/Lifetime Effects

Under the current proposal, the perfect asserts the existence of a stative situation/property that is "held" by the derived subject of predication (here, the "highest" argument of the dependent situation). There are two features of this derived situation that give rise to very particular pragmatic effects and felicity conditions. One is that the subject of the property must be an instantiated individual at the time the situation is asserted to exist. This is essentially the same intuition described by Smith (1991), updated for the situational analysis. Under the view being explored here, events and relations to participants do not require either the event description or the participant nominal description to be instantiated; but once a relationship is established at the level of situations (events with temporal and worldly instantiation), then actuality entailments follow the application of existential closure for both nominal and verbal extended projections. I assume that Smith's intuition, and its analogue here, is what is responsible for the infelicity of the examples in (34).

(34) a. ??Gutenberg has discovered the printing press.
      b. ??Shakespeare has written *Hamlet*.

However, if the names of historical characters are construed as abstract subject matter or labels in a more abstract list, then the perfect becomes felicitous again.

(35) Shakespeare has had a great influence on my life.

Next, we want to account for the intuition whereby the perfect seems to be felicitous only when it provides the "answer" to a salient at-issue question raised by the discourse, as in the analyses of Inoue (1979), Portner (2003), and many others. The problem with the notion of discourse relevance here is that it is hard to falsify, and to the extent that it holds, it is hard to distinguish from general Gricean maxims of cooperation that are independent of the perfect per se. For example, if we consider the discourses in (36) and (37), an overt at-issue question concerning either John or the ball can be answered by a transitive main clause either in the perfect or in the simple past.

(36) A: Where's the ball?
      B: John has thrown it on the roof.
      B′:   John threw it on the roof.
      B″:   It's on the roof.
      B‴:   ??John hurt his arm throwing the ball on the roof.

My intuition about (36) is that all the B responses except B‴, where *the ball* is in a subordinate clause, are felicitous answers to A. Similarly, when A asks a question about John, as in (37), my intuition is that both the B and B′ responses are mildly deviant to the same extent. B″ is completely strange because it doesn't mention John at all. The best answer is of course B‴.

(37) A: What's up with John?
      B: ?He has just thrown the ball on the roof.
      B′:   ?He just threw the ball on the roof.
      B″:   ??The ball is on the roof.
      B‴:   He hurt his arm throwing the ball on the roof.

The point is that the perfect and the simple past responses in (36) and (37) (B and B′, respectively) are good or bad to the same extent. This is worrying if the pragmatic presupposition here is supposed to distinguish the perfect from the simple past. In terms of explicit discourse felicity for an explicit question, pronominalization and main clause vs. adjunct clause seem to be the only factors that are strongly implicated. Therefore, it seems to me that the notion of discourse relevance does not have much bite here, over and above general Gricean considerations. Add this to the fact that there are clearly (i) situations where the state in question *does* have discourse relevance but the example is ungrammatical (38a) and (ii) situations where the perfect can be uttered out of the blue (38b), and it becomes very unclear whether we need to build discourse relevance into the meaning of the perfect at all.[6]

(38) a. ??Gutenberg has discovered the printing press.
      b.   The Orioles have won!

However, we still need to capture the real differences between the use of the perfect and the simple past in some intuitive way. It is here that we can exploit the second feature of the derived situation that gives rise to pragmatic effects under the present account, namely, the fact that it is a state that gives *evidence* for the existence of the embedded event. In the case of accomplishments, the s′ that is asserted often seems to be the same as the result state of the corresponding verb. In such cases, the difference between the perfect and the simple past is that in the latter, the result state might no longer hold (39b). But in the perfect (39a), the result state is precisely the state that is asserted to exist at the utterance time. The result state is in fact a prototype example of an Evidential State since its existence entails the existence of the dynamic event portion that leads to it.

(39) a. John has thrown the ball on the roof.
      b. John threw the ball on the roof.

However, the result state of an eventuality is not the only kind of Evidential State that could be asserted. In cases where the event description has no result state described within it, as in activities, the Evidential State needs to be more contextually constructed/inferred. In (40a) and (40b), we infer that there is some property acquired by John as a result of his having driven a truck and by Mary as a result of her having read *Middlemarch*. This can be as non-specific as simply the experience of "having driven a truck" or as specific as "knowing something about George Eliot's style," depending on the context. Importantly, because the Evidential State is constructed at the level of situations, it need not be something that is built into the event description—it just needs to be something that can be inferred by the listener as existing (in context) by virtue of the fact that the dependent situation exists.

(40) a. John has driven a truck.
      b. Mary has read *Middlemarch*.

So there *is* an important contextual component to the meaning of the perfect here. The interlocutor must infer the relevant Evidential State on the basis of real-world knowledge, common ground, and the particular issues under discussion. As noted earlier, this is what is called the *experiential perfect*, a cover term for the kind of situation-based Evidential State that needs to be inferred from context. I assume that the event-internal result state, when it exists, always counts as giving rise to a potential Evidential State, but it is only possible for ResP verbs. On the other hand, the experiential perfect is constructed via situations directly and is available for all types of verbs (including statives), as long as the dependent situation in question is now over and has had *contextual consequences*.

(41) a. John has driven a truck.
      b. Mary has eaten sushi.
      c. The deer has left tracks in the snow.

This obviously also gives a handle on the evidential flavor of the perfect in cases such as the deer track example in (22), repeated here.

(42) A: How did you find the wounded deer?
      B: The poor animal left bloody tracks in the snow.
      B′: ??The poor animal has left bloody tracks in the snow.

Notice that response B′ is clearly *relevant* to answering the question in some sense, but the present tense ascription of a stative property to the deer, that of having left tracks in the snow, does not seem felicitous. This is because the perfect in response B′ reports a criterial state as *evidence* of response B. If the event is already completed, as A's question shows, then we already know the truth of response B directly. Response B′ is only felicitous when it is precisely that state that is present and apparent to the interlocutors and not the entailed event itself (by general Gricean principles of relevance). Thus, if the deer has not been found yet and all we see is the snow before us, the following discourse is perfectly felicitous.

(43) A. How will we find the deer?
      B. No problem. Fortunately, it has left tracks in the snow.

The fact that a downstream Evidential State is what is being directly asserted, rather than the event itself, is what is directly responsible for the evidential flavor of the perfect that is very salient in certain contexts (see also Pancheva 2003).

   I conclude therefore that my proposal regarding Evidential State constructions fares no worse with respect to the general pragmatic restrictions on the perfect than many of the other proposals in the literature, and in many cases holds the promise of doing better. However, detailed examination of these constraints is beyond the scope of the present monograph.

4.2.3 Temporal Modification and the Perfect

Finally, if the current analysis is to be convincing, it needs to account for the curious temporal properties of the perfect. I start with a brief demonstration of what I have asserted so far: that the perfect actually involves the assertion of a *stative* eventuality, which is the one marked with tense inflection. The evidence that the perfect has the external distribution of a state comes from the standard tests for stativity in English: (i) the perfect is good in the simple present tense without a habitual interpretation (44a); (ii) the perfect is good in the embedded complement of *turn out* (44b); (iii) when following a simple past tense utterance, the past of the perfect does not advance the discourse time in a simple narrative context (44c); (iv) the perfect allows epistemic readings under *must* (44d).[7]

(44) a. John has written a novel.
    b. John turned out to have written a novel.
    c. Mary entered suddenly. John had fallen off his chair.
    d. John must have written a novel.

The present proposal involves the compositional building up of two situations: s_0, a first property of (properties of) situational descriptions based on the event built by the *-en/ed* participle; and s', a second situation that is an Evidential State for s_0. Only the verb introducing the s' situation is directly tense-marked in the perfect. We would expect temporal modifiers to be able to modify this higher situation directly, and in (45a) and (45b) they seem to do so, for the present perfect and past perfect, respectively.

(45) a. John has done his homework now.
    b. John had done his homework already last Tuesday.

The present perfect puzzle consists in the observation that temporal modification of the embedded situation is possible in the case of the past perfect (46b) and nonfinite forms (46c), but not in the case of the present perfect (46a).

(46) a. *John has done his homework yesterday.
    b. John had done his homework the day before.
    c. Having done his homework the day before, John was free to go to the party.

To end up with a consistent description, we can either devise a system whereby only the outer situational variable can be temporally modified, or devise one in which both situations are accessible for temporal modification. It seems difficult to devise a system where in the present perfect only the outer variable can be temporally modified while in the past perfect and modal perfect the embedded situations are temporally modifiable. Solutions to the present perfect puzzle have included analyses in terms of definiteness of reference time feeding which eventuality descriptions get targeted by temporal modifiers (for discussion, see Alexiadou, Rathert, and von Stechow 2003a,b). The extended-now theories (after McCoard 1978) seem to capture an important empirical intuition here.

It is important to note that describing the present perfect as allowing only present "now" modification is not strictly accurate. In fact, the present perfect also seems happy with adverbials that frame the whole sentence, including the existence of both s′ and s_0. Compare the readings of (47a) with a perfect and (47b) with a simple state.

(47) a. John has written a novel this year.
     b. ?John is tired this year.

A simple present tense utterance of a state like (47b) is not good with a frame adverbial of this kind, unless the state in question holds *at every moment* during that interval. By contrast, the reading in (47a) is that the writing of the novel took place during the period of this year, and that at *some* point during the year John achieved the state of "having written a novel." Facts like these are also the starting point for Kamp, Reyle, and Rossdeutscher's (to appear) new proposal, which seeks to augment the result state analysis of Kamp and Reyle (1993) to account for these temporal properties, which seem at first blush to be at odds with the result state intuition.

Since the compositional reasons for retaining the result state representation for the perfect have not gone away, the solution is to rethink the relationship between temporal anchoring and temporal adverbials. To quote Kamp, Reyle, and Rossdeutscher (to appear, 16), "Linking to the time provided by tense and linking to the denotation of a temporal adverb are two distinct operations." The authors provide a detailed study showing that a systematic account of adverbial interpretation can indeed be given and that it is perfectly compatible with a result state analysis of the perfect, once the following assumption is dropped:

The semantics of a projection of the verb takes the form of a single eventuality (either a single event or a single state). It is this eventuality that gets linked both to the time t introduced by tense and to the time denoted by the temporal adverb in case there is one. (Kamp, Reyle, and Rossdeutscher to appear)

Like Kamp, Reyle, and Rossdeutscher's, my analysis of the perfect contains more than one eventuality. As in their analysis, the s′ eventuality is a generalized kind of result state—a state that allows the existence of the embedded eventuality to be inferred and that can indirectly locate it in space and time. Like these authors also, I propose to account for the curious modification properties by adjusting my assumptions about what is a possible target for temporal modification precisely in the case where a complex eventuality structure is present. Below, I present a brief and informal idea of how that would work for a few core cases in English, but a full treatment of all such temporal modification possibilities is beyond the scope of this monograph. For a more complete account, see Kamp, Reyle, and Rossdeutscher to appear.

Ideally, conditions on temporal modification of the perfect should be uniform for the present perfect, the past perfect, and nonfinite instantiations alike. I propose, therefore, that these conditions be stated quite generally as in (48).

(48) *Temporal modification of the perfect*
In the English perfect, temporal adverbials can modify *either* the
run-time of the reference situation s′ ((outer)situation modification) *or*
the whole interval containing both the run-time of s_0 and the run-time
of and s′ (frame modification).

We have seen how this works for the present perfect, but how does it play
out for the past perfect and the nonfinite perfect, where it has been claimed that
s_0 can be modified directly? The answer comes from the difference between
present tense and the other two cases. In the present, there is a contextually
precise and definite right edge to the interval that is modified in the frame
modification alternative (i.e., the utterance time). In the past, the reference
situation s′ does not have to be a point; rather, the past can have extended
reference starting right after the end of the dependent situation. This is because,
in the case of the past, s′ is not identified with the utterance moment, but is a
stative situation that occurred *before* the utterance moment. Thus, a stative
situation s′ *can* have a point as its temporal run-time; there is no requirement
that it *must*. As a concrete illustration, consider (49a–b).

(49) a. John had done his homework (already)[8] at 8 that
           morning.   *Time of s′*
      b. John had done his homework the day before.   *Time of s_0?*

It is usually assumed that (49a) expresses that the s′ of "having done his homework" held at 8 that morning, and that (49b) says that the s_0 of the "doing
homework" event happened the previous day. However, if the s′ of "having
done his homework" can potentially extend right from the moment of the culmination of s_0 as the denotation of Evidential State allows, then the adverbial
in (49b) could in fact be modifying s′.

If I am correct that the adverbials that have been treated as modifying the
embedded event are actually modifying the reference situation s′, then it should
not be possible to modify two separate time moments. Under the hypothesis
that the pluperfect allows both s′ and s_0 to be modified, (50b) should be grammatical; under the hypothesis that only s′ can be directly modified but that the
choice and location of s′ are more flexible in the case of the past perfect, (50b)
should be odd. To my ear, (50b) is infelicitous.

(50) a. When his mum arrived, John had (already) done his homework.
      b. ?When his mum arrived, John had done his homework at 8 that
           morning.

The same effects can be duplicated with nonfinite forms.

(51) a. Having (already) done his homework when his mum arrived, John
           was ready to leave.

b. ?Having done his homework at 8 that morning when his mum arrived later, John was ready to leave.

The compositionally built-up complex situation that we call the perfect therefore has quite regular modification properties, once we take the special property of the present tense into account (i.e., confining s' to a single moment). This is the opposite of the claim by the extended-now family of analyses that the present tense can be used to encompass a longer time interval starting from a contextually relevant moment and stretching up to include the "now." However, this intuition is recaptured in the present framework with the stipulation that the *framing* interval for s' and s_0 is what is available for modification. In the case of the past perfect and the nonfinite perfect, this interval can be described by *by*-phrases, and in the case of the universal perfect, by *since*-phrases (52). *Since*-phrases modify the left edge of a frame and *by*-phrases modify the right edge.

(52) a. John had done his homework by midnight.
  b. Having done his homework by midnight, he got at least seven hours of sleep before having to go to school.
  c. John has lived in Paris since 2005.

When it comes to other adverbials, the current system predicts that the above constraint on temporal modification will apply to properties of situations, and it does not say anything about other kinds of low adverbials. Specifically, I would assume that event modifiers would be able to unproblematically modify the e that gives rise to s_0. Since there is no other event-conceptual description in a perfect sentence, the current system does not predict any ambiguity when it comes to instrumental and manner adverbials. Moreover, unlike with temporal modifiers, we should be able to express manner modification of the event at the same time as temporal modification of s', as (53) shows.

(53) When his mum came home, John had already done his homework carefully/with a pen.

So it is the derived situation s'—the highest one, the one that is actually anchored by tense inflection—that can be directly temporally modified, and this is true for all versions of the perfect. It is only obvious in the present perfect, but it is true quite generally.

I conclude that a treatment in terms of derived Evidential States does at least as good a job as other available theories. In addition, it builds in the aktionsart sensitivity and evidential properties of the construction. Temporal modification seems to be constrained to the outer situational variable and possibly also to total framing adverbials, and it seems as though one could devise an analysis whereby lower temporal modification of the embedded situation alone is systematically disallowed. However, nothing in the overall proposal crucially depends on this; the system as proposed offers the same potentials for modification as others in the literature. I therefore leave a full treatment of temporal modification in the English perfect for further study.

4.3 Conclusion

In chapter 3 and here, I have set out to give a unified analysis of the *-en/ed* participle in English as it appears in both passive and perfect constructions. The factors that contribute to making these constructions different even though they all employ the same lexical item are (i) the height to which the participial span extends (see (54)) and (ii) the other functional material that merges subsequently. For the passive, the stative and the eventive passive spell out ResP and InitP, respectively, denoting within the D_μ domain, while the perfect is built from a participle that is formed by spelling out AspP and includes the external argument. More importantly, to complete the construction of a proposition the perfect participle then requires that a verbal head—*have*—merge in the situational domain. The construction of the derived evidential stative situation gives the temporal and other semantic properties of the perfect that have been described in the literature. In addition, the fact that the perfect is built over situations, which are particulars instantiated in time and world, gives rise to the special entailments for the participial description that we did not find when we were still manipulating objects of the D_μ semantic type.

(54) *Scope of spell-out for the* -en/ed *participle*

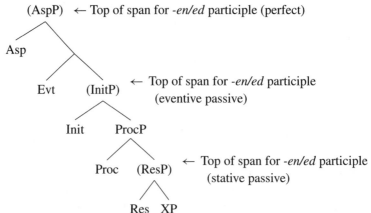

As we saw, the meaning of the *-en/ed* participle is extremely weak, essentially subtractive, in comparison to the corresponding main verb. Its role is to spell out subportions of the verbal denotation. While the passive participle form is clearly within the lowest symbolic conceptual domain of the clause, the perfect participle is higher, residing at the lowest point of the temporal-inflectional domain.

Given the differences we have noted between the *-en/ed* participle in passive constructions and the *-en/ed* participle in perfect constructions, then, to what extent can we see them as the "same" participle? Compared with the specification of the uninflected root, the passive participle is consistently a "stunted" version of that root. If we consider the larger inflected verbal form, though, a stunted version of that lexical item would include the possibility of what we have assumed for the perfect participle: a version with "agreement" and tense features missing. To unify the participle in English, then, we could say that it is a stunted version of the inflected verbal form. To account for the distinction as expressed in a language like Swedish, we could say that the passive participle is a stunted version of the verbal root only and that the supine is a stunted version of the inflected form of the corresponding verb.

This chapter has highlighted once again the difference between the event concept domain, which traffics in verbal symbols expressing partial properties of events generalized to abstract away from time and place, and the situational domain, which involves the addition of spatiotemporal information and the assertion that these event properties describe an instantiated event. To summarize the differences between these two distinct zones of linguistic structuring:

- *Relations in the event concept domain give rise to pseudointensionality*
  Event descriptions and derived event descriptions are related to each other at an essential level and do not entail or require mutual instantiation in the real world. We saw this with the creation of stative result participles that are semantically related to the corresponding events that have ResPs but do not have real-world "event" implications. Crucially, this cannot be captured in a model that builds possible worlds on top of an extensional reality. The abstract property is a primitive, arrived at by abstraction from experience. Relations in this domain have the flavor of classical intensionality, but are not intensional in the sense of requiring reference to possible worlds.
- *Relations in the situational domain give rise to real-world entailments*
  Situational descriptions have world and time parameters; existentially binding these variables entails actual instantiation of these situations at some time and world. For the perfect, I introduced a reference situation, such that

the existence of an evidential situation s′ for another situation s_0 entails the existence of that dependent situation by definition.

- *Relations found in the event concept domain are in competition with lexical verb forms*
  The event domain builds basic event descriptions with all their force-dynamical specificity and basic argument relations. Formatives within this domain can be sensitive to verbal subclass because they can select for domain-internal structure or undergo competition for insertion at this spell out cycle. This is the domain where elements of D_μ are first merged directly. One could think of this first phase of event building as the domain of lexical syntax in the sense of Hale and Keyser (1993). Formatives that merge outside this domain—for example, the auxiliary *have*—can never be selectively blocked by verb class. Thus, the progressive and the passive (both eventive and stative) have verb-class-specific distributions, while the perfect in English applies to all verb classes.

- *Relations at the situational level can be modified by temporal adverbs*
  The situational domain builds properties of situations that have temporal and worldly aspects. They can therefore be modified by temporal adverbials. By hypothesis, constituents in the lower event domain do not host temporal adverbs, although they do allow adverbials of manner and instrument. The zonal hypothesis is therefore also intended to feed ordering restrictions on adverbial modification, much as in Ernst 2002.

Another important result of the investigation so far involves blocking. Unlike standard DM theorists, I have employed a general system of phrasal blocking, whereby a simple nonauxiliated verbal lexicalization always blocks the auxiliated version that spells out the same representation. Since otherwise my starting assumptions are rather different from the ones found in DM, it is not clear that the prohibition against phrasal blocking found there (see Embick and Marantz 2008) is something that I should expect to carry over to the present system. Phrasal blocking is a coherent option for the system I am assuming here, where lexical verbs are specified with category features and span chunks of phrasal projections (see also Bye and Svenonius 2012, Svenonius 2012). It remains to be seen how a DM-like system would cope with the patterns and generalizations that my system captures with phrasal blocking. To the extent that this intuition fails to translate in a similarly elegant way in DM, it would be an argument in favor of the kind of phrasal spell-out system I have been assuming. In chapter 2, I also assumed a blocking mechanism to prevent *-ing* from applying to stative verbs, although this was not blocking under strict phrase structural identity, but more of an economy condition penalizing less economical lexicalization of identical structural semantic content. I summarize the blocking facts in (55) and state a general descriptive principle in (56).

(55) a. Attach -*ing* to any complete event structure and fill in with the dummy verb *be*.
        Blocked by stative verbs
    b. Spell out ResP as the -*en/ed* participle and spell out Evt with the dummy verb *be*.
        Blocked by adjectives in the case of deadjectival verbs
    c. Spell out ProcP as the -*en/ed* participle and spell out Evt with the dummy verb *be*.
        Blocked by unaccusative verbs

(56) *Blocking of auxiliation*
    In cases where a single verbal lexical item generates the same event description as an auxiliary structure, expression by means of an auxiliary is blocked.

The principle in (56), together with the unified denotations I have assumed for -*ing* and the -*en/ed* participle, allow us to avoid any specific constraint against applying the progressive to stative verbs, or against applying the passive to unaccusatives, or against forming stative passives from verbs like *empty* and *open*.

One major difference between the -*en/ed* participle and the -*ing* participle in English lies in whether the participle involves Merge of an additional head or not. In the case of -*ing*, I argued that a distinct Evt head -*ing* is merged and has the specific semantic effect of constructing a derived Identifying State. The -*ing* participle is then built by spell-out of the bare root followed by the suffix -*ing*. In contrast, the -*en/ed* participle cannot be decomposed in this way—it *is* the spell-out of a span of structure, one that is systematically related to the span spelled out by the corresponding main verb in lacking uninterpretable T features (much as in Kratzer's (2000) original intuition). Moreover, in order to capture the unity of the -*en/ed* participle, I argued that it is associated with all subchunks of the syntactic and semantic specification of the root verb. The bare uninflected verbal form in English also differs from the -*en/ed* participle in that the latter must be morphologically specified to prohibit further suffixation.[9]

The syntactic specifications for the lexical items used so far are repeated in (57), with the addition of uT (for uninterpretable T features) where relevant, and the inclusion of the perfect participle.

(57) a. *Inflectable transitive verb*
     <Asp (plus uT), Evt, Init, Proc, Res>
   b. *Bare root form*
     <Evt, Init, Proc, Res>
   c. *Participle in -en/ed*
     <(((Asp (without uT), Evt), Init), Proc), Res>
   d. *Dummy* be
     <T, Asp, Evt>
   e. *Perfect* have
     <T, Asp>

Finally, the denotation for HAVE is repeated in (58).

(58) $[\![have]\!] = \lambda Q \lambda x \lambda f' \lambda d \exists s' \exists f[Q(f)(d) \wedge State(s') \wedge \text{HOLDER}(s') = x \wedge f = \lambda s \lambda d[s'$ gives evidence for the spatiotemporal relation between s and d in the same world as $s'] \wedge f'(s')(d)]$

Identifying State, built by *-ing* in the event property zone, and Evidential State$_{sit}$, built by *have* in the situational zone, are similar, but different in a way predicted by their different zonal positions. In both cases, we get stative derivative versions that preserve identity: in the event concept zone, the stative derivative preserves essential properties of the event concept; in the situational zone, it gives actual evidence for the existence of the embedded event. The definitions of Identifying State and Evidential State are repeated here.

(59) *Identifying State (Definition)*
     For every event description P, an *Identifying State* for P is a stative
     eventuality that manifests sufficient cognitive/perceptual identifiers of
     the event property P.

(60) *Evidential State (Definition)*
     For all situational descriptions s_0, s′, s′ is an Evidential State for s_0 iff s′
     is a stative situation (i.e., a situation that can have a moment as its
     temporal parameter) that is a salient situation that provides *criterial*
     evidence for the existence of s_0 in the same world as s′. The existence of
     s′ always entails the existence of s_0.

The Evidential State construction built by *have* has different consequences for situations built from different event types. This is because of the meaning postulates relating event types to their possible instantiations. We used these meaning postulates to understand the asymmetric entailment relation between the progressive and a simple verb form (i.e., the simple verb form in the past will entail the progressive in the past, but not the other way around). These

meaning postulates also do the work of deriving the different semantic properties of the perfect when attached to verbs of different aktionsart types. The
meaning postulates given in box 2.3 are repeated here (again, adapted from
Taylor 1977).

Box 4.3
Temporal properties of different event types

1. *Temporal properties of simple dynamic events*
   A process event must have a temporal parameter longer than a moment. If a
   simple process is true at an interval I, then it is true at every subinterval of
   that interval larger than a moment.
2. *Temporal properties of states*
   A state can have a moment as its temporal parameter. If a state is true at an
   interval I, then it is true at every subinterval of that interval, including at each
   moment.
3. *Temporal properties of complex events*
   An event with complex subevental structure must have temporal run-times
   corresponding to *each* of the subevents in that structure. If a complex event
   is true at an interval I, then we cannot guarantee that there is any subinterval
   of I at which the complex event is true.

At this point, the fact that the stative proxies are constructed so liberally in
English in both of the zones we have looked at is a description—a consequence
of the empirical ground we have had to account for. These proposed derived
states (whether identificational or evidential) create a stative proxy while maintaining truth conditions. I speculate that its liberal use in English could be due
to the feature of the present tense in English that requires identification with the
speech moment. Following Taylor (1977), I have assumed that it is only stative
situations that can be identified with a single utterance moment. If anchoring in
English is set up so that the present only works via identity, then the operation
of converting extended situations to snapshot versions of themselves will be
an important and pervasive device. Thus, English has the kind of present tense
that it does, and also has rich auxiliation.[10]

Generally, I have been building up a view of the phrase structure of the
extended verbal projection in which the syntactic zones of the clause are
matched in the semantic ontology with entities of different "sorts." The intuition that an extended projection is rooted in a particular lexical category and is
adorned with successive layers of functional structure (see Grimshaw 1979) is
articulated here in the idea that the first phase is the zone where symbols of the
language are combined and then deployed to make a propositional assertion

about the world. We have moved into zone 2 in this chapter, where we have discussed the perfect and its temporal characteristics. Zones 1 and 2 differ in that zone 1 combines only elements of D_μ to give elements of D_μ, while zone 2 denotes spatiotemporal properties of events and elements of zone 2 combine with elements of D_μ to build more specified spatiotemporal properties of events.

In the next two chapters, I will look at other auxiliary verbs that operate within the situational zone: namely, the modals, both circumstantial and epistemic. The circumstantial modals interact with the aspectual zone in interesting ways, and the epistemic modals interact with tense information and general anchoring. Once again, I will focus on English and on giving explicit denotations for English auxiliary forms, although the nature of the analysis that emerges should reveal properties of the universal spine (see Wiltschko 2014) more generally.

5 Modals and the Spatiotemporal Domain

5.1 Introduction

The view I am pursuing here is that in natural language, propositions are cumulatively built up from lexicalized event properties that are essentially atemporal, subsequently elaborated with spatiotemporal specification, and then anchored to the context in order to create a proposition that is evaluable with respect to truth about the world. With the treatment of the perfect developed in the previous chapter, we are now well into the realm of temporally specified situations. In this chapter and the next, I look at the auxiliary elements in English that can never be embedded under another auxiliary (i.e., those that are always the topmost auxiliary form whenever they are present): the modals, both circumstantial and epistemic, and, more abstractly, "tense." I will assume that these elements all have as one part of their function the job of relating the situational description being built up to the utterance context, thereby anchoring the proposition and making it evaluable with respect to truth.

However, this is not all that the modals do. I will also need to present a specific semantics for modal expressions that does justice to their interpretations with respect to judgments of necessity and possibility. Importantly for this project, which is intimately concerned with relating syntactic and semantic generalizations, I need to account for the fact that many modals in English (and many other languages; see Nauze 2008 for examples) are ambiguous between deontic and epistemic interpretations. Moreover, it is a robust fact about natural languages that epistemic elements are systematically "higher" in the phrase structure representation than deontic ones (see, e.g., Cinque 2005, Narrog 2012).

The purpose of this monograph is not to address all the interesting puzzles and patterns that modality presents, for that would be impossible. However, as in previous chapters, we are in a good position to build on some of the knowledge and insights gained from previous work, and to integrate those results as desiderata into the present framework.

Modal meanings are found in all human languages, but for semanticists and philosophers they present a special kind of challenge because they occur in utterances where we humans make assertions about hypothetical, counterfactual, or future events and, in short, reason explicitly about things that are "not actual." The tool usually used to formalize reference to the nonactual is the notion of a world parameter, which allows us to toggle between the real world (annotated here as w*) and other "possible" but nonactual worlds when expressing meanings. Possible-worlds semantics, as formalized by Kripke (1959, 1963) and Lewis (1973, 1986) and later modified by Kratzer (1977, 1981, 1991) for a formal semantics for natural language modals, is an important backdrop to all formal work on modality. I will be helping myself to world variables in my own formal analysis, but they will be integrated in a rather different way.[1]

The purpose of this chapter is to provide a starting point for a treatment of tense and modality that is consistent with the new ontology and framework being proposed in this monograph. As with the previous chapters, this new set of desiderata will necessitate a shift in thinking. This might seem unnecessary to those satisfied with present theories of modality, but it is crucial if the agenda being pursued here is to be viable. My task, therefore, is to rethink modal semantics in a way that is consistent with the picture I have built up so far, but does justice to the gains and insights already made in this domain within the classical model (essentially Kratzer 1977, 1981, 1991). In some cases, I will argue that my rethink simply packages the domain differently and makes some different choices with respect to the division of labor between syntax-semantics and pragmatics, but is intertranslatable in terms of the things it can express and account for. In other cases, the rethink will give us a new purchase on old puzzles, making some things easier and some things harder. This will be the most interesting aspect of the enterprise. Regardless, the rethink itself is imposed from above by the demands of the new compositional framework and by constraints regarding the interface that I have argued to be independently desirable, so I will simply pursue it to see where it takes us.

The chapter is organized as follows. In section 5.2, I lay out the basics of modal interpretation from the descriptive and syntactic literature, aiming for a fairly theory-neutral description of what any new treatment needs to account for. In section 5.3, I take up the interaction of modal interpretation with negation—an important empirical domain that the proposed analysis will also take into account. In section 5.4, I give an overview of the most important semantic properties in the modal domain and state generalizations in a relatively theory-neutral fashion. In section 5.5, I propose a formal analysis of circumstantial modality designed to fit in with the framework of this monograph. I will show that circumstantial modality and the perfect auxiliary essentially interleave in this inflectional domain and that their effect on the situational description is actually rather similar semantically. They both involve the introduction of a reference situation (something that has been called the "perspectival situation" in modal semantics), therefore establishing an indirect (though systematic) temporal relationship between the event situation and the context.

5.2 What We Know: Syntax

Modal auxiliaries modulate a situational description so that it does not assert the existence of that situation in the world but rather states its *potential* or likelihood for existence, given certain constraints. The two flavors of potentiality encoded by natural language modals appear to be virtual certainty or necessity (as in English *must*) and mere possibility (as in *might, can, could*).

Several different types of modality have been distinguished. *Deontic* modality involves notions of obligation and permission. Some state of affairs is asserted to be "required" or "permitted" by virtue of some regulation or the imposed will of another, often left implicit. The subject of a deontic sentence is often the Actor whose potential for action is being constrained in this way. In (1a), the subject is obligated to go to the party; in (1b), the subject is permitted to go to the party. However, this is not always the case. In (1c) and (1d), the Actor obligated to bring about the described eventuality is left implicit; it could possibly be the hearer.

(1) a. Mary must go to the party.   *Obligation*
    b. Mary may go to the party.   *Permission*
    c. The books must all be on the shelves by noon.   *Obligation*
    d. Flip-flops may be worn in this restaurant.   *Permission*

In *dynamic* modality, the subject's hypothetical possibilities are constrained by the subject's own internal characteristics. Here the subject is always involved.[2]

(2) a. Mary will cheat at Monopoly if she gets the chance.   *Disposition*
    b. Mary can swim.   *Ability*

We can thus say that in the case of dynamic modality, we are dealing with *de se* potentials rather than circumstantial potentials.

Epistemic modality involves potentials that arise because of incomplete knowledge on the part of the speaker. In (3a), the speaker thinks that by virtue

Table 5.1
Modals in English (from Brennan 1993, 8)

	Root	Epistemic
may	Permission	Possibility relative to speaker's knowledge
must	Obligation	Necessity relative to speaker's knowledge
can	(a) Ability (b) Permission	Possibility relative to speaker's knowledge
will	Disposition to behave in a certain way (frequently used with future sense)	Necessity relative to speaker's knowledge

of other things she knows, she can *infer* the truth of the situation described, although she doesn't know it directly; in (3b), the speaker assesses that the situation is merely possible given what she knows.

(3) a. Mary must be in her office now.   *Epistemic necessity*
     b. Mary might be in her office now.   *Epistemic possibility*

Basically, as my descriptions have indicated, what all of these modal uses have in common is that they assert potentials rather than "facts of the matter."

The different modals in English and in particular the epistemic/deontic split have been described and analyzed carefully in many works going back to the 1960s and 1970s (e.g., Perlmutter 1971, Jackendoff 1972, Groenendijk and Stokhof 1975, Palmer 1986, Iatridou 1990, Brennan 1993, Portner 2009).

Consider, for example, Brennan's (1993, 8) analysis in table 5.1. In this table, Root is a category that collapses the nonepistemic readings of a modal; it can include dynamic and quantificational modal readings. Note also that Brennan has chosen to analyze *will* as a modal in its future "tense" use. In this chapter, I will also take the position that there is no meaningful way of distinguishing between *will* and the traditional modals either syntactically or semantically. To this list, I will add the English modals *might*, *should*, *could*, and *would*, which show moribund past tense morphology. Putting aside the morphology for a moment and concentrating on the possible readings, I augment table 5.1 with the forms in table 5.2.

Examples demonstrating epistemic, root, and dynamic meanings for the English modals are given in (4), (5), and (6), respectively.[3]

(4) *Epistemic readings for the English modals*
     a. Mary may be tired after all that swimming, since she is not used to exercise.

Table 5.2
Modals in English (addendum)

	Root	Epistemic
might	Permission in the past[a]	Possibility relative to speaker's knowledge
should	Obligation	Necessity relative to speaker's knowledge
could	Ability in the past	Possibility relative to speaker's knowledge
would	Disposition in the past to behave in a certain way	Hypothetical prediction relative to speaker's knowledge

[a]Archaic

    b. Mary must be tired after all that swimming, since she is not used to exercise.
    c. Mary can't be tired after all that swimming, since she is quite used to exercise.
    d. Mary will be tired after all that swimming, since she is not used to exercise.
    e. Mary might be tired after all that swimming, since she is not used to exercise.
    f. Mary should be tired after all that swimming, since she is not used to exercise.
    g. Mary could be tired after all that swimming, since she is not used to exercise.
    h. (If she had really gone to the pool), Mary would be tired now.

(5) *Root readings for the English modals*
    a. Mary may go to the party since she has done her homework.
    b. Mary must go to the party since she gave John her promise.
    c. Mary can go to the party since she has done her homework.
    d. Mary should go to the party since she gave John her promise.

(6) *Dynamic readings for the English modals*
    a. Mary can swim.
    b. Mary will swim any chance she gets.

How should we characterize the differences between these categories of modality semantically? And once we have a satisfactory semantic characterization, do the semantic types correlate in any way with the syntax? In other words, are there different syntactic representations corresponding to different semantic types?

In what follows, I summarize what I take to be the broad modern consensus for what we know about modality both syntactically and semantically. These are the properties and generalizations that will form the basis of my own analysis.

5.2.1   Thematic Relations: "Raising" vs. "Control"

Early work on the root vs. epistemic distinction argued that there was a lexical difference between the two types, with root and epistemic meanings involving subcategorization frames that included both NP and S and just S, respectively.

(7) $modal_{root}$: (NP) (S) (where NP is some NP in S)
     $modal_{epistemic}$: (S)
     (Jackendoff 1972, cited in Brennan 1993, 61)

Jackendoff (1972) argues that epistemic modals have the distribution of "speaker"-oriented adverbials while root modals have the distribution of "subject"-oriented adverbials. Another popular view has been that modals are a species of main verb and that root modals are transitive (control) predicates while epistemic modals are intransitive (raising) predicates (Ross 1969, Perlmutter 1971, Huddleston 1974). The raising vs. control analysis of epistemic vs. root modality is grounded in the intuition that in root sentences an actual thematic role is assigned to the subject, whereas in epistemic sentences no such role is assigned. This can be seen clearly in the possibility of expletive subjects in epistemic sentences like (8a–b), where the two sentences do not seem to differ in meaning.

(8) a. Mary must be really tired right now.
     b. It must be the case that Mary is really tired right now.

On the other hand, the ability reading of *can* in (9a) is paraphrasable by (9b) but crucially not by (9c).

(9) a.   Mary can swim.
     b.   Mary is capable of swimming.
     c.   *It is capable that Mary swims.

When it comes to deontic readings, however, the situation is more subtle. Certainly, on the most common usage of these modals, there is a failure of paraphrase akin to the dynamic case in (9), indicating a definitive thematic role for the subject. In (10a), the subject is the one who is obligated to perform the act in question. The paraphrase in (10b) is grammatical, but the one in (10c) is not.

(10) a. Mary must pay the extra fees herself.
   b. Mary is obliged to pay the extra fees herself.
   c. *It is obliged that Mary pay the extra fees herself.

However, as mentioned above, there are many "deontic" uses of modals where the subject is *not* the obliged (or "permitted") Actor; instead, the situation as a whole is what is forced or allowed, and the person who is to bring it about is left contextually implicit. In such cases, the deontic modal can be paraphrased perfectly well with a construction that contains an expletive subject for the modal adjective.

(11) a. The shirts must be clean and colorful.
   b. It is required that the shirts be clean and colorful.

(12) a. The exam may be handed in before the deadline.
   b. It is allowed that the exam be handed in before the deadline.

Thus, while it seems right to analyze epistemic readings as taking a single sentential argument syntactically, and dynamic readings as expressing a relationship between a subject and a VP predicate, deontic interpretations seem to be found in both kinds of syntactic subcategorization pattern. While deontic interpretations always do require some sort of Actor who is being obliged or permitted, that individual need not be expressed syntactically.

   Brennan (1993) gives examples of both epistemic modals and deontic modals with expletive subjects, demonstrating that they, unlike dynamic modals, do not obligatorily select for an external argument.

(13) *Epistemic*
   a. It may be raining.
   b. There may be some eggs in the refrigerator.
   c. It must be obvious that I have dyed my hair.
   d. There must be somebody drumming on the roof of the car.

(14) *Deontic*
   a. There may be up to five cars in the lot at one time.
   b. It must be quiet in the reading room at all times.
   c. There must be three lifeguards on duty.

The intermediate position of deontic modality with respect to this diagnostic is paralleled by the subject scope diagnostic described next.

5.2.2 Scope with Respect to a Quantified Subject

Brennan (1993) presents data regarding the relative scope of a quantified subject and the modal force that shows the same pattern as the paraphrase test above. Specifically, when it comes to epistemic readings, a modal can always take scope over the quantified subject, whereas in dynamic readings it may not. To see this, consider (15) and (16) (from Brennan 1993, 115–116). In (15), we find both a contradictory epistemic reading and a noncontradictory one. On the noncontradictory reading, the modal takes wide scope over the quantified subject.

(15) Every radio may get Chicago stations and no radio may get Chicago stations.
Contradictory reading: $\forall x \Diamond [\text{radio}'(x) \rightarrow \text{get-Chicago-stations}(x)]$
$\land \neg \exists x \Diamond [\text{radio}'(x) \land \text{get-Chicago-stations}(x)]$
Noncontradictory reading: $\Diamond [\forall x [\text{radio}'(x) \rightarrow \text{get-Chicago-stations}(x)]]$
$\land \Diamond [\neg \exists x [\text{radio}'(x) \land \text{get-Chicago-stations}(x)]]$

If we instead use a dynamic modal, the ability modal *can*, the sentence has only the contradictory reading.

(16) Every radio can get Chicago stations and no radio can get Chicago stations.

With deontic modals, both contradictory and noncontradictory readings are possible, as in the epistemic case. (As Brennan does not give an example of this case, I have provided my own.)

(17) Every child can be invited and no child can be invited, but you are not allowed to play favorites!

See also Bobaljik and Wurmbrand 1999 for detailed arguments that both deontic and epistemic modals need to be seen as raising predicates.

5.2.3 Modals and Symmetric Predicates

Finally, Brennan (1993) gives an interesting argument from symmetric predicates that indicates once again that the dynamic modals clearly modulate the event concept and affect the thematic role for the external argument, while epistemic modals do not. A symmetric (or reflexive) predicate R is one for which $R(x, y)$ entails $R(y, x)$. Examples in English are *shake hands with* and *get the same score as*. For example, (18a) entails (18b) and (19a) entails (19b).

(18) a. The governor shook hands with all the prisoners.
     b. All the prisoners shook hands with the governor.

(19) a. Peter got the same score as Joan.
     b. Joan got the same score as Peter.

If we add modal auxiliaries to these sentences, the entailment is clearly disturbed under dynamic interpretations. (20a) does not entail (20b). Peter might have the ability to get the same score as Joan no matter how high she scores, but the same might not be true of Joan with respect to Peter.

(20) a. Peter can get the same score as Joan.
   b. Joan can get the same score as Peter.

On the epistemic reading of the modal *might*, the entailments of symmetric predicates remain completely undisturbed, however. For example, (21a) and (21b) are mutually entailing.

(21) a. The governor might shake hands with all the prisoners.
   b. All the prisoners might shake hands with the governor.

   When it comes to deontic readings, in the cases where the subject is also the Actor whose actions are being manipulated by permissions and prohibitions, the entailment is also clearly disturbed. In the situation in (22), I may have given the governor permission to shake hands with whomever he or she likes, but not have allowed the prisoners themselves to make any such overtures, so that (22a) does not entail (22b).

(22) a. The governor may shake hands with all the prisoners.
   b. All the prisoners may shake hands with the governor.

However, if we construct a deontic sentence where the locus of the permission is not explicitly represented in the sentence, as in (23), then it seems that the entailment in fact goes through. If, for example, you are told that in the interests of keeping the peace, you must make sure that the situation in (23) comes to pass, then (23a) expresses exactly the same prescription as (23b).

(23) a. The girls must get the same score as the boys.
   b. The boys must get the same score as the girls.

   Thus, once again, when the subject is the locus of permission or prohibition, deontic modals pattern with dynamic modals, and they pattern with the epistemic modals otherwise. The classification and the diagnostics are summarized in table 5.3.

5.2.4 Ordering and Typology

We have already noted that regardless of its interpretation, an English modal always ends up in the highest position of the clause it appears in. Thus, from the surface position of an English modal it is not easy to see that there actually exist ordering patterns that have fairly robust typological support.

   If we look at Swedish, which is quite similar to English in many respects, but which has modals that can occur in nonfinite forms, a more fine-grained pattern emerges.[4]

Table 5.3
Major subtypes of modals and their properties

	Semantic role for subject	Modal scope with respect to subject	Persistence of symmetry
Dynamic	Yes	Modal low	No
Deontic	Yes/No	Ambiguous	No/Yes
Epistemic	No	Ambiguous	Yes

The first thing to observe is that the modal 'can' in its dynamic meaning in Swedish, referring to ability, can appear inflected directly for past tense.

(24) Han kunde   skriva   klart   sin uppsats.
     he   can.PAST write.INF finished/ready his article
     'He was able to finish his article.' (PAST > Dynamic modal)

When we look at the interaction of the dynamic modal with the perfect auxiliary 'have', we find that it can be successfully embedded under 'have' to give (25). The other order, shown in (26), is not possible.

(25) Han har kunnat   skriva   klart   sin uppsats.
     he   has can.PASTPART write.INF finished/ready his article
     'He was able to finish his article.' (HAVE > Dynamic modal)

(26) Han kan ha   skrivit   klart   sin uppsats.
     he   can have.INF write.PASTPART finished/ready his article
     '*It is capable that he has finished his article.' (*Dynamic modal > HAVE)

Turning to the epistemic version of 'can', we find the opposite ordering with respect to the auxiliary 'have'. It is perfectly possible to embed 'have' under the epistemic modal, as the grammatical interpretation for (26) shows.

(27) Han kan ha   skrivit   klart   sin uppsats.
     he   can have.INF write.PASTPART finished/ready his article
     'It is possible that he has finished his article.' (Epistemic modal > HAVE)

Turning finally to deontic modality, the modal auxiliary 'must' can receive a deontic reading of obligation, and under this reading it can embed the perfect auxiliary 'have', as in (28).[5]

(28) Han måste   ha   gört   leksan   innan Fredag.
     he   must.PRES have.INF do.PASTPART the.homework within Friday
     'He must have the homework done by Friday.' (Deontic modal >
     HAVE)

Unfortunately, in Swedish 'must' is a modal that has no nonfinite form (like
the English modals), so to check whether deontic modality can be embedded
under 'have', we need to choose a more inflectionally flexible deontic modal.
The clearest possibility deontic modal in Swedish is *få*, which is the most
common verb for expressing permission. In their most natural order, the perfect
auxiliary takes scope over this modal, as in (29).

(29) Han har fått   göra   det hele   sitt liv.
     he   has got.PASTPART do.INF that whole his life
     'He has been allowed to do that his whole life.' (HAVE > Deontic
     modal)

Finally, when two modals cooccur, the epistemic modal is always higher than
the root modal.

(30) Han måste   kunnat   skriva   klart   sin uppsats.
     he   must.PAST can.PASTPART write.INF finished/ready his article
     'He must have been able to finish writing his article.' (Epistemic
     model > Dynamic modal)

As these data show, then, 'have' in Swedish is higher than dynamic modality
and lower than epistemic modality, but it seems to be in principle interleavable
with deontic modality. I will assume that this is true for English *have* also, and
accordingly I place the base position for deontic meanings within the same
zone as the perfect auxiliary discussed in chapter 4.

This pattern is found quite generally crosslinguistically (see, e.g., Nauze
2008). Nauze (2008) finds broad support for the following hierarchy, proposed
also by Cinque (2005).

(31) Epistemic modality < Circumstantial modality < Dynamic modality

In English, however, word order never gives direct evidence for this hierarchical order, although the above diagnostics concerning the subject position and
scope give indirect evidence for it.

Another piece of evidence that might suggest hierarchical differences in
the base position of modals even in English comes from the taxonomy of
modals themselves, which seem to be in an interesting implicational relation with respect to the readings they allow. If we list the three types of

reading—dynamic, circumstantial, and epistemic—according to the height established via crosslinguistic typology, we can see that if a modal has a "lower" reading in English, then it also has all the corresponding higher readings, but the reverse implication does not hold.

(32) *Dynamic*   *Circumstantial*   *Epistemic*
      can/could   can/could   can't/could
      will/would   will/would   will/would
                       may   may
                       must   must
                       should   should
                                           might

In terms of closeness to the root, it should also be noted that the suffix *-able*, which creates adjectives with a "modal" flavor from verbal roots, is confined to dynamic meanings, the lowest of the three possibilities, where the internal properties of the subject are what are at stake.

(33) a. The book can be read.   *Circumstantial or dynamic*
     b. The book is readable.   *Dynamic: Inherent property*

The same seems to be true of the suffix *-er*, which creates nouns with a generic/type sense with the flavor of dynamic dispositional modality.

(34) a. John will cheat at Monopoly.   *Dispositional or futurate*
     b. John is a cheater.   *Dispositional only*

5.2.5 Taking Stock

The syntactic literature thus suggests that the different classes of modal—dynamic, deontic, and epistemic—correlate systematically with different syntactic behaviors that all implicate height of attachment. First, there seems to be a major zonal rift between dynamic modality and the other two categories. Table 5.4 shows that the properties of dynamic modality strongly implicate the lowest domain of nonspatiotemporal eventive properties as expressed by elements of D_μ. Dynamic modulations are difficult in principle to separate from the event description itself, they show no scopal ambiguity with respect to higher elements, and they can be expressed by derivational suffixes such as *-able* and *-er*.

We can also motivate a syntactic height distinction within the higher category that includes circumstantial and epistemic modality. The differences I will assume to hold between these two higher categories are listed in table 5.5.

It is still important to keep in mind, however, that English modals actually show no difference in *surface* height. These facts hold for all the English

Table 5.4
Distinguishing dynamic modality

Dynamic Participant-internal modality	Circumstantial/Epistemic Participant-external modality
Cannot have expletive subjects	Can have expletive subjects
Disrupts symmetry in symmetric argument structures	Variable
Occurs lowest in a sequence of modals crosslinguistically	Variable
Scopes low with respect to (polar) negation	Variable
Scopes low with respect to subject position	Variable
Can be expressed by derivational suffixation in English	Cannot be expressed by derivational suffixation in English

Table 5.5
Distinguishing circumstantial from epistemic modality

Circumstantial modality	Epistemic modality
Is lower than epistemics under cooccurrence	Is higher than circumstantials under cooccurrence
Can be past-shifted with regular tense morphology in some languages	Morphological past cannot shift modal state
Can take scope under the subject	Never takes scope under the subject
Cannot interaction with speaker-oriented meanings	Is speaker-oriented

modals: a modal never cooccurs with any other modal (35a); when a modal occurs, it is always the highest auxiliary (35b); modals invert in questions (35c) and can form tags; modals can host clitic negation (35d).

(35) a. *John must can do that.
      b. John must be teasing the cat.
      c. Must John always tease the cat?
      d. John mustn't tease the cat.

This does not mean that modal interpretations cannot be correlated with height of attachment in English. It means only that whatever the initial Merge position of a modal is, in English it obligatorily raises to the position that used to be called Infl. I will discuss the role of modals as anchoring elements in Wiltschko's (2014) sense in chapter 6.

5.3   Interaction with Negation

In this section, I examine the scope of modal meaning with respect to the scope of negation in English. This is an area that could potentially provide semantic evidence for the base position of different modal elements, if a clear pattern could be found. The first problem we will encounter in evaluating the data, however, is that the position of negation itself is less clear and reliable from a typological point of view than that of the other verbal elements discussed so far in this monograph. This problem is compounded by the fact that different types of negation have been distinguished: constituent negation, metalinguistic or "high" negation, and clausal polarity negation. Zanuttini (1992, 1997) argues for at least two possible positions for negation in Italian, even when just polarity negation is taken into account. Schwarz and Bhatt (2006) argue for "high" negation, which has different presuppositional properties from standard polarity negation.

(36)

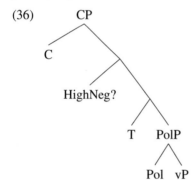

When examining the data, we must therefore take care to keep the type of negation under consideration fixed.

In this section, I first summarize the facts of English modals with respect to scope of negation, searching for a generalization. I then explore a purely semantic account of the patterns.

5.3.1   English Modals Are Idiosyncratic

Interestingly, most modals in English seem to categorically prefer one scope position with respect to polarity negation regardless of their flavor in any particular usage (see Cormack and Smith 2002).

(37) a. *Modals that scope over polarity negation*
        should, must, will, would, might, may   *Epistemic*
     b. *Modals that scope under polarity negation*
        dare, need, can, could, may   *Deontic*

The natural option for ranging these modals with respect to polarity is shown in (38).

(38)

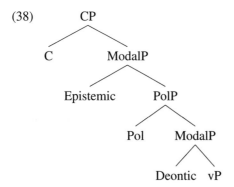

However, this picture is immediately falsified by *should* in its epistemic and deontic uses, which consistently scope above negation (39), and by *could* in its epistemic and circumstantial uses, both of which scope under negation (40).

(39) a. John shouldn't eat so much chocolate.   SHOULD > ¬
     b. John shouldn't miss his plane—he left early.   SHOULD > ¬

(40) a. John couldn't go to the party.   ¬ > COULD
     b. John couldn't be there yet—he left way too late.   ¬ > COULD

One might think that perhaps the ordering with respect to negation is more sensitive to the modal force of the modal in question and that the hierarchies are more semantic in nature. A first try at representing this ordering might be (41).

(41)

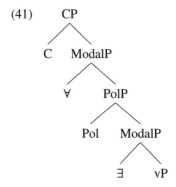

However, this doesn't work either because there are universal modals that scope under negation, as well as existential modals that scope above it.

Table 5.6
Microcomparison I between Swedish and English modals

Etymon	Force	Modal base	Scope with respect to negation	Nonfinites
måste	∀	Deontic/Epistemic	Below	No
must	∀	Deontic/Epistemic	Above	No

(42) a. John doesn't need to go to the party.   ¬ > NEED (∀)

     b. John might not go to the party.   MIGHT (∃) > ¬

To repeat, even when a modal has multiple readings (dynamic, deontic, epistemic), its scope with respect to negation carries over to all of them. This suggests that each of these "ambiguous" modals is a single lexical item, and that its requirements with respect to negation are an integral part of its meaning, regardless of "height" of attachment.[6]

But maybe English is especially rigid not because of something to do with modal meanings per se, but because the English modals all have a uniform final position in the sentence and none of them possess nonfinite morphological forms. While it is unclear what effect this might have, we can take a shortcut in our search for a linguistic generalization by comparing English with its closely related Germanic cousin, Swedish. Swedish has the modal *måste*, which is like English *must* in having both deontic and epistemic interpretations and in having no nonfinite forms.

(43) Nigel must not do that.

(44) Fredrik måste inte göra   det.
    Fredrik must not do.INF that
    'Fredrik doesn't have to do that.'   ¬ > ∀

Comparing (43) and (44) reveals that Swedish forces an interpretation where negation scopes above the modal *måste*, whereas in English as we have seen negation scopes consistently below *must* (see table 5.6).

Now, comparing the English *can* with Swedish *kunna*, we find that although *kunna* shows a variety of nonfinite forms and the freedom to occur under the perfect and under other modals, its scope with respect to negation is identical to that of *can* (see table 5.7).

(45) Nigel can't do that.

Table 5.7
Microcomparison II between Swedish and English modals

Etymon	Force	Modal base	Scope with respect to negation	Nonfinites
kunna	∃	Deontic/Epistemic	Below	Yes
can	∃	Deontic/Epistemic	Below	No

(46) Fredrik kan inte göra   det.
     Fredrik can not do.INF that
     'Fredrik can't do that.'   ¬ > ∃

This second microcomparison is summarized in table 5.7.

It seems as if there is no hope for a generalization based on the simple parameters of modal meaning or surface syntactic positioning. There are two sort-of generalizations that emerge from the data, although they are not easy to encode in a simple hierarchy.

(47) a. *Interpretational constraint:* *ALLOW-NOT
        There are no deontic, existential interpretations that scope over negation. (Iatridou and Zeijlstra (2013) also say they found none such.)
     b. *Lexical constraint:* *NOT-NECESSARY
        There are no universal modals that are *just* epistemic that scope under negation.

The status of generalizations differs slightly since the first is a constraint on interpretations, while the second is a constraint on modal lexical items.

I conclude that the failure to find a clean correlation here says something important about modal syntax and semantics. It looks like the data force an analysis whereby each modal *selects* for negation in its own idiosyncratic way. In what follows, I will propose that this is a form of *syntactic selection* (c-selection), which—although it has semantic implications—is not reducible to an independently establishable semantic property.

5.3.2 A Semantic Account of the Idiosyncrasy?

The puzzle of the interaction between modal quantificational meanings and negation has of course received attention in the semantic literature; see Israel 1996, Homer 2012, Iatridou and Zeijlstra 2013. The consensus reached in these works is that modal meanings come with a specific "polarity" sensitivity.

Table 5.8
Polarity classification of deontic modals in English (Iatridou and Zeijlstra 2013)

	PPIs	Neutral	NPIs
Universal	*must, should, ought to*	*have to, need to*	*need*
Existential		*can, may*	

To summarize Iatridou and Zeijlstra's (2013) proposal:

- Some modals are positive polarity items (PPIs), some are negative polarity items (NPIs), and some are neutral.
- All modals in English (regardless of flavor) are generated in a position below Infl and indeed below Neg.
- All modals in English (regardless of flavor) move to Infl because they are tensed.
- This movement reconstructs optionally depending on the polarity requirements of the particular modal.
- The reconstructed position is the default, and is the only one available for the neutral modals.
- The PPI modals are not allowed to reconstruct because of their polarity sensitivity and hence are interpreted only in the "high" position.

Iatridou and Zeijlstra only look specifically at deontic modality. Their classification of the modals in English with respect to polarity is shown in table 5.8.

Homer's (2012) analysis is similar to Iatridou and Zeijlstra's (2013) in that (i) the base position of all modals is below Polarity Phrase (PolP), and (ii) it is the PPIs like *must* that are special. In order to capture the PPI effects, in Homer's account a modal like *must* has to move out to take scope over negation.

However, the semantic analysis of PPI-ness is truly an *independent* explanation from the semantic side only if we can show that there is something about the semantics of these items that gives rise to their polarity behavior. In fact, formal semanticists know a lot about the meanings of PPIs and NPIs and the reasons why they behave the way they do. Unfortunately, even though "modal" PPIs share some distributional behavior with traditional NPIs and PPIs, many of the explanations and decompositions valid for those NPIs and PPIs do not seem to be independently verifiable for "modal" PPIs. (See Homer 2012 and Iatridou and Zeijlstra 2013.) As Iatridou and Zeijlstra put it:

How can we prove that *must* (and the other PPI modals) obligatorily introduce domain alternatives? In truth, we cannot. The reality is that, in general, the diagnostics for detecting whether some element introduces domain alternatives are very weak. ... The only thing that can be said is that if elements like *must* are assigned the ability to introduce alternatives, then it may be possible to express their PPI-hood in certain preexisting frameworks. Moreover, if such an analysis is correct, the question arises as to why *must* is banned only from antiadditive contexts and not from all downward entailing contexts.

Another problem that arises is this: since nothing specific in the discussion of polarity hinges on the choice of world variables instead of variables over individuals, we would expect there to be universal PPIs and existential NPIs in both domains of quantification. This is not the case, however. In the domain of individuals, PPIs and NPIs only seem to come with existential force; no polarity items with universal force over individuals seem to exist. However, when we look at deontic modals, PPIs and NPIs are found only among items with universal force. That is, among the deontic modals, no PPIs or NPIs with existential force have been reported. (Iatridou and Zeijlstra 2013, 557–558)

It is also notable that Homer at least is forced to stipulate an overt scopal movement for *must*. But this should be seen as quite striking and unusual, given all that is known about quantificational elements and their scopal interactions. Adverbial elements are interpreted in their "surface" structure position, assumed in these cases to be the same as their base-generated position; this is true of negation in particular. Quantificational DPs can often appear displaced from what is assumed to be their base position, and they also seem to give rise to ambiguity in their scopal relationship with other items.

So if modals are quantificational elements, do they pattern with negation or do they pattern with quantificational DPs in their scope-taking behavior? First of all, it seems as if the English modals do not surface in their base-generated position—not if we are going to tie differences in the modal base to height of first Merge. But they are not interpreted uniformly with respect to their base positions, nor are they interpreted uniformly with respect to their surface positions. Specifically, with respect to the semantic proposals discussed above, we could ask, why don't all modals scope under negation if they're base-generated there? Or similarly, why don't they all scope over negation if they all end up higher than polarity negation on the surface? Somehow, we have to say that modals like *must* do not reconstruct for scope under polarity negation, while modals like *can* obligatorily reconstruct. What is the independent *semantic* fact that guarantees this? Especially given the fact that English *must* and Swedish *måste* are otherwise identical in their range of interpretations, but differ with respect to PPI-ness. Further, why should head movement have an effect on scope, and then only for certain lexical items?

(48) *The difference between English* must *and Swedish* måste *under a reconstruction account*
Swedish: *Måste* obligatorily reconstructs for scope with respect to polarity negation.

English: *Must* cannot reconstruct for scope; instead, it must take scope in its surface position.

If we allow more ordering flexibility within the second-phase (situational) domain, and in particular allow PolP to attach freely within that domain, then there is an alternative way of stating the facts. Basically, the ordering of circumstantial modality and PolP is in principle free in this system, and the actual order found for each modal depends idiosyncratically on selection. In this version, the modals' behavior with respect to negation is due to syntactic selection under locality; no movement for scope taking is allowed or required.

(49) *The difference between English* must *and Swedish* måste *under a selection account*
Swedish: *Måste* selects for a polarity-neutral property of situational properties.
English: *Must* selects for PolP within the situational domain.

If we assume that *may* is actually two items, *may*₁ (deontic) and *may*₂ (epistemic), then the English modals have the selectional properties shown in box 5.1.

Box 5.1
Selectional properties of English modals

Polarity phrase	should, must, will, would, might
	may_2
Situational phrase	can, could, need
	may_1

When we compare this directly with the PPI account, the so-called PPI modals turn out to be those that *select for* PolP. Let us see how this selectional restatement, together with the following plausible assumptions about the functional sequence, gives the correct results.

• High negation is located in the left periphery (the extended C domain); low negation (constituent negation of verbs), in the first phase; and PolP, in the inflectional, second-phase zone of the clause. (PolP is the label I give to traditional clausal/polarity negation.)
• There can be only one PolP within the second phase. The positive setting of polarity does not correspond to an overt morpheme in English. Every inflectional domain/second phase must contain a PolP.

- PolP has no rigid place within the second phase.
- Interpretation of any element with respect to negation is based on its first Merge position.

If a modal selects for PolP, it will not be detectable when the polarity is positive, but it will scope above any expressed polarity negation. Modals that select for a polarity-neutral situational description will always have PolP merged above them at some stage; therefore, polarity negation will always scope over those modals. When polarity is negative, negation is always interpreted below *must* and above *can*. The classification is made lexical item by lexical item, not reading by reading, as is to be expected if this is a lexical c-selection property. The syntactic selection view also accounts for the locality of the effect and for the fact that it concerns polarity negation specifically, and not "high" negation.

The more explanatory question that we posed to the PPI account also needs to be posed to the selectional account. If this really is a matter of syntactic selection, why is there such a close selectional relationship between modal meanings and negation, and how does it affect the compositional semantics of these forms? I will address this question in section 5.5, but for now I merely note that circumstantial modality must interleave with PolP in the inflectional domain, and whether a particular modal combines with a polarity-specified projection or not seems to be a matter of lexical specification at the level of c-selection.

5.4   Semantic Properties of Modals: The Classical Theory

Up to this point, I have deliberately refrained from giving an introduction to the classical model for interpreting modal meanings in natural language, the Kratzerian model (Kratzer 1977, 1981, 1991). In this section, I offer a schematic introduction, concentrating on the intuitions and logical underpinnings of the system. (For a more step-by-step and technically explicit exposition, see for example Portner 2009.) My own analysis will not require engaging with the technical details of the classical model, but it is important to see how the two are related and how they differ.

For an understanding of the systems of logic underpinning modal reasoning, I am indebted to McNamara 2014, which has inspired some of the initial presentation and which supplies detailed references.

The formal tradition for thinking about the semantic properties of modals comes from philosophers and logicians. The latter were concerned first and foremost with logical relations among propositions and not with the inner workings of natural language, but in the realm of epistemic modality there

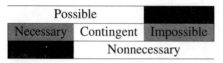

Figure 5.1
Alethic Modality

Necessary   Impossible

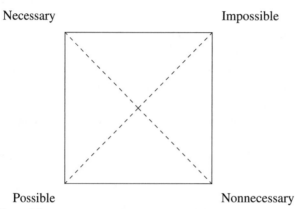

    Possible   Nonnecessary
Figure 5.2
Alethic Modality: Square of Oppositions

are clear natural language expressions that map nicely to these notions. Possibility and necessity (conventionally notated as $\diamond$ and $\square$, respectively) can be thought of as notions that can partition the domain of propositions into jointly exhaustive and mutually exclusive subclasses according to the schema shown in figure 5.1.

If we express this schema in terms of a square of oppositions, we get the diagram in figure 5.2. Here, the dashed lines represent the contradictories, entailments follow the vertical lines from top to bottom, the topmost horizontal line links contraries, and the bottommost horizontal line links subcontraries.

The logic is usually axiomatized on the basis of the "Necessary" primitive, from which all of the other notions can be defined with the help of negation.[7] In addition, it is usually assumed that the two statements in (50) hold.

(50) a. If $\square$p, then p
      (If a proposition is necessary, then it is true.)
   b. If p, then $\diamond$p
      (If a proposition is true, then it is possible.)

These indeed seem like rather unremarkable and harmless assumptions.

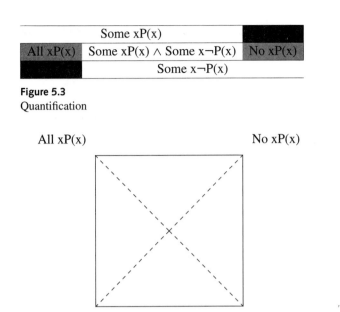

Some xP(x)		
All xP(x)	Some xP(x) ∧ Some x¬P(x)	No xP(x)
	Some x¬P(x)	

Figure 5.3
Quantification

All xP(x)   No xP(x)

Some xP(x)   Some x¬P(x)

Figure 5.4
Quantification: Square of oppositions

A natural analogy allows us to move from the alethic domain to the domain of quantification. Here, necessity has its parallel in universal quantification, and possibility, in existential quantification. In this case, the partition works out as shown in figure 5.3. The corresponding square of oppositions appears in figure 5.4.

The reason I am spelling this out in perhaps overly obvious detail is that I wish to highlight the fact that the classical model for interpreting modality in terms of possible worlds is a rewriting based on the success of the analogy between the quantificational square and the alethic square. As McNamara (2014, sec. 2.2) puts it, "These deep quantificational analogies reflect much of the inspiration behind 'possible world semantics' for such logics. Once the analogies are noticed, this sort of semantics seems all but inevitable."

Once the analogy is noticed, it is possible to give a (Kripkean) possible worlds semantics for modal logic in the following way. We assume a set of possible worlds W. We also assume a relation R relating worlds to worlds that have something in common. Formally, we can think of a model M as consisting of a pair W and R and a valuation function that assigns truth values to propositions in a particular world. (We assume that propositions are either true or false in a world, and never both.) We can call the set of all worlds v for which the relation R(w, v) holds, the set of all worlds that are *accessible* from w. Intuitively, the set of all accessible worlds from the base world will be the set that the modal operator quantifies over.

Formally, therefore, we can translate the notion of necessity into universal quantification in the following way, with definitions taken from Portner 2009. Skipping the standard axioms relating to the general propositional calculus, I cut to the chase and give the definitions for necessity modals and possibility modals in (51a) and (51b), respectively.

(51)   a. α is of the form $\Box\beta$ and for all v such that R(w, v), $[\![\beta]\!]^{v,M} = 1$.
           ($\Box\beta$ is true iff β is true in *all* members of W accessible from w.)
       b. α is of the form $\Diamond\beta$ and for some v such that R(w, v), $[\![\beta]\!]^{v,M} = 1$.
           ($\Box\beta$ is true iff β is true in *some* member of W accessible from w.)

The beauty and elegance of the Simple Modal Logic Hypothesis, as Portner calls it, is that "the meaning of every modal expression in natural language can be expressed in terms of only two properties: (a) whether it is a necessity or possibility modal, and (b) its accessibility relation R" (Portner 2009, 31). For example, we can imagine the epistemic frame shown in (52).

(52) *Epistemic frame*
      F = <W, R> is an epistemic frame iff for some individual i
      • W = the set of possible worlds conceivable by humans.
      • R = the relation that holds between two worlds w and w' iff everything that i knows in w is also true in w'.

We can extend the analogy to the deontic frame and posit a domain of quantification defined by the accessibility relation corresponding to the "rules" established by a certain context.

(53) *Deontic frame*
      F = <W, R> is a deontic frame iff for some system of rules r
      • W = the set of possible worlds conceivable by humans.
      • R = the relation that holds between two worlds w and w' iff all of the rules that r establishes in w are followed in w'.

In fact, there is no limit to the contextual specificity of the modal bases one could imagine. There could be subvarieties of deontic modal bases according to what kinds of laws or desiderata are involved, and these could be filled in by context. We could also imagine other modal bases such as *buletic* conversational backgrounds related to wishes and *teleological* conversational backgrounds related to aims.

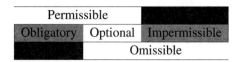

Figure 5.5
Deontic Modality

That the nature of R is flexible and subject to both contextual and linguistic modulation by means of framing adverbials has been amply demonstrated by Kratzer (1977). Two examples where the adverbial clause makes explicit the nature of the R that is being assumed are given in (54).

(54) a. In view of the laws of Massachusetts, drivers must yield to pedestrians.
  b. In view of the traditions of our famiily, you, as the youngest child, must read the story on Christmas Eve.

Because of the variability of deontic interpretations, which range all the way from explicit commands and permissions to general circumstantial facilitating and inhibiting conditions, I will follow Kratzer in referring to this class of modal interpretations as *circumstantial* modality.

However, there is some reason for disquiet. If we are explicit about the analogy between the alethic and quantificational schemas and the schema we would set up for permissions and obligations, we see that things do not work out quite as we would wish. Treatments of classical deontic logic do in fact operate with a schema parallel to the one shown in figure 5.1, with obligation (OB(p)) replacing necessity and permissibility (PE(p)) replacing possibility; see figure 5.5. As with the alethic case, these modal notions are assumed to partition the space of propositions exhaustively and are mutually exclusive. This partition gives rise to the square of oppositions in figure 5.6.

This seems all well and good except that unlike in the other two cases, the simple entailments that might be expected do not appear to go through.

(55) a. OB(p) does not entail p.
  b. p does not entail PE(p).

In other words, just because someone has an obligation to do something, it does not necessarily get done. And if p is the case, it might not actually have been permitted.

The original Kratzerian system has the advantage of modeling the unity behind the different meanings of the English modals in different instances of use, but it does this only if we choose to ignore the logical disanalogies between the quantificational system and the logic of permission and obligation.

Obligatory   Impermissible

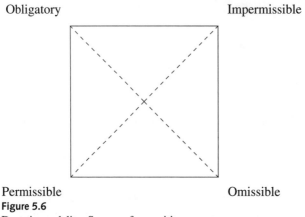

Permissible   Omissible
Figure 5.6
Deontic modality: Square of oppositions

In addition, the classical system fails to connect the systematic differences between circumstantial modality and epistemic modality with respect to syntactic height in the verbal extended projection.[8] As in the classical system, we want to build in the intuitive similarities and differences between epistemic and circumstantial flavors of modality, but quantification over different modal bases is not the only way to express those similiarities and differences between the different levels of modal expression. I will retain the use of possible worlds to express hypotheticality and potential in the semantic representation, but I will employ a semantics of "choice" rather than universal vs. existential quantification over possible worlds. Only in the case of logical choices will the two schemas be equivalent.

It is important to note that great strides have been made toward solving the problem of relativizing modal interpretation to height of attachment by Valentine Hacquard in her dissertation and many subsequent papers (Hacquard 2006, etc.). Hacquard makes an important and influential proposal extending the Kratzerian system to account for generalizations at the syntax-semantics interface. In particular, she is at pains to reconcile the elegance of the Kratzerian system, where a single underspecified meaning can handle both epistemic and root interpretations, with the results of linguistic typology (cartography), which suggest that epistemic readings attach higher in the clause, *outside* T, and that root meanings attach *inside* T. She proposes a system that ties particular types of interpretation to height in the structure. Her idea is to replace the base world from which the modal base is calculated with an event instead, and relate the semantic differences to differences in how that event is anchored. Anchoring in turn is sensitive to the height of the modal in question. Specifically, Hacquard claims that

- when the modal is speaker-oriented, it is keyed to the utterance time and receives an epistemic interpretation;
- when the modal is attitude holder–oriented, it is keyed to the attitude time and receives an epistemic interpretation; and
- when the modal is subject-oriented, it is keyed to the time provided by tense and receives a root interpretation.

Hacquard otherwise keeps intact the central structure of the Kratzerian solution: the idea that modals are functions from sets of possible worlds to sets of possible worlds; a restriction via contextually defined modal bases; ordering sources; existential vs. universal quantification.

Hacquard's proposal is important because it moves the formal apparatus into a position where it can operate in a way that makes it sensitive to syntactic context. It does so by making the contextual variable that determines the modal base bindable from within the sentence, depending on how high the modal is attached. Crucially, to make the proposal work, Hacquard must first modify the system so that it is an "event" that provides the base, not a world.

For the system being built up and defended in this monograph, the semantic type of a constituent varies systematically according to the particular zone it occurs in. Also, the zones correspond to the three main types of modal meaning. It seems natural, therefore, to try to derive the differences in interpretation directly from the *semantic properties of the complement* of the modal, rather than via the binding of a contextual variable as in Hacquard's system. I now turn to this task, for the circumstantial modals.

5.5 Circumstantial Modals as Modifiers of Spatiotemporal Properties

In the system I am proposing, spatiotemporal properties of the event being described are the elements denoted in the second, inflectional domain of the clause. I assume that a spatiotemporal relation between an event and a reference/perspectival situation also includes a specification of possible world. Thus, "accessibility" relations, encoded as R in Portner's (2009) schema, are in effect subtypes of f (properties of the event–anchor relationship), properties of which are the business of the second zone. It will make sense, then, that circumstantial modality in general is expressed in this domain. In contrast, dynamic modality seems to refer to inherent or intrinsic properties of the agent with respect to a particular event, and it will make sense to try to express these meanings in the first zone. Finally, epistemic modality is about the knowledge and choices of the speaker in seeking to make a truthful assertion. We should try to make that fall out from the fact that epistemic modals are attached even higher in the functional sequence than circumstantial modality. Once again, ideally we would like a unified denotation for modal meanings that underpins all three types of event modulation.

To preserve the insights of the classical model within the present system, we need to find a way to represent the flexibility of the modal base and tie it to height of attachment. We have assumed so far that the inflectional domain, the second zone, is characterized by the fact that it builds properties of anchored event properties. I repeat the denotation for something of the AspP type in (56).

(56) $[\![\text{AspP}]\!] = \lambda f \lambda d \exists e[\text{Utterance}(d) \wedge f(d)(e) \wedge \llcorner u \lrcorner (e)]$

In the case of the perfect, merging an auxiliary introduces a new situational variable that constitutes an intermediate reference situation for the ultimate anchoring relationship for the first-phase event. Specifically, *have* introduces a reference situation s' that is related to e and then serves as an intermediary in anchoring e to the utterance situation d.

(57) $[\![\text{have}]\!] = \lambda Q \lambda x \lambda f' \lambda d \exists s' \exists f[Q(f)(d) \wedge \text{State}(s') \wedge \text{HOLDER}(s') = x \wedge f =$
$\lambda s \lambda d[s' \text{gives evidence for the spatiotemporal relation between } s \text{ and}$
$d \text{ in the same world as } s'] \wedge f'(s')(d)]$

For the circumstantial modal auxiliary, I will assume something similar. The modal will introduce a perspectival situational variable s' with respect to which the situation denoted by the first-phase s_0 is oriented. While the perfect expresses an inferential relation between the reference situation and the prejacent situation, the modal will express a projective, predictive relation between the two.

The parallelism between the modal auxiliary and the perfect auxiliary is illustrated in figures 5.7 and 5.8. Figure 5.7 shows the schematic relationship for the perfect. The perfect auxiliary introduces an s' reference situation, which is the outer situational variable that will eventually be anchored to tense. The relationship between s' and s_0 is evidential/inferential, and s_0 is in the determined past with respect to s'. Figure 5.8 shows the corresponding picture for the circumstantial modal. The modal auxiliary also introduces an intermediate, or reference, or perspectival situation that is the outer situational variable eventually subject to anchoring. But now the relationship between s' and s_0 is projective instead of inferential.

Comparing the two figures, we can see that they express a metaphysical modal base schema (as described in Condoravdi 2002 and Werner 2006) in which worlds are strictly identical up to a given time (the actual world) and only diverge in the future of that given time. Within the metaphysical scheme,

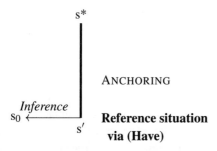

Figure 5.7
Schema for the perfect

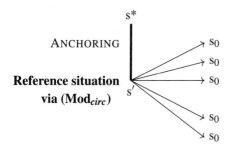

Figure 5.8
Schema for circumstantial modality

the perfect asserts the base situation to be in the determined past of the reference situation; the circumstantial modal asserts the base situation to be in the projective nondetermined future of the reference situation.

For circumstantial modality, therefore, I will express the primitive notion of circumstantial possibility in terms of open choices. Circumstantial choices are simply different possible future situations from a particular situational perspective. It cannot therefore have a time specification that is either present or past with respect to the perspectival situation. The modal combines with the constituent expressing properties of spatiotemporal properties of s_0 anchored at d, and states that such an f exists as a vector expressing s_0 as a choice from s'. The denotation for the circumstantial modal is thus as follows:

(58) $[\![\text{Mod}_{circ}]\!] = \lambda Q \lambda x \lambda f' \lambda d \exists s' \exists f [Q(f)(d) \wedge \text{State}(s') \wedge \text{HOLDER}(s') = $
        $x \wedge f = \lambda s \lambda d [s \text{ is located at a world-time pair that is a CHOICE for}$
        the perspectival topic in $s'] \wedge f'(s')(d)]$

That is, there is a perspectival stative situation s' for which s_0 (the situation characterized by the event property described in the first phase) is a live alternative for the topic argument. It is this perspectival stative situation that will eventually be anchored by the tense predicate. As a concrete example, consider (59).

(59) a. Vidar may eat the chocolate.

       b.   ModP $\lambda f' \lambda d \exists s' \exists f, s_0 [\llcorner u \lrcorner (s_0) \wedge \text{Topic}(s_0) = \text{Topic}(s') = \text{Vidar}$
                        $\wedge \text{'}s_0\text{-is-a-CHOICE-at-}s\text{''} \wedge f'(s')(d)]$

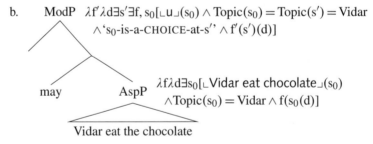

$\lambda f \lambda d \exists s_0 [\llcorner \text{Vidar eat chocolate} \lrcorner (s_0)$
$\wedge \text{Topic}(s_0) = \text{Vidar} \wedge f(s_0(d)]$

       may   AspP

                Vidar eat the chocolate

In (59b), *may* is merged in the second zone. The meaning built up is that 'eating the chocolate' is a live alternative for 'Vidar' in the present situation. The specific lexical item *may* contributes the presuppositional content that this is a possible alternative for him because of the permissions that have been accorded him.

The spatiotemporal relation between the perspectival situation and the prejacent situation performs intuitively the same role as the Kratzerian accessibility relation in terms of possible worlds, and it represents a vector distance with respect to a time and world from s' that is a "possibility" for the perspectival topic in s'.

Looked at from this viewpoint, the relationship that unifies the usage of various different modals appears to be the abstract notion of CHOICE among live alternatives. Intuitively, topic x is in a situation s′ in which she is faced with a set of live options or potentials. The modal expresses the idea that there is some degree of uncertainty in the characterization of the situation (as is the case in all instances of future prediction), and it specifies the prejacent as a CHOICE available to x in s′. This informal schema is laid out in box 5.2.

Box 5.2
Informal schema for modal denotations

> A modal meaning involves the assertion of a CHOICE within a set of live alternatives *for* a topic individual x *in* a perspectival situation s′. These alternatives are directly constructed from the constituent that the modal attaches to.

If AspP has built up a property of event properties based on the existence of an event e of a particular type, the effect of the CHOICE modal is to assert that the pivot argument is free to choose a situation that instantiates e. The reasons for that freedom can be permissions, circumstantial possibilities, or internal abilities. This specification I assume is contributed by context and the individual lexical presuppositions of the particular circumstantial modal.

The present proposal is intended to seriously build in the idea that modal assertions are made from a background of uncertainty; that is to say, there are a number of potential ways the world could be, but a particular choice among those potentials is being asserted as a possibility.

Moreover, as discussed in section 5.3, because of the polarity sensitivity of modals, we also need to assume that the modal sometimes combines with PolP in the syntax and that intuitively, both positive and negative alternatives are also explicitly members of the set of alternatives that are live from the perspective of s′.

Solving all the problems of representing negation in a model like this is beyond the scope of this monograph. I will simply stipulate here what seems to work in the context of the empirical facts. Recall that I have assumed that clausal (polarity) negation lies within the second zone and therefore combines with properties of spatiotemporal properties. I will assume therefore that polarity negation simply negates the existential quantifier binding the event variable that has been closed at Asp.

(60) a. $\llbracket \text{PolP}_{pos} \rrbracket = \lambda f \lambda d \exists e[\text{Utterance}(d) \wedge f(e)(d) \wedge \llcorner u \lrcorner(e)]$
     b. $\llbracket \text{PolP}_{neg} \rrbracket = \lambda f \lambda d \neg \exists e[\text{Utterance}(d) \wedge f(e)(d) \wedge \llcorner u \lrcorner(e)]$

When it comes to the assertion of a simple CHOICE for the pivot argument, whether the syntactic category of the complement is AspP or PolP
is immaterial to the circumstantial alternatives generated. The circumstantial
alternatives will be all the logically possible alternative states of affairs fanning
out from the perspectival situation at the relevant times in the future. These
will inevitably include some situations in which the prejacent eventuality takes
place and some in which it doesn't.

The only difference will lie in whether polarity negation can scope outside of
the modal meaning and negate it directly or not. If a modal selects AspP rather
than PolP, then polarity negation will be interpreted as negating the modal.
This means that if one wanted to assert the circumstantial possibility of *not*
doing something, then low constituent negation would have to be used, not
polarity negation. I assume that negation, like modality itself, has three zonal
manifestations, characterized informally as follows:

(61) a. *Constituent negation* for verbs is located within EvtP, the event ess-
        ences domain, and constructs an actual eventuality that manifests pos-
        itive properties that are the negation of the description deployed—an
        antievent, if you will.
     b. *Polarity negation* is located in the spatiotemporal properties domain
        and introduces a negative operator on the existential binding of e.
     c. *High negation* is located in the speech act domain and negates the
        accuracy of a particular deployed lexical item (subject to focus).

In fact, when it comes to deontic modals, there seems to be little difference
between the assertion that it is permitted that an event not exist and the assertion that the antievent exists. This is because the antievent is always stronger in
this kind of permission context. If instantiating the antievent is allowed, then
merely not instantiating the event with the relevant descriptive properties is
also allowed. This is because, to the extent that they differ, the two scenar-
ios seem to belong to the following kind of implicational scale of decreasing
likelihood of being permitted:

(62) Mary doesn't go to the party. > Mary makes a big dramatic point of
     visibly failing to show up at the party.

If something on a particular point of the scale is allowed, then everything
higher than that is allowed as well.

So the difference between AspP-selecting deontics and PolP-selecting deontics does not give rise to a serious difference in expressivity when it comes
to this aspect of the meaning of a modal. On the other hand, if a modal does
select PolP, then polarity negation can only be interpreted as negating the event

variable. In that case, negating the possibility itself would have to be handled by periphrasis. This seems like an expressive disadvantage. It is for this reason, I think, that deontic "existential" modals tend to scope under negation; that is, they tend to be non–PolP selectors. Thus, purely existential circumstantial modals do not tend to be PolP selectors in natural language quite generally. As Iatridou and Zeijlstra (2013) point out, languages do not seem to possess existential deontic modals that embed negation. The availability of low negation as a stronger version of the low scope polarity negation, and the clear communicative payoffs from being able to negate the permission itself via Pol, is probably what leads to this pattern.

The other point to consider here is that existential circumstantial modals often derive from a dynamic version located inside the event domain; in the case of *can*, this is the ability reading. I will assume that the dynamic verb is a species of Init, and like lexical verbs never scopes over any kind of negation at all—it is merged too low to scope over even low zone negation. Empirically, it seems that if a modal is used in more than one zone then whether it selects a negation/position projection or not carries over to all of its uses. Basically, this means that if the modal has any dynamic (low) use, then its scope with respect to negation will be consistently fixed as being *under* negation.

Before I give denotations for the circumstantial modals in English, I still need to capture the difference between "possibility" and "necessity" modals in the present kind of implementation. The existential binding of the f property relating s' to the prejacent situation as a valid live alternative is tantamount to existential assertion of possibility. The innovation needed here is not to introduce universal quantification over f for so-called universal modals; rather, it is to think of the circumstantial necessity modals *non*quantificationally in terms of *exclusive* choice. In the formula in (63b), I have replaced the simple CHOICE predicate with the one that goes with necessity modals: the unique *exclusive choice*.

(63) a. Jane must [$_{PolP}$[$_{AspP}$ <Jane> sing]].

   b. $[\![\text{Mod}_{circ\text{-}must}]\!] = \lambda Q \lambda x \lambda f' \lambda d \exists s' \exists f[Q(f)(d) \wedge \text{State}(s') \wedge \text{holder}(s') = x \wedge f = \lambda s \lambda d[s$ is located at a world-time pair that is the exclusive CHOICE for the perspectival topic in $s'] \wedge f'(s')(d)]$

Here, once again, the set of alternatives is all the different possible values of world-time vectors projected from s'.

When it comes to the "necessity" circumstantial modals, which express exclusive CHOICE, the difference between combining with a negative PolP and combining with a positive PolP gives quite distinct directive effects. Moreover, compelling a pivot to perform an antievent does not entail that one would be

Table 5.9
The circumstantial modals of English, notated with their polarity selection

Circumstantial modal	± Exclusive CHOICE	Presuppositional flavor	Zones
Pol_{can}	−	Facilitative	(ep) < circ < dyn
Pol_{may}	−	Permissive	circ
$will^{Pol}$	+	Predictive	ep < circ
$should^{Pol}$	+	Normative	ep < circ
$must^{Pol}$	+	Directive	ep < circ
Pol_{could}	−	Facilitative	(ep) < circ < dyn
$-Pol_{need}$	+	Omissive	ep < circ

content with her merely failing to perform an event of that type. In the scale set up in (62), if someone is forced to do the higher thing, then doing the lower thing is also fine—essentially the reverse of the simple CHOICE case. Thus, low negation does not give the same effects for the exclusive CHOICE deontic modals. "Necessity" circumstantial modals can therefore in principle have either selectional setting.

In table 5.9, I list the circumstantial modals of English and their selectional setting. Mod^{Pol} indicates that the modal in question selects for PolP and therefore always scopes over polarity negation when it exists; ^{Pol}Mod indicates that the modal in question selects for a non-polarity-marked AspP and therefore always scopes under polarity negation when it exists. Following Copley (2002), I assume that *will* is a modal in the circumstantial zone (as opposed to being a tense, or even an epistemic modal). The reason I think that future *will* is a circumstantial modal of prediction rather than an epistemic modal is that it is the purest instantiation of circumstantial choice projected into the future. In fact, there *is* an epistemic version of *will* that speakers spontaneously produce; it differs crucially from future *will* in that it is anchored to the utterance time and reports on the speaker's predictions about the current state of affairs based on her knowledge.

(64) a. John will go to the party.   *Predictive circumstantial modal*
     b. John will be in his office now (because I know his habits).   *Epistemic*

Finally, we note that modal verbs in English combine with the bare, "uninflected" form of the verb. We have already seen that the bare, uninflected root in English can lexicalize the full complement of verbal heads and thus, by hypothesis, lacks only tense or aspect information. Furthermore, it is the form that is morphologically eligible for suffixation. I will assume that the form that combines with modal verbs is this very same item, suffixed with an irrealis Asp head, which represents the infinitival ending (null in English).[9]

The system I have outlined proposes analyzing modals as expressing CHOICE over linguistically constructed live alternatives. But this is nothing more than "possibility" itself, relativized to a particular situational reality and topic. It has the same status as the notion of necessity or possibility in the axiomatization of modal logic, or as the notion of what is "possible" in the construction of possible worlds. It is the irreducible axiomatic part of the idea of potentials or hypotheticality in the domain of language. We have already established that human users of language employ a dimension of this kind in their daily expressivity, and it needs to be represented as one of the compositional building blocks. The only difference between the proposed system and the classical treatments lies in *where* the primitive notion of possibility is located in the axiomatization of the logic that modal meanings build on. The proposed system rejects the quantificational analogy, and the system is built on an analogy to CHOICE, generalizing from the deontic core cases instead. The primitive CHOICE relation asserts the freedom of the pivot within the space of hypothetical alternatives, from a particular situational vantage point. Simple CHOICE does nothing more than assert a particular freedom for the pivot, given the Grounds for constraining one's options contributed by the presuppositional content of the modal.

The pivot for the CHOICE is a crucial argument of the CHOICE relation and is the topic (either explicitly or implicitly) of the perspectival situation. Something can be a choice for a pivot x if it is one of the things x is able to do or is allowed to do, or if it is logically possible for x to do it. The important thing is that the choices are relativized to the involvement of x. In circumstantial modal constructions, this x argument is usually the highest or external argument of the event in the situational description, but it can also be other arguments or even filled in contextually.

There is an important role in these definitions for different presupposed information or pragmatic contextual information about the Grounds for why the pivot has the CHOICE in question. This framework is not intended to replace the contextual input to modal semantics. The Grounds for a CHOICE are contributed in part by the lexical presupposition of the modal itself and in part by the linguistic context and other contextual factors.

(65) *Grounds for CHOICE coming from discourse context*
    A: Oh no, I have a meeting at 9 tomorrow morning!
    B: Then you must get up before 8 for once.

(66) *Grounds for* CHOICE *coming from adverbial modification*
      If you want to make that meeting, you must get up before 8.

5.6   Conclusion

In this chapter, the specific meaning contribution of circumstantial modals in English turned out to be similar in an interesting way to the function of the *have* auxiliary, which resides in the same domain. As argued in chapter 4, the *have* auxiliary introduces a proxy or intermediate situational variable s′ bearing a particular relation to the core situational description s_0. This intermediate situational variable is equivalent to the one that has been called the reference situation in linguistic work on aspect (e.g., Reichenbach 1947, Klein 1994). In the view taken in this chapter, it is also equivalent to the perspectival situation invoked in work on modality (Condoravdi 2002). The intermediate situational variable is the one that is eventually anchored to tense. It is a special case of the spatiotemporal property of s_0, the core situational variable existentially bound at the edge of the first phase, which is then anchored only indirectly to d. Like perfect auxiliaries, circumstantial modals introduce an intermediate situational variable in relation to the core event. However, instead of being in a relation of entailment to s_0, s′ is in a relation of prediction. Specifically, modals assert

Table 5.10
The CHOICE and classical models for modal semantics compared

	Classical model (Kratzer 1977)	CHOICE semantics for modality in the quotational quantificational system
Quantificational force	∃	CHOICE
	∀	Exclusive CHOICE
Modal base (primary effects)	Dynamic	Syntactic height: within EvtP
	Circumstantial	Syntactic height: between EvtP and TP
	Epistemic	Syntactic height: above TP
Modal base (secondary effects) plus ordering source	Deontic, buletic, teleological, etc.	Presuppositional content from modal concerning nature of Grounds for CHOICE
Modal base (secondary effects)	Contextual and linguistic factors constraining modal base	Contextual and linguistic factors regarding Grounds for CHOICE

choice among live alternatives as part of their lexical semantics. They divide into the ones where the choice is a simple CHOICE among many (the existential modals) and the ones where the CHOICE is assessed to be the *only* option the pivot is faced with (the universal modals).

In changing the compositional semantics for modals away from the classical model, the idea is not to deny the different components of meaning isolated in that tradition or to deny the work done by contextual factors. Rather, changing the architecture results in the kind of mapping between the syntax and the semantics that will allow us to integrate modality more naturally with temporal interpretation and to unify the modals' denotations across domains. In table 5.10, I compare the classical system, with its parameters of (i) quantificational force, (ii) modal base, and (iii) ordering source (as in Kratzer 1977), with the proposal made in this chapter.

In the next chapter, I will extend the account to epistemic interpretations which by hypothesis are built higher up in the phrase structure. In addition, I will establish what happens at the level of T and how situational anchoring is achieved in this system.

6 Modals and Generalized Anchoring

In the previous chapter, I introduced the issue of modal meanings and showed how circumstantial modal interpretations are captured in a framework that models the second zone of the clause as denoting spatiotemporal properties of event properties. We saw that like the auxiliary *have*, circumstantial modal meanings introduce an intermediate reference situation, which in the case of modals is the *perspective* with respect to which the most deeply embedded event is located. While the auxiliary *have* locates the embedded event in its own "realistic" past, the modal auxiliaries introduce a reference situation that has the embedded event in its own "predicted" (i.e., nonreal) future. In this chapter, I focus first on another aspect of modal meaning that is an important semantic component of the extended verbal projection: temporal anchoring.

Whatever situational description has been built up in the second zone, whether simple (no intermediate reference situation) or auxiliated (with intermediate "reference" situation), the outermost situational variable needs to be explicitly related to the contextual anchor point, the utterance time, in order to create something that has actual truth conditions. This is classically seen as the job of tense, but in modal constructions, it is the modal itself that occupies the T position and therefore, by hypothesis, also contributes information related to anchoring. In what follows, I summarize the patterns of anchoring interpretation found with modals in English. It should be clear from the discussion that anchoring information is indeed modal-specific in an important way. Once the patterns are established, I will propose an account of the anchoring contribution of modals in terms that mirror the anchoring contribution of tense, and I will propose how that meaning is integrated into the denotations I have built up so far.

Finally, I will turn to epistemic modal interpretations and propose how these are constructed from the basic building blocks we have already seen. I will argue that epistemic meanings emerge precisely when they attach to constituents whose temporal parameter has already been fixed. In addition, they do not introduce a new reference situation; rather, they use the utterance-situational variable d as their "perspectival" situation.

6.1   Temporal Properties of Modals

Interesting generalizations emerge from a careful description of the relation-ship between the modal assertion and temporal properties. In discussing these, I take my lead from Condoravdi (2002).

Condoravdi (2002) points out clearly the need to distinguish between the temporal perspective of a modal and its temporal orientation. In the system proposed here, the perspectival situation is s', introduced by the modal itself. The event time is the spatiotemporal position of the embedded event e, as built up by the first zone. For example, in modal sentence (1a) the event of "going to the party" is in the future relative to the utterance time, in (1b), the event of John "being in his office" is contemporaneous with the utterance time, and in (1c) the event of "winning the race" is previous to the utterance time.

(1) a. John might go to the party.
    b. John might be in his office.
    c. John might have won the race.

One way to capture this is to specify the semantics for MIGHT directly in two versions, one forward shifting and the other nonshifting with respect to the possible worlds considered. One might even stipulate a third composite modal, MIGHT-HAVE, that requires the possible worlds to precede the utterance time. Condoravdi gives the three possible denotations in (2) corresponding to such a view (although, as will become clear, she herself proposes a more compositional treatment and unified conception of *might*). (In the following denotations, *MB* designates the modal base that a modal depends on for its interpretation; Kratzer 1977.)

(2) a. *Forward-shifting modals*
       MIGHT$^1_{MB}$ ϕ is true at $<w, t>$ iff there exist w', t' such that w' in MB(w, t), $t \prec t'$ and ϕ is true at $<w', t'>$.
    b. *Nonshifting modals*
       MIGHT$^2_{MB}$ ϕ is true at $<w, t>$ iff there is w' *in* MB(w, t), such that ϕ is true at $<w', t>$.
    c. *Backward-shifting modals*
       MIGHT-HAVE$^1_{MB}$ ϕ is true at $<w, t>$ iff there exist w', t' such that w' in MB(w, t), $t' \prec t$ and ϕ is true at $<w', t'>$.
       (Condoravdi 2002, 61)

These three interpretations all take the present utterance time as the perspective, but this too is independently modifiable. In certain contexts, the perspective of the modal can be shifted backward to say that at a particular point in time in the past, a modal statement was true. These cases are particularly clear when we look at dynamic modality, where intuitively the moribund past tense on *could* actually seems to do some transparent semantic work.

(3) In those days, John could easily swim two kilometers.

But past perspective for the modal is also possible in embedded sentences for (future-meaning) *would* (4a), (epistemic) *might* (4b), and the circumstantial version of *could* (4c).[1]

(4) a. Last year, John told me that he would quit his job.
     b. Last year, John told me that he might quit his job.
     c. Last year, John told me that he could take a vacation any time he
         wanted.

To distinguish between these two different aspects of the temporality of modal meaning, Condoravdi uses the terms *perspectival time* and *evaluation time*. The perspectival time is the time at which the *potential* for the prejacent event is asserted, and the evaluation time is the time of the prejacent event itself. This corresponds directly, as I have said, to the perspectival situation s' and the embedded situation s_0, respectively. We can see already that it is not a simple matter of inspecting the morphology or the lexical items in question to know how the perspectival time and the evaluation time are configured in any particular case.

Condoravdi provides some important generalizations with respect to this patterning, which I demonstrate here. First, deontic modality always forward-shifts, even with stative predicates. Consider (5a–b) using *can* with the meaning corresponding to circumstantial possibility.

(5) a. John can go to the party (if he does his homework).   *Forward-shifted*
     b. John can be in London by noon (if he takes the early flight).

                                                               Forward-shifted

Epistemic modality is variable, but is sensitive to aktionsart: dynamic predicates induce forward shifting, while stative predicates produce nonshifted readings.[2]

(6) a. John might go to the party, but I wouldn't count on it. *Forward-shifted*
     b. John might be in his office, but I wouldn't count on it.

                                                      Nonshifted or forward-shifted

In my proposal for circumstantial modality in chapter 5, the forward-shifting property of circumstantial modals arises obligatorily because of the notion of live alternatives, which simply are not defined for times simultaneous with or previous to the perspectival situation.

Finally, backward shifting seems to be possible only in the context of additional linguistic material: addition of the perfect auxiliary *have* or embedding under a past tense matrix predicate. In the former case, we find only epistemic modals.

(7) a. John must have won the race.
    b. John might have won the race.
    c. John could have won the race.
    d. John may have won the race.

In the latter case, we find deontics and dynamics in addition to epistemics, but only a lexical subset of them (basically those with moribund past tense morphology).

(8) a. John said that he would go to the party.
    b. John said that he could swim two kilometers.
    c. John said that he could take a vacation whenever he wanted.
    d. John said that he might go to the party.
    e. John said that I should go to the party.
    f. ?John said that he must go to the party.
    g. ?John said that he may go to the party.
    h. ?John said that he will go to the party.
    i. ?John said that he can go to the party.

The question marks on (8f–i) indicate that they seem to be good only on the equivalent of a kind of double access reading for the modal perspective.

The generalizations we have made from examining the interaction of English modal meanings with temporal information and aktionsart are summarized in tables 6.1 and 6.2. Given the agenda of this monograph, these patterns should be made to fall out from a compositional treatment of modal meaning in construction with the properties of the constituents the modals combine with.

I separate the generalizations concerning evaluation time from those concerning perspectival time. In the case of evaluation time, the generalizations depend on the type of modality and the aktionsart of the prejacent (see table 6.1). In the case of perspectival time, the generalizations depend on the particular modal and the kind of morphology it possesses (see table 6.2).

Under the classical view of anchoring, the T head combines with a situational description (the topic situation) and establishes a relationship between it

Table 6.1
Evaluation time

	Forward-shifted	Nonshifted	Backward-shifted
Epistemic	Yes	Yes (states only)	Yes (with *have* only)
Circumstantial	Yes	No	No

Table 6.2
Perspectival time

	Present	Past
must	Yes	No
may	Yes	No
can	Yes	No
will	Yes	No
might	Yes	Yes (under embedding)
could	Yes	Yes (under embedding)
should	Yes	Yes (under embedding)
would	Yes	Yes (under embedding)

and the utterance situation (see (9)). I assume that tense relationships are just one possible instantiation of the anchoring relation (see Ritter and Wiltschko 2009).

(9) *TP as the locus of generalized situational anchoring*

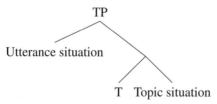

The present framework will be designed to express the very same basic intuition. The topic situation is the situational description provided by the main verb (in the case of nonauxiliated structures) or by the reference situation introduced by an auxiliary. In general, the time parameter of the topic situation is constrained by the establishment of a relation between it and the time parameter of d. This relational information is what is assumed to reside in T (I will continue to use the label *T* for the node that contributes this relation). This is thus a straightforward extension of neo-Reichenbachian theories of tense/aspect whereby a reference time or topic time (see Klein 1994, Demirdache and Uribe-Etxebarria 2008) is the intermediary between the utterance time and the event, with the difference that I only invoke intermediate situations in the case of auxiliary structures. In what follows, I will also use the * notation to indicate the parameters of the utterance situation d: t^* = anchor time and w^* = anchor world.[3]

As is uncontroversial, the temporal predicate PAST establishes a temporal relation of precedence between the topic situation (the situational description denoted by the complement to T) and the utterance situation.

In my terms, anchoring will simply be the existential closure of spatiotemporal location for the outermost situational variable, achieved by relating it explicitly to the utterance situation. The proposition is thus identical to the existential closure of the f variable. What results is a constituent that denotes a property of the current utterance. The utterance d has the arguments Speaker and Hearer that (like the utterance situation itself) are indexically bound.

Constituents larger than TP in the clause will be properties of the utterance situation and will be written according to the following schema:

(10) $\lambda d \exists f \exists Q[Q(f)(d) \wedge \text{Source}(d) = \text{'Speaker'} \wedge \text{Goal}(d) = \text{'Hearer'}]$
     where Q stands for the predicate of situational properties already built
     up by the second phase

As a concrete example without auxiliaries, consider the sentence *Vidar ate the chocolate*. I assume that the final AspP (maximal constituent in the second zone) for that sentence has the following denotation:

(11) $[\![\text{AspP}]\!] = \lambda f \lambda d \exists e[\text{Utterance}(d) \wedge f(d)(e) \wedge {}_\llcorner \text{Vidar eat chocolate}_\lrcorner(e)]$

The temporal predicate PAST contributed by the morphology anchors the situation to the utterance as shown in (12).

(12) $[\![\text{TP}_{past}]\!] = \lambda d \exists f \exists e[\text{Utterance}(d) \wedge f(d)(e) \wedge \text{PAST}(f) \wedge {}_\llcorner \text{Vidar}$
     $\text{eat chocolate}_\lrcorner(e) \wedge \text{Source}(d) = \text{'Speaker'} \wedge \text{Goal}(d) = \text{'Hearer'}]$

In this framework, PAST must be a predicate over spatiotemporal properties rooted in d, f. It can be specified informally as in (13).

(13) $\forall$ eventualities e and speech events d, such that f(d)(e), PAST(f) is true iff
     the temporal parameter of e *precedes* the temporal parameter of d.

Turning now to present tense, I will assume (for reasons that will be obvious as we proceed) that it contributes the information that the outermost situational variable is anchored to the utterance time via identity, and that the utterance time is abstractly represented as a moment, not as an interval. This is because the English present has the peculiar property that it only combines felicitously with states, and I will continue following Taylor (1977) in assuming that the crucial distinguishing property of states is that they are able to be true at a single moment. Thus, the present tense sentence *Vidar likes sushi* will have the denotation in (14).

(14) $[\![TP_{pres}]\!] = \lambda d \exists f \exists e [\text{Utterance}(d) \wedge f(d)(e) \wedge \text{PRESENT}(f) \wedge {}_{\llcorner}\text{Vidar}$
like sushi$_{\lrcorner}(e) \wedge \text{Source}(d) = \text{'Speaker'} \wedge \text{Goal}(d) = \text{'Hearer'}]$

In this framework, PRESENT is a property of f, a relation between e and d, defined informally as follows:

(15) ∀ eventualities e and speech events d, such that f(d)(e), PRESENT(f) is true iff the temporal parameter of e *is identified with* the temporal parameter of d, the moment of speech.

In the case of perfect and modalized sentences, the same tense semantics applies: the innermost situational variable only gets anchored *via* the reference situation s′, which is the one that is directly affected by the tense predicate.

In English, temporal information such as PAST or PRES performs the shift from properties of situational properties to properties of the utterance. But as we also know, modals in English all behave distributionally as if they end up high in the clause: they invert in questions, they precede negation, they do not require *do*-support, and only one can appear in a given clause. I take these facts at face value and assume that, wherever the modal is actually base-generated, it always ends up in the equivalent of Infl. Moreover, I assume that it is the job of the T head to establish a relationship between the reference situation s′ and the situational anchor of the clause d. The natural assumption then is that modals also must be endowed with information that establishes such a relationship. I assume moreover that this anchoring property of Infl, suitably generalized, is a universal property of natural language sentences, plausibly driven by constraints at the interpretational interface (Ritter and Wiltschko 2009). I will assume therefore that modals also anchor the situation, but do so by relating the situational description to the anchor *world* or time, or both.

To accommodate the modals, I will need to generalize my approach to tense slightly. I will assume that anchoring comes in two main flavors: the kind we saw with the past tense where a constraint is placed on the denotation of the temporal interval in relation to the utterance time, and the kind where the situation is directly indexically *identified* with the utterance situation (see the informal definitions in box 6.1). In the former case, some kind of discourse or anaphoric binding of the temporal variable is necessary to provide the actual value of the temporal variable.

Box 6.1
Types of anchoring

> 1. ∀ eventualities e and speech events d, such that f(d)(e), INDEX(f) is true iff
>   the temporal parameter of e is strictly identified with the temporal parameter
>   of d, the utterance time.
> 2. ∀ eventualities e and speech events d, such that f(d)(e), ANAPH(f) is true iff
>   the temporal parameter of e is resolved *anaphorically*, either by reference to
>   something in the linguistic context or by reference to some purely discourse
>   contextual topic time or world.

Under this view, past tense in English is in the "anaphoric" camp, while present tense is clearly indexical.[4] The idea that modals in some sense do the same job as tense has echoes in Iatridou's (2000) proposal (see also Isard 1974) that past tense morphology is not a primitive tense category, but is one manifestation of a more general semantic category (REMOTE, in Iatridou's terms). According to Iatridou, the REMOTE relation can relate worlds as well as times, accounting for some cases of past morphology on modals. My proposal is different from Iatridou's in that I take INDEXICAL vs. ANAPHORIC to be the primary relational distinction, not IDENTITY vs. REMOTE, although I think the guiding intuition is the same.[5]

There is also a tense auxiliary in English, *do*, and a monograph on English auxiliaries would not be complete without mentioning it. I assume that *do* can be inserted directly in T in English to spell out the temporal features ANAPHORIC and INDEXICAL (*did* and *does*), respectively. However, the conditions under which *do*-insertion is allowed and/or forced in competition with the simple past tense would take us too far afield here.

Turning then to anchoring by modals, I will argue that they too come in two distinct varieties, the indexical and the anaphoric, depending on the relationship they establish between the perspectival situation s′ and the anchor context d.

Recall the two strong generalizations we noted earlier regarding the tense interpretation of modals: namely, that circumstantial modality is obligatorily forward-shifted while epistemic modality needn't be, and that some modals introduce a perspectival time that is obligatorily identified with the utterance time, while other modals are more flexible. The hallmark of these modals' extra flexibility is the ability to have their perspectival situation identified with an attitude in the matrix under embedding, as (16a–d) illustrate.

(16) a. Vidar thought that he could win the race.
     b. Vidar thought that he should get a prize.

    c. Vidar thought that he would win the race.

    d. Vidar thought that he might get a prize.

The modals in (17a–d) do not allow this kind of perspectival anaphoricity; they give rise to a feeling akin to the double access reading when present tense is embedded under past, as in (17e).

(17) a. ?Vidar thought that he may win a prize.

    b. ?Vidar thought that he must win a prize.

    c. ?Vidar thought that he can win the race.

    d. ?Vidar thought that he will win the race.

    e. ?Vidar thought that he is deserving of a prize.

The idea here is that the modals in (17a–d) share with the present tense the property of being indexically bound to the utterance time. The other modals, in (16), are anaphoric in the sense defined above. Note that anaphoric reference in this sense covers many different modes of reference resolution (being essentially negative); it is intended to mirror the cut in the pronoun system between indexical forms like *I/you* and nonindexical ones like *he/she/it*. As is well known, this is the cut that is almost universally instantiated crosslinguistically within pronoun systems. It means that the actual reference assigned to the temporal variable can be achieved by binding at the discourse level or within the sentence; crucially, though, reference needs to be resolved since it is not automatically identified with a parameter of the context as it is in the indexical case.

    Thus, in addition to their CHOICE semantics, modals in English possess information that anchors the external situational variable. Some modals (e.g., *must*) have indexical anchoring specification, while others (e.g., *might*) have anaphoric anchoring information. This distinction cuts across the epistemic/circumstantial divide. Thus, we must now augment our modal denotations with this extra information. Since *must* is an indexical modal, it will provide information anchoring the perspectival situation obligatorily to the speech situational parameters. (18) shows the denotation of the TP headed by the circumstantial *must* (abstracting away for now from the argument structure information and from the CHOICE component of the epistemic modal's meaning).

(18) $[\![\text{TP}_{must}]\!] = \lambda d \exists f' \exists s' \exists f \exists s_0 [\text{Utterance}(d) \wedge \text{State}(s') \wedge f(d)(s_0)$
$\wedge \llcorner u \lrcorner(s_0) \wedge f'(d)(s') \wedge \text{INDEX}(f') \wedge \ldots]$

This means that the base perspectival situation introduced by *must* is always the same as the utterance time. In contrast, *should* is not indexical in this sense, but anaphoric, and the world and time variables in the perspectival world may be anaphorically resolved to a salient discourse interval, or identified with some linguistically present time via binding.

(19) $[\![TP_{should}]\!] = \lambda d \exists f' \exists s' \exists f \exists s_0[\text{Utterance}(d) \wedge \text{State}(s') \wedge f(d)(s_0)$
$\wedge \llcorner u \lrcorner(s_0) \wedge f'(d)(s') \wedge \text{ANAPH}(f') \wedge ...]$

Returning to embedded contexts, as we might expect anaphoric modals pattern with the simple past tense in English in allowing the time of the embedded situation to be bound by the matrix situation.

(20) John: "I can go to the party."
John said that he could go to the party.

(21) John: "I may go to the party."
John said that he might go to the party.

(22) John: "I will go to the party."
John said that he would go to the party.

On the other hand, the indexical modals *can*, *may*, and *will*, and the singleton *must*, are a little strange in embedded contexts and have the flavor of a double access reading, much like the English present tense when embedded under past.

(23) a. John said that he can go to the party.

Ability must still be current

b. John said that he may go to the party.

Permission must still be current

c. John said that he will go to the party.

Party cannot have happened yet

d. John said that he must go the party.

Obligation must still be current

Certain questions naturally arise here concerning the behavior of the quotational quantificational system in embedded contexts, in particular concerning the reference of the embedded d eventuality. I will assume that quite generally there are two options for the d variable of an embedded sentence: it can be identified either with the higher d of the matrix verb, giving rise to indexical effects, or with the situational variable of the matrix verb itself if it happens to be a verb of communication. While this mimics in broad outlines the possibilities for anchoring assumed in the literature, an exploration of the specific consequences and predictions of this system as compared to others when it comes to indexical shift must be left for future research. It is worth noting in passing, though, that the quotational quantificational system, possibly uniquely, predicts a preferential status for verbs of *saying* in allowing indexical shift (as opposed to attitude predicates more generally).

6.2   Epistemic Modality

6.2.1   Epistemic Modals as Modifiers of Assertions

In chapter 5, I proposed denotations for the possibility and necessity modals in the realm of circumstantial modality, and I have now been explicit about the anchoring properties of both tense and modals. The outer situational variable introduced by the modal meaning is anchored to the utterance via the modal's temporal setting and asserted as being either identified with the utterance situation d or not.

But what about epistemic modality, as in (24)?

(24) a. Jane might be in Edinburgh.
      b. Jane must be in Edinburgh.

In this case, the notion of uncertainty or potential seems to lie in a different dimension. As Condoravdi (2002) notes, epistemic modality involves quantification over "worlds" that occur at the same time as the perspectival world. Epistemic modality is not necessarily forward-oriented in the way that circumstantial modality is.

I propose that the source of epistemic readings is precisely that the modal attaches *after* the situation is anchored to the utterance, as f has already been resolved and no circumstantial alternatives could be generated. Since we have already had to assume that modals carry both an anchoring specification and a modal meaning in English, let us see what happens if the modal merges first at T.

Let us start with *must*. If *must* lexicalizes T, it will contribute indexical information with regard to the temporal variable of the situational description constructed up to that point. According to the denotations given so far, the AspP constructed up to that point would look like this:

(25) $[\![\text{AspP}]\!] = \lambda f \lambda d \exists e[\text{Utterance}(d) \wedge f(d)(e) \wedge \llcorner u \lrcorner(e)]$

An indexical specification of f would give rise to the TP in (26).

(26) $[\![\text{TP}_{pres}]\!] = \lambda d \exists f \exists e[\text{Utterance}(d) \wedge \text{INDEX}(f) \wedge f(d)(e) \wedge \llcorner u \lrcorner(e)$
      $\wedge \text{Source}(d) = \text{'Speaker'} \wedge \text{Goal}(d) = \text{'Hearer'}]$

Now, we also want the epistemic interpretation of *must* to be related in a systematic way to the interpretation already given for circumstantial *must* in terms of unique CHOICE among live alternatives. The difference between the circumstantial modal meaning of must and the epistemic one is that the former involves a set of circumstantial alternatives for a topic/pivot participant in the situation, while the latter involves alternatives for the speaker herself because of her incomplete direct knowledge of the facts. This is expressed intuitively in (27).

(27) *Epistemic* must
     The proposition expressed is the *exclusive* CHOICE for the speaker in the utterance situation d, given the alternatives open to her, consistent with her knowledge.

Crucially, the speaker *is* faced with live alternatives because she does not have complete experiential evidence for what she is about to say; however, what knowledge she does have is consistent only with the assertion made (and not, for instance, its opposite). Once epistemic meanings are described in this way, we see that one of their defining features is that the alternatives with respect to which a CHOICE is being made are not alternatives related to ways in which the world might unfold in the future, but alternatives related to what the fact of the matter is at a particular world and time. The alternatives are at least in part due to ignorance, not to the radical indeterminacy of the future. Also, there is no separate introduction of a perspectival situation here—the perspectival situation is the utterance situation itself, d.

I propose that the reason the epistemic modal can be inserted directly in T and not in the second zone is that one does not need to introduce a reference situation variable to construct the epistemic meaning. The perspectival situation is d itself, and the modal meaning can be expressed without intermediary as the relationship between d and the embedded situation. Or, put the other way around, if the modal does not introduce a novel reference situation by being merged in the spatiotemporal zone, then the CHOICE-among-live-alternatives meaning must be applied to d as the perspective situation. In the absence of an intermediate perspectival situation, the world and time of the core situational variable are fixed to the present actual world by the anchoring conditions of *must*. The modal's CHOICE semantics is now confined to the alternatives generated by the speaker's lack of direct knowledge concerning the truth ofthe proposition. Against this background, the speaker asserts her choice of alternatives, based on her best indirect evidence and inferential powers. This seems like the right meaning for epistemic *must* in this context. The contextual opening for different Grounds for making the choice is what gives epistemic modality its evidential flavor. The fact that the speaker nevertheless has grounds for choosing p over ¬p reflects the fact that she has good evidence, or has inferred on the basis of other information, that it is correct. But the existence of the set of uncertainties ensures that this meaning will never be equivalent to a plain assertion.

The modal contribution of *must* in its epistemic use should be essentially the same as the denotation for circumstantial *must* except for the fact that there is no intermediate perspectival situation s'. The CHOICE governs alternatives for the topic of d, by assumption the speaker. Here, f for the depicted event is temporally anchored to the here and now, and the modal therefore asserts that the actuality of the situation in question is the speaker's only choice given her knowledge. But what are the alternatives here? The world and time parameters of f in this case are not "up for grabs," since by hypothesis they have been specified by the anchoring contribution of *must*. But this is not surprising, since our intuition here is that epistemic modality is not about circumstances, and by hypothesis it does not traffic in spatiotemporal properties.

Of course, in principle, the speaker's choice of what to assert about the world is completely open. She could choose to say *I am hungry* or *It is snowing like crazy outside*, or she could choose to say *Jane must be in Edinburgh*. Her alternatives are in principle endless, and this cannot be what the CHOICE predicate of the modal meaning is operating over. It seems to me that the "alternatives" here must be the simple assertoric options related to the Question under Discussion (QUD) related to the discourse.

I express the meaning of epistemic *must* more fully, then, as in (28).

(28) $[\![TP_{ep-must}]\!] = \lambda d\exists f\exists e[\text{Utterance}(d) \wedge \text{State}(e) \wedge f(d)(e) \wedge \llcorner u\lrcorner(e)$
$\wedge \text{INDEX}(f) \wedge e$ is the exclusive assertoric CHOICE for the speaker of d]
where the live alternatives for the speaker are the different assertions possible given the discourse QUD.

The epistemic modal force of a modal like *must* can indeed vary drastically given the discourse context, even when confined as it is to making an assertion about the current world and time. Consider the following minidialogues:

(29) A: Is Mary in her office?
      B: Yes, she must be.

(30) A: Who is in the office now?
      B: Mary must be. She always gets there by 8.

(31) A: Where is Mary?
      B: She must be in the office.

Thus, when it comes to epistemic modality, the alternatives we are operating over are plausibly the same kinds of Roothian alternatives that are necessary for the construction of focus meanings. I consider this to be a positive aspect of the journey toward reconfiguring modal semantics to be sensitive to syntactic structure in the sense that the proposed system employs semantic notions already known to be independently necessary in the description of natural language meanings.

The denotation for the TP headed by *must* is just like the present tense except for the addition of some content related to the notion of speaker CHOICE among alternatives. One conservative position would be simply to say that this content comes from the lexical presuppositional information contributed by the specific modal and that it does not in fact stem from any higher structural position in the clause. If this were true, then epistemic modals would simply be versions of the modals that lexicalize only T, leaving the Asp feature unassociated (something allowed in principle in the spell-out system I have been assuming). However, the presuppositional content in this case does not go away; instead, it applies to the utterance variable as situational perspective. There are reasons to think, though, that as a systematic synchronic possibility of this system always allowing underassociation of the Asp feature might seriously overgenerate. After all, across languages not *all* circumstantial modals have an epistemic counterpart, although such polysemy is a common phenomenon. I will assume that the epistemic modal lexicalizes only T (suitably generalized) and that its relation to the lower, circumstantial version is fed by grammaticalization. Further discussion of this issue is unfortunately beyond the scope of this monograph.

6.2.2   Aktionsart Sensitivity of Epistemic Modals

However, we do have additional evidence that the temporal specification of *must* is being employed at the TP level and does not require the introduction of an intermediate reference variable. As noted in Ramchand 2014a, under its epistemic reading *must* is confined to stative prejacents. Consider the data in (32). While all kinds of stative prejacents including derived states such as the progressive (32b) give rise to perfectly good epistemic readings, a dynamic verb phrase such as *write that book* gives rise only to a deontic interpretation either in the active (32c) or in the passive (32d).

(32) a. Jane must be in Edinburgh.   *Epistemic and deontic*
     b. Jane must be writing her book.   *Epistemic and deontic*
     c. Jane must write that book.   *Deontic only*
     d. That book must be written.   *Deontic only*

This pattern is totally expected under the hypothesis that the indexical temporal specification of *must* applies to the first-phase situational description itself under the epistemic reading (without the introduction of an intermediate reference stiuation), and this has the effect of constraining the situational descriptions to be those that can be true "at a moment." Consider again the dynamic eventive vs. stative meaning postulate given in (33) (inspired by Taylor 1977).

(33) *Events vs. states*
   a. If α is a *stative* predicate, then $\alpha(x)$ is true at an interval I just in case $\alpha(x)$ is true at all moments within I.
   b. If α is an *eventive* predicate, then $\alpha(x)$ is only true at an interval larger than a moment.

We know that the English present tense is special in requiring a stative complement, and now we know further that this property carries over to *must*, but only on the epistemic reading where it lexicalizes T and combines directly with the verbal prejacent.[6]

Now, let us see if the proposed system predicts the right meanings for an epistemic modal with anaphoric anchoring specification. The epistemic modal *might* has an anaphoric and not indexical specification for worlds and time; it also differs from *must* in asserting simple CHOICE, not exclusive CHOICE.

(34) Jane might be in Edinburgh.

Intuitively, under this kind of system we want the meaning in (35) for epistemic *might*.

(35) *Epistemic* might
   The proposition expressed is one assertoric CHOICE for the speaker at a contextually salient world-time pair $<w, t>$, given the alternatives open to her, consistent with her knowledge.

This means that the speaker has grounds for thinking that the proposition has a chance of being true, although she does not know it directly. But now the proposition that is being entertained is not actually constrained to be one that holds at the utterance time. This predicts in particular that epistemic uncertainty with *might* can be asserted of propositions involving situations at any time at all distinct from the real world. As pointed out in Ramchand 2014a, this is in fact the case, contrasting sharply with what we found for *must*. So, epistemic readings are possible for states (36a) *and* dynamic events (36b) in the future.

(36) a. Jane might be in Edinburgh.   *Epistemic*
     b. Jane might go to the party.   *Epistemic*

It is important to emphasize here that the difference between (36b) and (32c) cannot be ascribed to epistemicity per se; it must also be related to the different anchoring properties of the two modals *must* and *might*. Given this, the denotation for an epistemic modal TP involving *might* should look like (37).

Table 6.3
Epistemic modals in Engilsh

Epistemic modal	±Exclusive Choice	Anchoring
$must^{Pol}$	+	INDEXICAL
$might^{Pol}$	−	ANAPHORIC
$should^{Pol}$	+	ANAPHORIC
$^{Pol}could$	−	ANAPHORIC
$will^{Pol}$	+	INDEXICAL
$would^{Pol}$	+	ANAPHORIC
^{-Pol}can	−	INDEXICAL

As with epistemic *must*, I assume that the alternatives in question arise from the assertoric alternatives generated by the QUD.

(37) $[\![TP_{ep-might}]\!] = \lambda d \exists f \exists e[\text{Utterance}(d) \wedge \text{State}(e) \wedge f(d)(e) \wedge \llcorner u \lrcorner(e)$
$\wedge \text{ANAPH}(f) \wedge e$ is one assertoric CHOICE for the speaker of d]
where the live alternatives for the speaker are the different assertions possible given the discourse QUD.

Thus, the epistemic modals in English come in both anaphoric and indexical flavors and are characterized by the fact that they express either simple or exhaustive CHOICE with respect to the assertoric alternatives open to the speaker when faced with the QUD.

I summarize the epistemic modal meanings, their classification, and their selection with respect to negation in table 6.3.

Note that *may* is absent from the table. Permission *may* is listed as ^{Pol}may in table 5.9 of circumstantial modals, but there is a question about how to classify the version of *may* found in (38).

(38) a. If things go according to plan, John may well go to that party after all.
b. John may not end up passing the exam.

Two observations are relevant here. First, *may* is the only modal in the English inventory that is not consistent in its choice of scope with respect to polarity negation. Second, the use of *may* in (38a–b) is very similar to the use of future *will*, which I argued to be a pure circumstantial. In fact, *may* looks like the simple CHOICE version of exclusive CHOICE *will* in these contexts.

(39) a. If things go according to plan, John will maybe go to that party after all.
b. John will maybe not end up passing the exam.

The parallelism suggests that if *will* is a prediction circumstantial, then so is *may*. Classifying this *may* as a prediction circumstantial means that there are two circumstantial *may*s in English. I will call these may_1 (permission *may*) and may_2 (prediction *may*) and assume that we are dealing with two lexical items. Given this assumption, *may* is no longer a counterexample to the generalization that modals are specified for selection with respect to negation. The decision to classify may_2 as a prediction circumstantial also makes sense of the fact that this reading is not confined to stative prejacents, even though *may* in all its uses has an indexical specification.

This completes my discussion of the general proposal for epistemic meanings. In what follows, I look at further extensions and predictions of the model.

6.2.3 Modals Embedding the Perfect

In this section, I look at what happens when a modal like *might* or *must* embeds the perfect. Since this monograph is about auxiliaries and ordering in English, we need to examine each auxiliary not just on its own but also in concert with others (where such combinations are possible). In fact, the interpretation of epistemic modals embedding the perfect has been the topic of much recent work in semantics because of the interesting different readings that arise (Condoravdi 2002, Stowell 2004, Demirdache and Uribe-Etxebarria 2008). Consider the sentence in (40), which is claimed to have at least two and possibly three different readings.

(40) John could have won the race.
     a. ... let's go and find out.   *Past epistemic reading*
     b. ... but he didn't in the end.   *Counterfactual reading*
     c. ... (still) at that point.   *Backshifted or metaphysical reading*

The question is whether the compositional system proposed here can generate these readings and their restrictions. In the literature, the past epistemic reading in (40a) is treated by assuming that the PAST operator contributed by the perfect auxiliary takes scope over the modal. However, I have already committed myself to an analysis of the perfect auxiliary according to which it introduces an intermediate situational variable related to the lower situation by a relation of inferential prediction. Consider (41), where *must* embeds the perfect.

(41) John must have won the race.

The representation built by the perfect auxiliary is a stative situation with inferential force, not a semantic PAST operator. Therefore, by assumption, the meaning generated for (41) is that there is a current situation s' that gives evidence for the event of 'John winning the race'. The situation s' is current because we have assumed that epistemic *must* contributes a "present" tense temporal relation to the verbal extended projection. The epistemic modal meaning of *must* now attaches to assert that s' is epistemically forced on the speaker. Thus, it seems that the current system already generates the epistemic uncertainty reading for (41), which is good. And it does so without assuming anything special or different about the perfect auxiliary in this construction.

What about the counterfactual reading or the backshifted, metaphysical reading of (41)? How do we generate those? Well, here the data get interesting, because for (41) no such readings exist. (41) thus contrasts with (40), where those readings naturally emerge. In fact, the generalization is that modals with an indexical specification do not give rise to the other two readings at all. This should give us a clue to correctly analyzing those forms. In (42a–b), the epistemic indexicals *cannot* and *may* embed the perfect; no counterfactual or backshifted reading for those sentences exists.

(42) a. John can't have won the race.
    b. John may have won the race.

So, in fact, scope reversal involving a PAST operator overgenerates empirically. The counterfactual and backshifted possibilities are shown by the very modals that exhibit *anaphoric* anchoring behavior in allowing embedding under a past tense operator.

(43) a. John could have won the race.
                        Counterfactual/backshifted reading possible
    b. John might have won the race.
                        Counterfactual/backshifted reading possible
    c. John should have won the race.
                        Counterfactual/backshifted reading possible

One would hope that the difference between anaphoric and indexical anchoring for the perspectival situation would also be able to account for the existence of the counterfactual reading.

We have seen that the epistemic ('past') reading is already straightforwardly accounted for under the present system, where PerfP denotes a derived state that "gives evidence for the previous existence of the dynamic eventive situation." To build the epistemic uncertainty reading for the anaphoric modal anchorers, we need only assume that the temporal moment can indeed accidentally overlap with the utterance time but is not identified with that single moment. This means that all three modals in (43) can build 'past' epistemic readings by asserting that the s' inferential state built by the perfect holds at some interval overlapping the utterance time.

However, we need to build the other two readings as well, using the anaphoric flexibility of the above type of modal. Recall, it is the reference situation s' that gives evidence for the past event of 'winning'. It is this situation that is being judged as epistemically possible using the epistemic modals *might* and *could*; crucially, though, under the epistemic reading it is s' that is anchored using the modal's anchoring information. So, whereas in the case of the epistemic modal *must* s' had to be current, in the case of *might* and *could* the spatiotemporal location s' can be anaphorically resolved.

Thus, *John might have won* says that an s' situation giving evidence for John winning is an assertoric choice for the speaker at some possible world and time as determined by the discourse. Since *might* is not indexical, we can assume that the choice of world is not confined to the actual one and that any salient enough, and even hypothetical, world-time pair can be chosen. If we assume this, then if we identify the location of situation s' anaphorically with some nonactual $<w, t^*>$ pair, then the situation that gives evidence that 'John win the race' could be located now, but at *some nonactual world*. This will give the straightforward counterfactual reading. If the location of s' is identified as the hypothetical future from a particular point in the past (as in *At that point, he could have still won the race*), then we derive the metaphysical reading, although this one, I think, involves a circumstantial reading of the modal. It is the flexibility of the anchoring properties of the nonindexical modals that allows this kind of contextual sensitivity and gives what looks like a multiplicity of distinct readings. But there seems to be no necessity in this kind of model to describe this in terms of scope reversal. Crucially, none of the possibilities for anchoring the world-time pair of the situation introduced by the perfect are possible for the indexically anchored modals.

Note that the proposed system also predicts that deontic modals can embed the perfect, since they inhabit the same zone. But here, the predicted reading is that the inferential perfect state s' is projected as a possibility or exclusive possibility for the agent. The forward projection of the prejacent event has already been built into the semantics of circumstantial modality via the idea of circumstantial live alternatives. It is easy to see that these combinations are also licit and result in the predicted meaning (although in certain cases some contextualizing is needed, as with all deontic modulations of "statives").

(44) a. John must have his homework done by noon.
   b. The applicant may have completed her degree at the time of application.

This ends the discussion of epistemic modality per se. I have proposed that epistemic modals are anchoring elements that, unlike the perfect and the circumstantial modals, do *not* introduce a reference or perspectival situation; instead, they express the semantics of choice parasitic on the utterance situation itself and the assertoric choices of the speaker. This, intuitively, is the same conclusion reached by Hacquard (2006) in her seminal work on the differences between circumstantial and epistemic modality. The differences are implementational: the present system involves reification of the utterance situation in the shape of the situational variable d already introduced at the edge of the first zone. Other major differences revolve around reconceiving the general nature of modal meanings as involving CHOICE among live alternatives and tying the nature of those alternatives to the denotation of the prejacent. In this sense, the connection to the compositional system proposed here applies to the analogue of the modal base in addition to the analogue of the perspectival situation.

6.3   Evidence for CHOICE among Live Alternatives as Basic to Modal Meaning

In this section, I stand back and assess what the shift away from quantificational meanings for modals has done and whether such a drastic move has any further desirable consequences. I am aware that given the pedigree of quantificational analyses of modal meanings, a number of payoffs are needed if the alternative is to be entertained. The first payoff is that under this account, dynamic, circumstantial, and epistemic modal meanings can be related straightforwardly to the three domains of the clause that seem to be semantically necessary for independent reasons. The second is that the notion of CHOICE among alternatives makes sense of some long-standing traditional puzzles concerning (i) the weakness of universal modal meanings and (ii) the interaction of deontic modals with overt disjunction. I take up these points in turn.

6.3.1   Dynamic Modal Interpretations

Under a quantificational account of modal meanings, the difference between the lexical modals and the auxiliary modals reflects a lexical vs. functional distinction in the grammar. The circumstantial and epistemic modals are uniformly argued to be quantificational, while the meaning of the lexical/dynamic modals seems to live in the domain of lexical semantics. As we have seen, an individual modal doesn't have to have a corresponding lexical alternant, so maybe it's all right if the two types are analyzed quite differently. However, it is true that at least in English, a lexical modal meaning does always coexist with a quantificational version. Let us see how the present account would treat the dynamic modal *can*.

Recall that I have argued that the dynamic modals show all the syntactic hallmarks of first Merge attachment within the lowest event structure domain. This is because they affect the argument roles of the predicate that they combine with and they are able to scope under a quantificational subject. Consider (45a). Since the modal is in the domain of D_μ, where event properties are confined to those that are abstractions over space and time, whatever we say about John's alternatives here must not depend on any actual swimming events either before now or in the future. I am forced to conclude that the notion of ability and the notion of disposition are primitive event properties that can compose with other event properties to create 'the ability to V' and 'the disposition to V', respectively. I suspect that the English habitual as in (45b) is in fact the default specification of the latter meaning.

(45) a. John can swim. *Dynamic*
    'John possesses the property of having <*Johnswim*> in his abilities to put in train.'
  b. John swims. *Habitual*
    'John possesses the property of having <*Johnswim*> in his disposition to put in train.'

It is tempting to think of the causal relationships among subevents as the analogue of the flow of time in the domain of particulars. Basically, ability to effect a change in the force-dynamical domain is paralleled by circumstantial facilitation in the spatiotemporal domain. The relation to higher modal meanings is that these primitive cognitive concepts are reused in the higher domains via metaphoricization to encode more abstract situational versions of these basic meanings. The metaphor involves the relativization of the notion of potentiality and disposition to situational live options, or epistemic options.

Whether or not the dynamic version of the modal *can* in English is the very same lexical item in the grammar of a native speaker, the location of the meaning of modality in the domain of live alternatives is a classification that starts to make sense of the reasons such polysemies or historically derived homonymies arise in the first place.

Notice that when derivational morphemes such as *-er* or *able* apply to verbal root symbols, the meanings generated have precisely the kind of pseudointensionality that we have come to expect from the first zone. They are further evidence that the basic meanings of potential and disposition are available at the level of lexical concept formation, which crucially abstracts away from real-world instantiations.

(46) a. John is a swimmer./John is a smoker. *Disposition*
  b. This avocado is edible./This movie is unbearable. *Potential*

6.3.2   The Semantic "Weakness" of Universal Modals

There is an intuition among speakers that a modal statement is weaker than a simple assertion of fact. However, the formal semantics of modals like *must* as involving universal quantification over possible worlds makes it seem like a *stronger* reading than the simple assertion of factuality in the actual world. This puzzle has come to the fore again through the work of von Fintel and Gillies (2010), who dub the intuition about the weakness of *must* "The Mantra." Consider the following two utterances:

(47) a. It is raining outside.
      b. It must be raining outside.

A speaker in full possession of the facts would be uncooperative in the extreme not to utter (47a) if it were true. Sentence (47b) feels like a hedge. However, the classical account in terms of possible worlds involves universal quantification over all worlds in the modal base, including presumably the actual one. Thus, it seems as if (47b) should be saying something that is *even stronger* than (47a), contrary to our intuitions.

One way to fix this is to weaken the modal meaning somehow—for example, by saying that the possible worlds in the modal base here contain a hedge to the effect that the real world might *not* be one of the worlds of the modal base consistent with the speaker's knowledge. This is the view taken overwhelmingly in the literature starting with Karttunen (1972), who first discussed the problem (see also Groenendijk and Stokhof 1975, Kratzer 1991).

Despite the intuition that *must* is somehow weaker than plain assertion, von Fintel and Gillies (2010) support the strong view, maintaining that *must* indeed represents universal quantification over a realistic modal base, and that Must ϕ really does entail ϕ and is strong in this sense. The illusion of weakness, they claim, arises because of a presupposition that *must* carries concerning the nature of the evidence that allows the speaker to assert that ϕ is true in all possible worlds. Essentially, *must* presupposes that the evidence is not direct or perceptual, and it is this evidential flavor that contributes to the pragmatic effect that the speaker is saying something weaker than a plain assertion.

It should be clear that the present proposal for *must* does not have the property of being *stronger* than the simple assertion. In fact, a modalized sentence and a simple assertion are not in any kind of entailment relation in either direction, so no scale of strength can be set up. However, the proposal for *must* does include the idea of live alternatives. This is only well defined in the context of some sort of factual uncertainty, where certain aspects of the situation or proposition are technically undecided. I have claimed that this is always the case when the speaker does not directly witness a situation. From this point of view, the proposed denotation is a direct translation of the intuition that modal statements, even those with the so-called universal modal *must*, are always statements made against a backdrop of factual uncertainty. Indeed, under the current proposal this intuition is built into their meaning.

6.3.3 The Puzzle of Deontic Modality and Its Interaction with Disjunction: The Paradox of Free Choice Disjunction

Another semantic puzzle regarding modals is relevant to the current proposal: namely, the problem of the interaction between deontic modality and disjunction. Deontic logics are well known for generating paradoxes when compared with the alethic inferential systems they are analogues of (see McNamara 2014 for discussion). This particular familiar problem has been taken up recently by Zimmerman (2000) and Aloni (2007), to whom I owe this presentation of the problem.

Consider the following sentences of English:

(48) a. Vincent is in Paris or in London.
     b. ⇒ Vincent is in Paris or Vincent is in London.

(49) a. Vincent may be in Paris or in London.
     b. ⇒ Vincent may be in Paris or Vincent may be in London.
     c. ⇒ Vincent may be in Paris and Vincent may be in London.

The problem is that while (48a) entails (48b) in the expected way, and that while (49a) on one reading entails (49b), it is also true that under a narrow scope reading for the disjunction, (49a) entails (49c)!

It seems as if we want the following theorem to be true for permissibility (PE):

(50) $PE(p \lor q) \Rightarrow PE(p) \land PE(q)$

But (50) is not a theorem of standard deontic logics, and if we added it as an axiom for PE, then we would end up with an unacceptable system. Because $PE(p) \to PE(p \lor q)$ is already a theorem in the system, combining that theorem with (50) would have the unwelcome result that if anything at all is permitted, then everything is.

So, on the one hand, we want to preserve a standard logic for disjunction and a standard deontic logic. But, on the other hand, we cannot have them both and still generate the entailment in (49c). Zimmerman's (2000) solution is to modify the semantics for disjunction. Aloni's (2007) is to modify the semantics for modals.

Note that the problematic entailment does not arise for universal modals like *must*.

(51) a. Vincent must be in Paris or in London.

   b. ¬ ⇒ Vincent must be in Paris and Vincent must be in London.

In the present system, none of the standard paradoxes arise because deontic modality is not characterized in terms of the analogy to alethic modality. Rather, what I propose is a notion of "choice" as part of the central *lexical* content of a modal predicate itself. To address the problematic entailment, we need only notice that the natural language disjunction *or* is interpreted either as taking wide scope over the whole proposition to deliver the entailment in (49b) or as taking low scope under the CHOICE predicate. What is then expressed is that 'being in Paris or London' is a possible choice for Vincent under the possible circumstantial alternatives. I assume that this means that *or* lies within in the event domain on this reading, and we need to construct a *single* event property corresponding to 'being in Paris or London'. All we need to assume here is that a composite event property of this sort has the following characteristic:

(52) *Disjoint properties and event instantiation*
      Any event that instantiates property 'A or B' must always have
      mereological subparts corresponding to an event instantiating A and an
      event instantiating B.

The reason (52) holds is that because the property is an essential (not contingent) property, a feature due to our assumptions about the lowest event zone, the two disjuncts must be essentially present in all true instantiations of that property. This means that any deontic modal statement that offers the pivot a CHOICE consisting of the situation instantiating the complex property 'A or B' will automatically have a situational choice that contains situations instantiating A and B as mereological subparts. This entails that A is a CHOICE for the pivot *and* B is a CHOICE for the pivot.

6.4   Conclusion

In this chapter, I have made specific proposals about the way modal and temporal interpretation is integrated into the clause. I have argued that temporal modification is only possible at the level of the second zone, which has the semantic type of properties of spatiotemporal event properties. This is the zone where the spatiotemporal properties of s_0 can be further specified and modified, and where ultimately the anchoring information is expressed. The anchoring information is, specifically, identity or nonidentity with some parameter of the utterance situation, d. I argued that present tense in English expresses indexical anchoring in this sense (identity with the temporal moment

of the utterance situation) and that past tense expresses nonidentity, thus opening up the temporal interval of the described situation to anaphoric resolution.
I showed that modals too express either indexical or anaphoric anchoring properties as part of their lexical specification, and that by and large the anaphoric
modals are the ones that still bear moribund "past" tense morphology in
English, probably not accidentally so. This classification is independent of the
types of domains that the modals can operate over and independent of whether
they are "universal" or "existential" in traditional terms—all English modals
are "finite" and have some anchoring specification for the perspectival situation
that they introduce.

With regard to modal meanings per se, I pursued an approach where by
the interpretation of a modal can be made sensitive to the denotational properties of its complement. I also argued against a quantificational approach
to modal meanings—an argument based in part on unexpected interactions
between modals and negation and on the desire to unify the lexical content of
modal meaning across zones as much as possible, and allow the final meaning
to be fed directly by the denotation of the prejacent. For this reason, I proposed a view of modality that centers on the notion of live alternatives and on
CHOICES for an individual within those up-for-grabs alternatives.[7] Under this
conception of things, the so-called existential modals correspond to a simple
assertion that something is *one* choice for the individual, while the so-called
universal modals correspond to the assertion that something is the *only* or
exclusive choice for that individual. I argued that this general lexical meaning is abstract enough to form the basis for particular modal meanings in all
three domains.

To summarize my proposal about modals' point of attachment: I have assumed that they combine semantically with projections in the zone that denotes
properties of elements of D_μ (dynamic modals), projections in the zone that
denote properties of spatiotemporal event properties (circumstantial modals),

Table 6.4
Relativization of modal interpretation

Zone	Choice pivot	Source of uncertainty	First merge
Conceptual (dynamic)	Actor	Inherent causal properties of Actor	Evt
Spatiotemporal (circumstantial)	Situational topic	Undecidedness of future circumstance	Asp
Assertoric (epistemic)	Speaker	Lack of complete knowledge	T

and projections in the zone that denote properties of the utterance (epistemic modals); see table 6.4. In addition, many modals select directly for PolP. I have assumed that selection for PolP must be stated on an item-by-item basis, but that selection for negation is maintained across polysemous uses of a modal even when these straddle zones.

The phrase structure trees in (53) and (54) show the possibilities for attaching epistemic and circumstantial modals, respectively. In the trees, spans are represented by dashed lines and @ is Brody's diacritic representing the position of linearization for a span.

(53) *Epistemic modal*

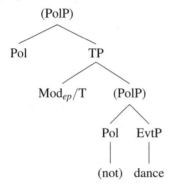

(54) *Circumstantial modal*

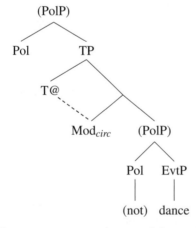

I have now come to the top of the auxiliation ladder and given an explicit treatment of anchoring elements like tense and epistemic modality. I have given semantic and syntactic specifications for all the elements that participate in rigid auxiliary ordering in English. I have done this in the context of a semantically zoned verbal extended projection, presumed to be universal, and with a view to unifying as far as possible the denotations of the individual pieces. My aim has been to construct a system in which (i) the typological generalizations of meaning compositions across languages fall out as a natural consequence of the zoning and (ii) the actual ordering of auxiliaries in English does not need to be stipulated by template. In chapter 7, I summarize the overall proposal and assess how it meets the goals set out at the beginning of this monograph.

7 Summary and Outlook

In this final chapter, I summarize the proposals I have made and then take a look at sentence (1) to see how the proposed system delivers the ordering that we find.

(1) Vidar might have been being chased.

Finally, I discuss extensions and implications of the proposed architecture, and lay out an agenda for further research.

7.1 Architecture and Semantic Zones

My overall architectural claim has been that the syntax-semantics mapping corresponding to the extended verbal projection delivers denotations in three distinct domains, corresponding to the three distinct hierarchically ordered domains for which robust evidence exists in syntax. Syntactic research tends to stipulate the $V < T < C$ hierarchy templatically, but if this monograph is on the right track, that hierarchy is underwritten by a particular ontology of semantic sorts. This in turn raises the possibility that the hierarchy of semantic sorts may be derived from something else. I suspect that the "something else" is a kind of developmental cognitive prioritizing, as well as third-factor considerations related to the reusability of symbols in declarative memory. It is not my purpose here to argue for a specific explanation in these terms. I have only been at pains to construct a system in which such questions can be asked and tested, where the primes of the semantic ontology are more commensurate with the primes and basic elements being discovered in psycholinguistic and neurolinguistic investigation. If we are to make any progress at all on the question of how much of the linguistic system is determined by constraints imposed by the properties of the mind/brain, then semantic ontology needs to be reconfigured from a less symbolic and more algorithmic perspective (to use Marr's (1982) terminology).

The zones I have proposed are the following. The first is a symbolic, conceptual zone where memorized elements of the system are deployed and composed. The idea here is that these lexical items are stored as <phonological string, syntactic features, semantics> triples and that the semantic part of this triple is confined by definition to partial event properties that are independent of temporal and worldly information. Therefore, the first zone is the one where elements of D_μ are composed. The second zone, inaugurated by Merge of an explicit quotational operator introducing the event variable for the utterance, d, is the domain of spatiotemporal event properties.[1] The idea is that spatiotemporal properties can only be stated in a context, where there is an anchoring eventuality, or origo, to construct such meanings. In terms of implementation, I close the event variable at the edge of vP (at the level of what I have called Evt), and the second phase becomes essentially the domain of properties not of events, but of event *properties*.[2] Finally, once the outermost f property variable is existentially bound at T, we are left with properties of d, or properties of assertions. This third zone of the clause is necessary to account for epistemic modal interpretations. I also assume that this is the zone where speaker-oriented meanings reside more generally. The proposed zones and their correspondence to the standard syntactic labels for the hierarchy are shown in (2).

(2) *Semantic zones and syntactic domains*

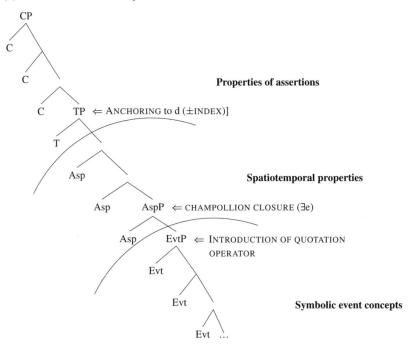

The proposed zones have certain clear diagnostic properties. The lowest, symbolic zone is characterized by meanings that have often been taken to be intensional or modal. I argued that all kinds of sublexical modality in this sense are really cases of "pseudointensionality" and that they stem from the fact that the symbolic zone manipulates event property abstractions. This zone has its own primitive relations related to identification and subevental relatedness, but does not require the machinery of possible worlds. In the second domain, the full toolbox of possible worlds and times is available; this is the domain where time and world parameters are manipulated. This domain also has the possibility of introducing a constrained set of reference situations (specifically in the case of the perfect and of circumstantial modality). I assume that the introduction of a reference situation is constrained by the fact that it needs to bear the kind of relation to the inner event that will allow specification of *its* spatiotemporal location to give spatiotemporal location to the dependent event. Finally, I have assumed that the edge of the spatiotemporal zone is the locus of anchoring information that explicitly relates the situation to the contextual parameters (I have labeled this *T* in the phrase structure diagrams, but it may be more suitable in the end to label it *Infl*, following Ritter and Wiltschko 2009). This final zone contains speaker-oriented adverbs, metalinguistic negation, and possibly other things like evidentiality markers. Boxes 7.1–7.3 schematize this summary and locate the relevant verbal formatives in their respective zones, as proposed in the previous chapters.

Box 7.1
Symbolic event concepts zone

> Verb root; participle in *-en/ed*
> *-ing*
> Dummy *be*
> Dynamic modality
> "Constituent" negation
> Manner and instrumental adverbs

Box 7.2
Spatiotemporal properties zone

> Clausal polarity
> Circumstantial modality
> Perfect *have*
> Temporal adverbs

Box 7.3
Properties of assertions zone

"High" negation
Epistemic modality
Speaker-oriented adverbs

7.2 Insertion: Lexical vs. Functional Items

In capturing the connection between lexical items and the syntax, I have adopted a view of the lexicon that involves spell-out of spans (Williams 2003, Adger, Harbour, and Watkins 2009, Adger 2010, Bye and Svenonius 2012): that is, vocabulary items are specified with a list of category features from the universal spine, and they realize spans corresponding to those features. Vocabulary items cannot realize noncontiguous spans, nor can they realize structures for which they bear no feature. In constrained circumstances, underassociation of category features is allowed, but underassociation is not freely available. This implementation is designed to transparently enforce the kind of mapping between lexical spell-out, morphological structure, and syntactic hierarchy that captures the facts traditionally captured by the Mirror Principle (Baker 1985). A transparent system like this is necessary if the zonal ontology is to have any effect at all on morphological patterns and typological word order patterns. However, this has not been a monograph about theories of lexical insertion, and I leave it open that an equivalently Mirror Theory–respecting alternative could also deliver the correct results. Crucially, in using zones to account for order, I have tried to avoid morphology-internal devices that might threaten the mapping between morphology and syntax.

In frameworks such as Distributed Morphology (DM), the root is the receptacle for conceptual content but is devoid of syntactic information. The functional structure of the clause is both syntactic and the locus of structural semantic information. In my system, too, I assume that the nodes of the syntactic tree are associated with formal semantic denotations that represent the structural semantics of the clause. However, these abstract functional meanings are supplemented, or clothed, with the conceptual content associated with roots, or contentful lexical items.

However, the classical DM model differs in certain ways from the system I have presented here and that I have advocated more generally in earlier work (Ramchand 2008, 2014b). One big difference is that the distinction between conceptual content and structural semantic content is not serial as in the DM architecture, but parallel. Moreover, the contentful lexical item is not devoid of syntactic information; rather, it is quite explicitly a triple containing syntactic as well as phonological and semantic information. The syntactic information provides the link between the lexical item's conceptual and phonological properties and governs its conditions of deployment.[3] In chapters 2–4, I specified in some detail what kinds of relations and structural semantics I think belong in the first phase (they involve causation and property predication, for example). The structural semantics associated with, say, Init, Proc, or Res is assumed therefore to be *unified* with the conceptual content provided by particular lexical verbs such as *run* vs. *jump*. In other words, *run* provides conceptual content allowing the identification of a process event of 'running' and of the initiation of 'running', while *jump* invokes the perceptual and cognitive properties of 'jumping' as applied to an initiated process. The process is quite general, and not formally intractable, although it is in tension with our standard means of writing the denotations of lexical items.

However, there is one respect in which the DM strategy of separating roots from vocabulary items has echoes in the system proposed here: in both cases, the lowest domain is special. Elements of D_μ are triples, as I have said, and they can be "deployed" explicitly by the speaker. The most sensible way to think about the building of this part of the verbal projection seems to be that the elements of D_μ themselves merge to build structure. This indeed is what I have assumed. The move to include symbolic elements of the language as part of the domain has the consequence of establishing a real rift between elements of D_μ, which can be deployed in the first phase, and functional vocabulary items that are not members of D_μ, which can be thought of as undergoing late insertion as exponents (contributing phonology and in some cases certain conceptual content in the form of presuppositions). In both cases, syntactic contribution and conceptual-phonological matter are separated, but only functional items (i.e., those that are not members of D_μ) can be modeled by late insertion in this system. The D_μ domain is structured, productive, and syntactic just as in the constructivist ideal. But it is also similar to the intuition behind roots within DM in that it is encapsulated and merged early. The closest historical antecedent, in spirit, is probably the lexical syntax of Hale and Keyser (2002).

In setting up this system, I have used the toolbox that seems to me the most transparent for expressing the generalizations that emerge from natural language data, and the most compatible with my own cherished beliefs. If there were a toolbox that I could have just taken off the shelf to implement the agenda of this monograph, I would have done so. Part of the point of this monograph has been to build an architecture with the right properties to meet my desiderata. On the other hand, the architecture I have used has certain properties that are surely contingent and could have been done another way. The difficulty of capturing the intuition behind event kinds/concepts/essences in a semiformalized system has been the most difficult constraint to satisfy. I think it is interesting that the latter challenge has led me to a system that enforces a stronger distinction between lexical and functional items than I had hitherto assumed, more in line with the position always held by DM. However, because of my aim of providing denotations for lexical items as polysemous items of representational integrity, I have been forced into a more piece-based, Lego-style approach[4] to the construction of linguistic representation. This in turn makes it easier to see what predictions this kind of compositional system provides for the storing and processing of lexical items in the production and comprehension of natural language propositions.

7.3 Summary of the Pieces

In this section, I summarize the syntactic and semantic denotations of the core players in the analysis of the English auxiliary system that has emerged from this study.

The lexical item *-ing* is a member of D_μ and has the denotation in (3), where Identifying State (ID-State) is defined as in box 7.4. Its syntax is simply specified as <Evt>.

(3) $\llcorner u_V\text{-}ing\lrcorner = \lambda x \lambda e[\text{State}(e) \wedge \text{ID-State}(e, \llcorner u_V \lrcorner) \wedge \text{HOLDER}(e) = x]$

Box 7.4
Identifying State: Definition

> For every event description P, an *Identifying State* for P is a stative eventuality that manifests sufficient cognitive/perceptual identifiers of the event property P.

The participle in *-en/ed* is the realization corresponding to systematic nonprojection of the features <Asp, Evt, Init, …> of the corresponding past tense verb. The nonprojection is rooted at the bottom of the span, as shown in tree (4).

(4) *Scope of spell-out for the* -en/ed *participle*

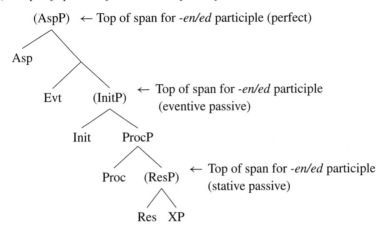

     (AspP)   ← Top of span for *-en/ed* participle (perfect)

Asp

     Evt   (InitP)   ← Top of span for *-en/ed* participle
                           (eventive passive)

       Init   ProcP

          Proc   (ResP)   ← Top of span for *-en/ed* participle
                              (stative passive)

            Res XP

The blocking facts are summarized in (5), and the blocking principle for auxiliation is stated in (6).

(5) a. Attach *-ing* to any complete event structure and fill in with the dummy verb *be*.
   Blocked by stative verbs
   b. Realize ResP as the *-en/ed* participle and realize Evt with the dummy verb *be*.
   Blocked by adjectives in the case of deadjectival verbs
   c. Realize ProcP as the *-en/ed* participle and realize Evt with the dummy verb *be*.
   Blocked by unaccusative verbs

(6) *Blocking of auxiliation*
   In cases where a single verbal lexical item generates the same event description as an auxiliary structure, expression by means of an auxiliary is blocked.

We move now to the second zone, the domain of properties of spatiotemporal event properties. *Have* has the syntactic specification <Asp> and the semantic denotation in (7). It introduces a reference state s′, the Evidential State, from which the most embedded event is inferrable. The definition of Evidential State is given in box 7.5.

(7) $[\![\text{have}]\!] = \lambda Q \lambda x \lambda f' \, \lambda d \exists s' \exists f[Q(f)(d) \wedge \text{State}(s') \wedge \text{HOLDER}(s') = x$
   $\wedge f = \lambda s \lambda d \, [s' \text{ gives evidence for the spatiotemporal relation between s}$
   and d in the same world as s′] $\wedge f'(s')(d)]$

Box 7.5
Evidential State (Definition)

> For all situational descriptions s_0, s', s' is an Evidential State for s_0 iff s', is a stative situation (i.e. which can have a moment as its temporal parameter) which is a salient situation that provides *criterial evidence for the existence of* s_0. The existence of s' always entails the existence of s_0 in the same world as s'.

Circumstantial modal meanings are also merged in the second zone. They modify spatiotemporal properties of the embedded event by introducing a perspectival intermediate situation with respect to which the embedded event is said to be a CHOICE (either simple or exclusive) among live alternatives. Denotations for the simple choice circumstantial modal and the exclusive choice circumstantial modal are shown in (8) and (9), respectively.

(8) $[\![\text{Mod}_{circ-may}]\!] = \lambda Q\lambda x\lambda f'\,\lambda d\exists s'\exists f[Q(f)(d) \wedge \text{State}(s') \wedge \text{HOLDER}(s') = x \wedge f = \lambda s\lambda d[s$ is located at a world-time pair that is a CHOICE for the perspectival topic in $s'] \wedge f'(s')(d)]$

(9) $[\![\text{Mod}_{circ-must}]\!] = \lambda Q\lambda x\lambda f'\,\lambda d\exists s'\exists f[Q(f)(d) \wedge \text{State}(s') \wedge \text{HOLDER}(s') = x \wedge f = \lambda s\lambda d[s$ is located at a world-time pair that is the exclusive CHOICE for the perspectival topic in $s'] \wedge f'(s')(d)]$

The general schema for modal meanings is informally characterized as in box 7.6.

Box 7.6
Informal schema for modal denotations

> A modal meaning involves the assertion of a CHOICE within a set of live alternatives *for* a topic individual x *in* a perspectival situation s'. These alternatives are directly constructed from the constituent that the modal attaches to.

Both the perfect and circumstantial modality involve modification of properties of spatiotemporal properties of events. They have an extremely similar semantic contribution: they introduce a perspective situation s' that provides an intermediate reference situation between the depicted event and d. This is shown schematically in figures 7.1 and 7.2. In figure 7.1, we see that the perspective situation introduced by the perfect auxiliary follows the embedded situation s_0; figure 7.2 shows that the perspective situation introduced

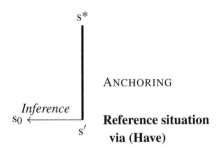

ANCHORING

Inference

Reference situation
via (Have)

Decided   Undecided

Figure 7.1
Schema for the perfect

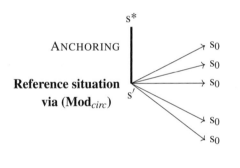

ANCHORING

Reference situation
via (Mod$_{circ}$)

Live Alternatives

Decided   Undecided

Figure 7.2
Schema for circumstantial modality

by the circumstantial modal precedes the embedded situation s_0. In the case of the perfect, the perspectival situation s' is related to the embedded situation by entailment; in the case of the circumstantial modal, by projection. In both cases, the reference situational variable s' is the one that will be directly anchored to the context via the T relation. In both cases, the anchoring of the intermediate reference situation is enough to spatiotemporally specify the embedded situational variable s_0.

At the T position of the clausal spine, anchoring to the context takes place. I have argued that there are two basic forms of anchoring; see box 7.7. The representations of present and past in English are given in (10) and (11), respectively.

Box 7.7
Types of anchoring

1. $\forall$ eventualities e and speech events d, such that f(d)(e), INDEX(f) is true iff the temporal parameter of e is strictly identified with the temporal parameter of d, the utterance time.
2. $\forall$ eventualities e and speech events d, such that f(d)(e), ANAPH(f) is true iff the temporal parameter of e is resolved *anaphorically*, either by reference to something in the linguistic context or by reference to some purely discourse contextual topic time or world.

(10) $[\![\text{TP}_{pres}]\!] = \lambda d \exists f \exists e [\text{Utterance}(d) \wedge \text{INDEX}(f) \wedge f(d)(e) \wedge \llcorner u \lrcorner(e)$
$\wedge \text{Source}(d) = \text{'Speaker'} \wedge \text{Goal}(d) = \text{'Hearer'}]$

(11) $[\![\text{TP}_{past}]\!] = \lambda d \exists f \exists e [\text{Utterance}(d) \wedge f(d)(e) \wedge \text{ANAPH}(f) \wedge \llcorner u \lrcorner(e)$
$\wedge \text{Source}(d) = \text{'Speaker'} \wedge \text{Goal}(d) = \text{'Hearer'}]$

All modals in English carry anchoring information. In (12), I give the TP corresponding to circumstantial modal *must*, which is anchored indexically, combined with its circumstantial modal meaning.

(12) $[\![\text{TP}_{must}]\!] = \lambda d \exists f' \exists s' \exists f \exists s_0 [\text{Utterance}(d) \wedge \text{State}(s') \wedge f(d)(s_0) \wedge \llcorner u \lrcorner(s_0)$
$\wedge \text{INDEX}(f') \wedge f = \lambda s \lambda d [s$ is located at a world-time pair that is the exclusive CHOICE for the perspectival topic in $s'] \wedge f'(d)(s')]$

Finally, epistemic modality occurs when the modal spells out only at T and applies the CHOICE semantics to d as its perspectival situation. Here the live alternatives come from the speaker's different assertoric choices given her knowledge and the Question under Discussion (QUD).

(13) $[\![\text{TP}_{ep-must}]\!] = \lambda d \exists f \exists e [\text{Utterance}(d) \wedge \text{State}(e) \wedge f(d)(e) \wedge \llcorner u \lrcorner(e)$
$\wedge \text{INDEX}(f) \wedge e$ is the exclusive assertoric CHOICE for the speaker of d]
where the live alternatives for the speaker are the different assertions possible given the discourse QUD.

(14) $[\![\text{TP}_{ep-might}]\!] = \lambda d \exists f \exists e [\text{Utterance}(d) \wedge \text{State}(e) \wedge f(d)(e) \wedge \llcorner u \lrcorner(e)$
$\wedge \text{ANAPH}(f) \wedge e$ is one assertoric CHOICE for the speaker of d]
where the live alternatives for the speaker are the different assertions possible given the discourse QUD.

7.4 Auxiliary Ordering Revisited

From a basic empirical perspective, auxiliary ordering in English (which has been our test case all along) now looks like it can be made to follow from zonal properties and ontological classification of denotations rather than from detailed selectional mechanisms for particular morphological endings. The goal has been unified syntactic denotations for all the formatives employed in the auxiliary system, and this has largely, been achieved. It is time to put all the pieces together, and assess the costs and stipulations that this particular model has required.

As a way of focusing the discussion, let us look at sentence (1), repeated here, which displays the full complement of auxiliaries in the English system.

(15) Vidar might have been being chased.

The tree for the VP of this sentence is shown in (16).

(16) Maximal auxiliation in English

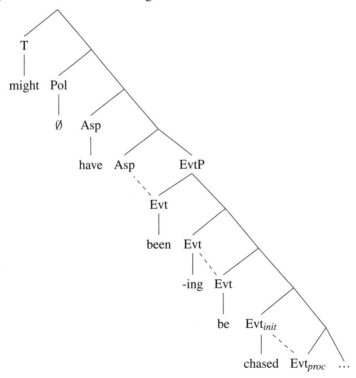

Chase is a verb with the syntactic specification <Asp, Evt, Init, Proc>, and its *-en/ed* participle has the specification <Init, Proc>. *Be* inserts in Evt followed by *-ing* and then another instance of *be* in the higher Evt. Could the ordering be otherwise? Let us consider the possibilities.

The progressive cannot occur before the passive because the participle involves the spell-out of a contiguous span based on the root's specification. Merging *-ing* would close off the domain that can be spelled out by the participle. The suffix *-ing* cannot attach to the participle itself since the participle cannot accept a suffix. The progressive *-ing* can only attach to the bare root, which also spells out the full span (minus Asp). Nor would it help to spell out the dummy verb *be* as the participial form. We could do that, but since *be* has no category features other than Evt (and Asp and T), spelling the dummy *be* out as *been* would only affect its ability to enter the situational zone; another *be* would have to be inserted and tensed in any case, and the redundant *been* would be blocked. In any event, it would not give any kind of passivization effect. In fact, as we have seen, it is possible to generate an *-en/ed* participle above the progressive, but it goes on to grow into the *perfect*, since spelling out the participle at this height will inevitably mean that no argument has been removed. Similarly, the perfect cannot occur below the progressive, the passive, or dynamic modality since (i) perfect *have* merges in the higher situational domain (by stipulation) and (ii) the effect of nonremoval of an argument comes from the very height of the participial span that feeds the perfect. A more truncated participle would not retain the external argument, and so a perfect could never be built.

Could dynamic modality occur before the progressive? No, this is ruled out by the same semantic economy rule that prohibits the progressivization of stative verbs. In fact, an English-specific factor already rules out any kind of modal embedding: namely that in English, modals have only one lexical entry, the one that contains both Asp and T features. There simply are no participial or bare forms for the English modals in the standard dialect.

Turning to the situational zone, could the perfect occur above circumstantial modality instead of below it? I assume that this is possible in principle, but that the above-mentioned language-specific fact about English modals prevents it. In languages where modals have nonfinite forms, the circumstantial modal can remain in Asp and in principle an epistemic modal could merge to spell out T (as in Swedish or Norwegian). However, in English, the epistemic and circumstantial modals simply cannot cooccur.

7.5 Open Questions and Further Research

7.5.1 The Nominal Domain
So far, I have said nothing about nouns. Considerable work on the cartography of the nominal extended projection shows that here, too, there is an intriguing

typologically robust order to the construction of DPs from base lexical items (Zamparelli 2000, Cinque 2005, Borer 2005, Dékaný 2012, Pfaff 2015). I assume that nominal projections too are partitioned into a symbolic D_μ domain and a higher domain of instantiation, where I assume both reference and case reside.

Apart from investigating a similar kind of hypothesis in the nominal domain, however, further research must be specific about how nominal arguments are merged/integrated with the verbal functional sequence in the course of building up a proposition. To gain the advantages of Champollion closure at EvtP for the interaction with quantification more generally, we need to assume crucially that quantified nominal projections are not merged in complete form within the EvtP. I believe that to understand the relationship between the two extended projections, we need to adopt a view of phrase structure that involves merging of minimal nominal structures in the lowest minimal part of the verbal extended projection together with higher copies that contain more and more functional information. Thus, I would argue, the part of an argument that is merged in the first phase is actually not a full-fledged referential projection or phase; rather, it is the lower portion of the nominal argument, which contributes its conceptual semantics to the buildup of the D_μ domain before the deployment operator is merged. Only later on are such arguments given referential status, existentially bound, or quantified. There is some evidence that the direct complements to V should be just Ns, not DPs (Williams 2003, Svenonius 2004, Sportiche 2005). Taking this result seriously and integrating it into a coherent theory of Merge and linearization is entirely possible and is likely to be warranted on independent grounds anyway. One way of implementing the idea would involve the multidominance of the banyan trees proposed by Svenonius (2004). However, a detailed exposition building propositions via the interleaving of nominal and verbal functional sequences is beyond the scope of this monograph, and I leave it for future research.

7.5.2 On the Universal vs. the Language Specific

The zones should be universal, since they are designed to account for robust crosslinguistic generalizations in the first place. However, a number of features of the auxiliary-ordering analysis in English are clearly language specific.

The presuppositional/conceptual semantics of the language-particular lexical items that spell out the zones is of course up to each language. In particular, the spans spelled out by individual lexical items are specific to the language and the particular vocabulary item. For example, idiosyncrasies about English include the fact that all modals have a T feature and do not have corresponding uninflected entries. The English present tense also turns out to be special, and

I have speculated that this is one reason why the language makes such liberal use of auxiliation in building derived states for anchoring.

In principle, under this system we expect ordering constraints and patterns because of the universal hierarchical ordering of the three semantic zones of the clause. Within this broad expectation, individual languages might impose even stricter and more fine-grained orderings because of language-specific items. Thus, the fact that there are only three zones in this system does not derive all of the full richness of orderings reported in the cartographic literature. However, language-specific selectional facts may sit on top of the more minimalistic universal spine in this sense (see Ramchand and Svenonius 2014 and Wiltschko 2014 for discussion of the same general idea).

7.5.3 The Future and the Search for Explanations

The new ontology proposed here offers hope of a more systematic connection between grammatical theory on the one hand and psycholinguistics and neurolinguistics on the other. Specifically, the new ontology is formulated in such a way as to make possible predictions about what we might find in those subfields. Specifically, the existence of elements of D_μ as symbolic generalizations located in declarative memory is taken seriously in this model. As linguists, we are also interested in the idea of how the linguistic system is constrained by the more general properties of the mind/brain. Language in turn is interesting to those other domains of inquiry because it offers insight into one of the most complicated things that human minds do—namely, the processing of hierarchical symbolic structures.

Though many details and consequences remain to be explored, in this monograph I have hoped to give a proof of concept that a system created with such a radically different ontology can meet basic descriptive desiderata and indeed be made to work.

Notes

Chapter 1

1. For example, they contain at most one force-dynamical change, at most one direct causer, and at most one specified result state. See Ramchand 2008 for discussion.

2. Kratzer uses loose verification for the relationship between situations and propositions, as opposed to the exact verification system of Fine-an truthmaker semantics (Fine, 2014). For this reason, exemplification is necessary in order to create minimal situations that verify a proposition.

3. As a simplification, and for the purposes of exposition, I translate all Zoggian forms into IPA notation and use descriptive terms from human linguistics. In fact, Zoggian does utilize an auditory channel, but one that is not perceptible to the human ear.

4. This is absolutely not to disparage representations with clear and precise truth conditions; rather, my intent is to take into account the fact that syntactic representations simpliciter may in fact underdetermine those more explicit representations, depending on the division of labor between grammatical ingredients and contextual and pragmatic effects. The methodology I will adopt is conservative in what it ascribes to the grammatical system.

5. In the *World Atlas of Linguistic Structures* database (Dryer and Haspelmath 2013), only 31 out of 201 typologically distributed languages have no past, future, or aspectual inflection on the verb. (Whether a language has tense marking or aspect marking turns out to be two independent properties, contrary to folk belief.) See also Julien 2002 for a typological description of the relative ordering of voice and cause morphology with respect to tense and aspect.

6. I will have nothing to say about linearization in this monograph.

7. Eckhardt's (2012) use of the Davidsonian event variable corresponding to a performative verb also bears a close relationship to this idea. For Eckhardt, this variable (which she labels ε) denotes the ongoing act of information transfer. The existence of this variable is necessary for the analysis of performatives and adverbials like *hereby*, although it is not sufficient, since the analysis of performatives also requires an explicit definition by the speaker of what her utterance is doing. In my own system, d is represented explicitly as the ongoing act of information transfer, and does not require an explicit performative verb for its introduction. One could see the quotational system as a

hybrid version of an analysis where every utterance is preceded by an implicit performative: *John is tall* is really *I ASSERT THAT John is tall*, except that no literal embedding or deletion is taking place. Rather, the claim will be that a representation of the eventuality corresponding to the ongoing utterance event is explicit in the compositional semantics, and is necessary to convert the usage of symbols of D_μ into something that has explicit truth conditions.

8. There is an important caveat here: namely, that I am working with a decomposition of the verb phrase and Champollion assumes a single V head. For Champollion, the "lexical" nature of event closure means that the event variable is bound before the argument DPs are introduced. My approach to verbal lexical meaning, on the other hand, operates with a rather decomposed event structure in which arguments are interleaved in specifier positions at various heights. This means that introducing event closure at the edge of the first phase does not necessarily have the happy outcomes for quantification that are natural consequences of Champollion's original proposal. Nevertheless, I maintain that the idea here is essentially the same as Champollion's, but in a syntactically updated sense. Getting the results concerning the interaction with quantificational arguments requires being more specific about how nominal arguments are merged the proposition is being built up. In brief, I assume that nominal projections too are partitioned into a symbolic D_μ domain and a higher domain of instantiation, or reference. The part of the argument that is merged in the first phase is actually not a full-fledged referential projection or phase; rather, it is the lower portion of the nominal argument, which contributes its conceptual semantics to the building up of the D_μ domain before the deployment operator is merged. Only later on are these arguments given referential status, existentially bound, or quantified. Thus, all quantification lies systematically *outside* the level of event closure, as in Champollion's system. However, a detailed exposition of the way nominal and verbal functional sequences interleave to build the proposition is beyond the scope of this monograph, and will have to remain the major promissory note of this work.

9. As is well known, the gerundive actually encompasses a host of subtypes. Since this monograph deals with verbal extended projections, I will not examine these in any detail, although I will try to provide a motivation for the existence of this family of more nominal-like expressions built around *-ing* forms.

10. See Caha 2009 for an explication of the equivalence between DM's version of the Elsewhere principle in terms of underspecification (the Subset Principle) and the version required by the spanning approach (the Superset Principle).

11. In fact, in previous work (Ramchand 2011, 2016) I have argued that there are aspects of this template that should not need to be stipulated; rather, they follow from the recursive deployment of a number of primitive relations that operate over event properties as a matter of human cognition. Subevental embedding corresponds as a matter of general principle to the cause/leads-to relation. I propose to limit recursion to structures with a maximum of one dynamic predication per event phase. This is a constraint that comes from our general cognitive relationship to event perception: independently perceived dynamic change corresponds in interpretation to a *distinct* event. For a set of subevents to be conceptualized as a single unified event, there can only be one independently represented dynamic core. Finally, the thematic roles are restricted to the holding of either a static property or a changing property. They do not need to

be "selected"; rather, they are introduced via predication at each level of subevental description. These are abstract properties of the cognitive glue that puts events and their participants together, and they are patterns in the abstract system of grid lines that underwrites and organizes the verbal lexical labels we then learn.

12. Caha's (2009) nanosyntactic approach recognizes nonterminal spell-out, and also recognizes "treelets" as the syntactic part of a lexical item's specification. However, in that system, trees are built not by the direct merger of lexical items themselves, but by a rewriting process based on "match." The nanosyntactic approach further differs from the present one in that syntactic "movements" can be triggered in order to feed lexicalization under "match."

13. Poser blocking is so-called after the first close examination of cases where expression in terms of a single form blocks expression in terms of multiple words (Poser 1992). This kind of blocking is effectively disallowed in a system like DM, where the competition for lexical insertion plays out only in the domain of single terminals. The operations of fusion and selection, which implicate adjacent heads, can allow the result of competition to include information from directly adjacent heads in the phrase structure, but not from heads any further away. (for discussion, see Embick and Marantz 2008). The grounding assumptions of DM are so different from the assumptions underlying this monograph that it is not immediately obvious to me whether the generalizations that underlie the use of blocking in chapters 2 and 3 can or cannot be captured in a DM framework using different principles. Poser blocking and its role in participle constructions are also anticipated strongly in the work of Lundquist (2008), to whom the ideas behind the treatment in chapter 3 are indebted.

Chapter 2

1. Note that the mismatched reading in (10), where *do* is construed as substituting for a main verb in nonfinite form after the modal auxiliary, is marginally possible; however, it is irrelevant and I will ignore it in what follows. The reading where *do* substitutes for the auxiliary phrase is robustly ungrammatical.

2. Note that Baltin (2006) shows that British *do*-substitution does pattern like a proform, rather than like ellipsis, with respect to the tests in Hankamer and Sag 1976.

3. It is equally well known that there are a number of systematic exceptions to this generalization. In one class of exceptions, normally stative verbs are coerced into a more dynamic sense, as in *John is being good today* or *I am really loving this pizza*. Another class of exceptions concerns positional statives such as *sit*, *stand*, and *lie*, which regularly occur in the progressive with nondynamic interpretations. I will not discuss the latter class here.

4. This leads to a problem with accomplishment predicates, which Hallman solves by assuming that the telos for accomplishment predicates is *added* by a null telicizing operator that is in complementary distribution with the English progressivizing operator.

5. This is essentially a version of the "multiple choice paradox" later discussed and explored by Bonomi (1997): the progressive of a disjunctive set of options can be true in contexts where none of the progressivized versions of the individual options would be judged true.

6. As in Ramchand 2008, I will assume that DPs that undergo A-movement from one argument position to another simply accrue argument entailments additively.

7. The details of the interleaving of the extended projections of DP and VP are beyond the scope of this monograph, however. I assume that even though the nominal projection is encapsulated away from the extended verbal projection, the existence of higher levels of functional structure that are not interpreted at the lower levels is what drives movement to the higher domains of the verbal functional sequence.

8. This is essentially an extension of the phenomenon of Poser blocking (Poser 1992). See also Lundquist 2008 on the formation of the equivalent of *-ing* participles in Swedish, and their various polysemies, including a discussion of blocking. For Lundquist, the Swedish equivalent of *-ing* is simply a nominal gender feature that can attach to structures of various sizes.

9. I leave technical details of implementation aside here.

10. One could assume further that the inflectional information present on main verbs in English is placed there by downward Agree from higher interpretable heads. Alternatively, one might say that the main verb does indeed bear T, but that the spell-out diacritic for the T-Asp-Evt-etc. span in English is always located at Asp.

11. The object of a stative verb is part of the event description of the state. It is in what I elsewhere (Ramchand 2008) call "rhematic" position.

12. This is in contrast to the *-en/ed* participle, which always abstracts over the internal argument of the related active verb when used attributively.

13. When the *-ing* participle appears, it appears first without the auxiliary verb *be*. It seems to occur first with telic verbs and then is gradually extended to verbs without salient endpoints. It is apparently never overextended to stative verbs.

Chapter 3

1. In Swedish, a Germanic language closely related to English, the same form is not used for both passive and perfect. Swedish has a dedicated participial form, the supine, which is used in the perfect construction, showing at least that the lexical choice for this kind of participle *can* be different from the passive. For this reason, it has perhaps seemed less urgent to bake in a formal unity between the two forms in a language like English.

2. Starke's own framework involves spell-out of constituents instead of spans, which makes it very difficult to construct a system that will integrate the participle with the auxiliaries, especially cases of multiple auxiliaries. For this reason, Starke had to abandon the cleanest and simplest implementation of his intuition (pers. comm., class seminars). My account will use spans, allowing a more direct version of Starke's earliest intuition, which I believe to be the correct one.

3. I will use the term *passive participle* informally to refer to the use of the participle in contexts where the external argument is not expressed. This should not be taken to imply that I think the passive participle is a distinct lexical item from the perfect participle.

4. This is similar to a point made by Alexiadou and Anagnostopoulou (2008). In Greek, participles in *-menos* can be both target state and resultant state in Kratzer's terms, but always have event implications. Participles in *-tos*, on the other hand, do not have event implications. Alexiadou and Anagnostopoulou also make a distinction between event-implicating participles that include Voice and those that do not.

5. The test is not perfect, because, as Kratzer (2000) explains, 'still' could also fail to be felicitous because the target state is not reversible. For failure to combine with 'still' to truly diagnose a resultant state, one must exclude the possibility that the failure happens for trivial real-world reasons.

6. I assume that the simple perfect in German is grammatical as well. However, since the simple perfect has taken over the function of the past tense in many dialects, it is plausible that it does not have the same "resultant state" semantic analysis as the English perfect anyway. (See Löbner 2001 for discussion of the semantics of the German present perfect.)

7. How the proposed decompositions match up with individual morphemes, particles, and suffixes is a separate question. In the case of German, it seems as if the causative suffix that derives the verb *leeren* 'empty' from the corresponding adjective does not give rise to a target state, while the abstract prefix *auf* does. I assume this is because the causative suffix is actually located in Init, while the prefix *is* the licensor of Res despite its rather abstract semantics in *aufpumpen*.

8. In the normal case also, the finite verb inflects for tense and agreement information, and I will assume that this means that the inflected forms actually include Asp and T in their span information. But in this chapter we will not be directly concerned with these syntactic features.

9. In point of fact, the tensed verb in English probably only spans as far as Asp. I will assume this means that instead of having a T feature in its syntactic span, it has a uT feature that enters into agreement with T.

10. That certain low adverbs can modify target states without event implications is also noted by Anagnostopoulou (2003) and Alexiadou and Anagnostopoulou (2008) for Greek.

11. However, given that the derivation takes place at the level of D_μ and that a new D_μ is actually built, the system predicts that it would be possible for the two D_μs to be reanalyzed as not belonging to the same paradigm of forms. If a participle were reanalyzed in this way and drifted from its association with the verb it was derived from, it could eventually be cut free and reanalyzed by speakers as an independent adjective. I assume this has happened in the history of English, witness, for example, the adjective *accomplished* in *She is an accomplished musician.*

12. German is known to differ from English when it comes to the meanings and distribution of the verb *sein* 'be' and the properties of present tense. Present tense in English is incompatible with dynamic eventualities, except under special readings such as the habitual or the vivid narrative. My attempts to judge a sentence like *The dog is chased* are analogous to trying to interpret an event in the present tense, since for me *be chased* can only be an eventive passive. However, it may well be that German is quite different in this regard, and that there is in fact a third category in between the stative passive and

the eventive passive. As my concern in this monograph is just English, I intend to make claims only about what is built in the English system, not about potential typology.

13. In Ramchand 2008, I argued that English labile causative/inchoative verbs should be built in the syntax via a null causative head. For the purposes of the present system using spanning and its relationship to the participle in -*en/ed*, I have to assume that the entry for verbs like *melt* actually has an optional Init feature. This will mean that the participial spell-out of a Proc, Res structure may either have an existentially bound external argument or not. In the latter case, passive will be blocked by the simple unaccusative form and will never surface. Only the participle version of the full InitP structure will feed eventive passive formation.

14. Instead of assuming a separate Voice head with a causal flavor, I will assume for concreteness that the Evt head can host derived external arguments and is not necessarily tied to a particular event structure role, although when an argument is base-generated there it is interpreted as bearing the causer or agent role depending on the encyclopedic semantics of the verbal root phrase InitP.

15. Throughout this chapter and chapter 2, I have been assuming that we can distinguish in a deep and primitive way between events and states, which then interact in distinct ways in the temporal calculus. We can either encode this assumption as a primitive property of eventuality arguments that can be invoked in meaning postulate statements, or reify it as a sortal difference in the ontology itself. I do not know how to distinguish between these two options, and I have simply been assuming the former mechanism implicitly, without making the ontology for events more fine grained. However, it does not seem to me that the other aktionsart categories (i.e., achievement, activity, accomplishment) need to be ontologically distinguished in this way since I think their behaviors emerge from the state vs. event distinction and factors of composition. (See Altshuler 2016 for discussion and for arguments that the state vs. event distinction *should* be expressed in the ontology.)

Chapter 4

1. I am assuming further that lexical entries with a set of category features cannot freely underassociate (contrary to what I assumed in Ramchand 2008), so a tensed form of *be* cannot be inserted directly in T in English.

2. Myler (2017) attempts to unify *have* in all three of its incarnations: lexical possession verb, light verb, and perfect auxiliary. In my system, only the first two can be synchronically related, because of the difference between functional and lexical items and the ontological system being proposed here. However, it is natural to think that the structural semantic properties of *have* at least carry over to all uses: stative situation with a single HOLDER argument filled by internal Merge. This would have to be the outcome of the way in which grammaticalization works, however, rather than a result of these forms' being the same vocabulary item.

3. The problem extends to the past perfect, backshifted to a moment in the past.

4. For descriptive purposes, the terms and definitions in this section are taken from Parsons 1990.

5. The independent temporal phenomena Portner (2003) notes are also relevant in some sense since they indicate the pervasive effects of these general properties in a number of empirical domains. I assume that the same general mechanisms are at work and give rise to sequence-of-tense aktionsart sensitivity and to discourse-sequencing aktionsart sensitivity as well. A detailed discussion of these particular constructions and the additional factors they contribute to the final constraints is beyond the scope of this monograph.

6. General Gricean considerations of relevance will always apply, but then we need to know exactly what situation/property is being asserted by the perfect to determine whether it is relevant in context. My claim in this section is that it is the Evidential State that is being asserted and that it holds of a particular participant.

7. The final diagnostic will be discussed in more detail in chapter 6.

8. Here and in the following examples, I use the adverb *already* to force the intended reading. The reading is available without the adverb, though.

9. While I have implemented the new architecture using a specific set of assumptions and tools, the purpose of this monograph is not to argue explicitly for a particular toolbox. My main concern is the ontological revisions I have proposed, and the morphological and spell-out implementations are offered for explicitness and to demonstrate proof of concept. I leave it open that other implementations of the new ontological commitments are possible.

10. I will take up tense specification and clausal anchoring in detail in chapter 6, where I will discuss tense auxiliaries and anchoring by modals.

Chapter 5

1. I eschewed possible worlds in the analysis of event essences and the intensionality supposedly found with the progressive, since I argued that the D_μ level can manipulate event properties in ways that do not involve invoking the existence of particulars. However, with modals we are now in the higher syntactic domain, where we are dealing with event particulars (also referred to as "situations") and where it is natural to appeal to a world parameter. (The only exception will be the case of dynamic modality, discussed in section 6.3.1.)

2. Brennan (1993) also isolates a class of quantificational modality, as illustrated in (i).

(i) A snake can bite.
   ('It is sometimes the case that a snake bites.')
   Though I will not explicitly account for this class here, I take it to be a subspecies of dynamic modality.

3. For reasons that are currently obscure, only negative and interrogative versions of the English modal *can* allow an epistemic interpretation.

4. The data in this section come from my own fieldwork with native speakers.

5. Note that here, the reading is that the perfect eventuality is obliged to hold sometime in the future. This is consistent with deontic modality in general, which is obligatorily forward-shifting with respect to the evaluation time. It is tricky to construct felicitous

versions of these sentences because some context is required to construct a situation where a perfect state will be relevant in the future.

6. The only exception to this generalization is the modal *may*, which does vary in scope with respect to negation depending on interpretation. I will assume that this means that at this point in the history of English, these have become two distinct lexical items. I will make a specific proposal for the two versions of *may* in section 6.2.1.

7. Necessity is classically chosen, but in fact any one of these modal notions can be taken as basic and the others derived from it with the help of negation.

8. Kratzer (1977) also introduces the idea of the ordering source on worlds, a third parameter that is needed to account for our judgments of the gradability or degrees of possibility and/or obligation. I will not make use of the ordering source or its equivalent. I note that the examples used to demonstrate the need for the ordering source come from modal expressions that are either nominal or adjectival. I suspect that the factor of gradability comes from the adjectival domain itself and is not a core property of verbal auxiliary modals. Investigating this idea is obviously beyond the scope of this monograph.

9. This null morpheme provides the presupposition that the verbal eventuality in question is located in a different world than the world of the perspectival situation.

Chapter 6

1. See Stowell 2004 for a discussion of these facts and an argument that moribund past tense morphology on English modals actually is grammatically interpretable.

2. What Condoravdi (2002, 69) actually says is, "The correct generalization is that modals for the present have a future orientation optionally with stative predicates and obligatorily with eventive predicates." She claims further that this fact is independent of the flavor of modality in question. I have reason to doubt the latter claim; hence, I relativize her statement to epistemic flavors. In the case of circumstantial modality, it seems to me that stative predicates obligatorily forward-shift just like dynamic ones.

3. This at least is the assumption for normal matrix situations, but I assume that it can be relativized to deal with embedded attitudes and free indirect discourse.

4. I put aside other interpretations of the present tense in English here. Under certain discourse conditions, additional meanings for the present include narrative past and planned future. I assume that habitual present involves the construction of a derived dispositional state in the first phase. I suspect that narrative past and planned future both involve the implicit building of a reference situation that is truly present, with a forward or backward inferential relation. However, since the correct analysis of these constructions would involve studying a great deal more data, I leave it for further work.

5. The difference between REMOTE and ANAPHORIC arises in cases where, for example, ANAPHORIC-type anchoring results in reference resolution overlapping the speech parameters. This would be disallowed by a REMOTE specification, but fine for a modal specified as ANAPHORIC. My choice of privative features reflects the fact that I think the latter type exists.

6. Note also that this interpretation of the present tense is consistent with the fact that both the perfect and the progressive create derived states, while the passive does not. This is what I have assumed to be the case in all the denotations given so far.

Another construction type that I have not considered in any detail is the use of the habitual present tense with English eventive predicates. I will assume that the habitual also requires the construction of a derived state. I think this is a quite plausible possibility on the surface, but working out the details is once again beyond my remit here.

7. The notion of alternatives is a primitive here, corresponding to the primitive of possible situations in a model such as Fine's truthmaker semantics (Fine 2014).

Chapter 7

1. Recall, the quotational operator was a move inspired by the semantic work on demonstrations (Davidson 2015, Henderson 2016) generalized to purely symbolic and nonideophonic lexical items.

2. Champollion (2015) also makes this move, for reasons involving the interaction of the event variable with quantification more generally. Regularizing such interactions is part of the payoff here as well, but now it is underpinned by more VP-internal reasons as well: the deployment of the quotational operator and the construction of the spatiotemporal property type.

3. In the end, I leave it open that in certain languages and/or for certain items, this syntactic information can be quite underspecified; however, it is still a required component of the triple that defines elements of D_μ. The alternative to this kind of syntactic information is the kind of postsyntactic frame of insertion proposed by Harley and Noyer (1999) to do the job of subcategorization.

4. Thanks to Sandra Ronai (pers. comm.) for suggesting the metaphor.

References

Abney, Steven. 1987. The English noun phrase in its sentential aspect. PhD diss., MIT.

Abusch, Dorit. 1985. On verbs and time. PhD diss., University of Massachusetts, Amherst.

Adelman, James, Gordon Brown, and José Quesada. 2006. Contextual diversity, not word frequency, determines word naming and lexical decision times. *Psychological Science* 17: 814–823.

Adger, David. 2010. Variability and grammatical architecture. Available at http:// ling.auf.net/lingBuzz/001176.

Adger, David, Daniel Harbour, and Laurel Watkins. 2009. *Mirrors and microparametric phrase structure beyond free word order*. Cambridge: Cambridge University Press.

Aelbrecht, Lobke, and Will Harwood. 2012. To be or not to be elided: VP ellipsis revisited. Ms., University of Ghent.

Åfarli, Tor A. 1989. Passive in Norwegian and in English. *Linguistic Inquiry* 20: 101–108.

Åfarli, Tor A. 1992. *The syntax of Norwegian passive constructions*. Amsterdam: John Benjamins.

Alexiadou, Artemis, and Elena Anagnostopoulou. 2008. Structuring participles. In *WCCFL 26*, edited by Charles B. Chang and Hannah J. Haynie, 33–41. Somerville, MA: Cascadilla Press.

Alexiadou, Artemis, Monika Rathert, and Arnim von Stechow. 2003a. Introduction: The modules of perfect constructions. In *Perfect explorations*, edited by Artemis Alexiadou, Monika Rathert, and Arnim von Stechow, vii–xxxviii. Berlin: Mouton de Guyter.

Alexiadou, Artemis, Monika Rathert, and Arnim von Stechow, eds. 2003b. *Perfect explorations*. Berlin: Mouton de Gruyter.

Aloni, Maria. 2007. Free choice, modals, and imperatives. *Natural Language Semantics* 15: 65–94.

Altshuler, Daniel. 2016. *Events, states and times*. Berlin: de Gruyter.

Anagnostopoulou, Elena. 2003. Participles and voice. In *Perfect explorations*, edited by Artemis Alexiadou, Monika Rathert, and Arnim von Stechow, 1–36. Berlin: Mouton de Gruyter.

Arsenijevic, Boban, and Wolfram Hinzen. 2012. On the absence of X-within-X recursion in human grammar. *Linguistic Inquiry* 43: 423–440.

Austin, J. L. 1950. *Truth: Philosophical papers.* Oxford: Oxford University Press.

Baayen, Harald R. 2010. Demythologizing the word frequency effect: A discriminative learning perspective. *The Mental Lexicon* 5: 436–461.

Baker, Mark C. 1985. The Mirror Principle and morphosyntactic explanation. *Linguistic Inquiry* 16: 373–415.

Baker, Mark C. 2003. *Lexical categories.* Cambridge: Cambridge University Press.

Baker, Mark C., Kyle Johnson, and Ian Roberts. 1989. Passive arguments raised. *Linguistic Inquiry* 20: 219–251.

Baltin, Mark R. 1989. Heads and projections. In *Alternative conceptions of phrase structure,* edited by Mark R. Baltin and Anthony S. Kroch, 1–16. Chicago: University of Chicago Press.

Baltin, Mark R. 2006. The non-unity of VP-preposing. *Language* 82: 734–766.

Barwise, Jon, and John Perry. 1983. *Situations and attitudes.* Cambridge, MA: MIT Press.

Beaver, David, and Cleo Condoravdi. 2007. On the logic of verbal modification. In *Proceedings of the 16th Amsterdam Colloquium,* edited by Paul Dekker, Maria Aloni, and Floris Roelofsen, 3–9. Amsterdam: University of Amsterdam.

Bhatt, Rajesh. 2008. Transitivity alternations and verbalization. Ms., University of Massachusetts, Amherst.

Bilgrami, Akeel. 1992. *Belief and meaning.* Oxford: Blackwell.

Bjorkman, Bronwyn. 2011. Be-ing default: The morphosyntax of auxiliaries. PhD diss., MIT.

Bobaljik, Jonathan David, and Susi Wurmbrand. 1999. Modals, raising and A-reconstruction. Ms., University of Connecticut.

Bonomi, Andrea. 1997. The progressive and the structure of events. *Journal of Semantics* 14: 173–205.

Borer, Hagit. 2005. *Structuring sense.* Vol. 1, *In name only.* Oxford: Oxford University Press.

Borer, Hagit. 2013. *Structuring sense.* Vol. 3, *Taking form.* Oxford: Oxford University Press.

Bošković, Željko. 2014. Now I'm a phase, now I'm not a phase. *Linguistic Inquiry* 45: 27–89.

Brennan, Virginia. 1993. Root and epistemic modal auxiliary verbs. PhD diss., University of Massachusetts, Amherst.

Bresnan, Joan. 1982. The passive in lexical theory. In *The mental representation of grammatical relations,* edited by Joan Bresnan, 3–86. Cambridge, MA: MIT Press.

Brody, Michael. 2000. Mirror Theory: Syntactic representation in perfect syntax. *Linguistic Inquiry* 31: 29–56.

Brown, Roger. 1973. *A first language: The early stages.* London: George Allen & Unwin.

Bruening, Benjamin. 2014. Word formation is syntactic: Adjectival passives in English. *Natural Language and Linguistic Theory* 32: 363–422.

Bye, Patrik, and Peter Svenonius. 2012. Non-concatenative morphology as an epiphenomenon. In *The morphology and phonology of exponence: The state of the art*, edited by Jochen Trommer, 427–495. Oxford: Oxford University Press.

Caha, Pavel. 2009. The nanosyntax of case. PhD diss., University of Tromsø.

Carrier, Jill, and Janet H. Randall. 1992. The argument structure and syntactic structure of resultatives. *Linguistic Inquiry* 23: 173–234.

Champollion, Lucas. 2015. The interaction of compositional semantics and event semantics. *Linguistics and Philosophy* 38: 31–66.

Chomsky, Noam. 1957. *Syntactic structures*. The Hague: Mouton.

Chomsky, Noam. 1970. Deep structure, surface structure, and semantic interpretation. In *Studies in general and Oriental linguistics*, edited by Roman Jakobson and Shigeo Kawamoto, 52–91. Tokyo: TEC.

Chomsky, Noam. 1981. *Lectures on government and binding*. Dordrecht: Foris.

Chomsky, Noam. 1995. Language and nature. *Mind* 104: 1–61.

Cinque, Guglielmo. 1999. *Adverbs and functional heads: A cross-linguistic perspective*. New York: Oxford University Press.

Cinque, Guglielmo. 2005. Deriving Greenberg's Universal 20 and its exceptions. *Linguistic Inquiry* 36: 315–332. University of Venice.

Cipria, Alicia, and Craige Roberts. 2000. Spanish imperfecto and pretérito: Truth conditions and aktionsart effects in a situation semantics. *Natural Language Semantics* 8: 297–347.

Condoravdi, Cleo. 2002. Temporal interpretation of modals: Modals for the present and for the past. In *The construction of meaning*, edited by Stefan Kaufmann, David Beaver, Luis Casillas, and Billy Clark, 59–87. Stanford, CA: CSLI Publications.

Copley, Bridget. 2002. The semantics of the future. PhD diss., MIT.

Copley, Bridget, and Heidi Harley. 2015. A force-theoretic framework for event structure. *Linguistics and Philosophy* 32: 103–158.

Cormack, Annabel, and Neil Smith. 2002. Modals and negation in English. In *Modality and its interaction with the verbal system*, edited by Sjef Barbiers, 143–173. Amsterdam: John Benjamins.

Davidson, Donald. 1967. The logical form of action sentences. In *The logic of decision and action*, edited by Nicholas Rescher, 81–95. Pittsburgh, PA: University of Pittsburgh Press.

Davidson, Kathryn. 2015. Quotation, demonstration and iconicity. *Linguistics and Philosophy* 38: 477–520.

Dékány, Eva. 2012. A profile of the Hungarian DP. PhD diss., University of Tromsø.

Demirdache, Hamida, and Myriam Uribe-Etxebarria. 2000. The primitives of temporal relations. In *Step by step: Essays on Minimalist syntax in honor of Howard Lasnik*, edited by Roger Martin, David Michaels, and Juan Uriagereka, 157–186. Cambridge, MA: MIT Press.

Demirdache, Hamida, and Myriam Uribe-Etxebarria. 2008. Scope and anaphora with time arguments: The case of 'perfect modals'. *Lingua* 118: 1790–1815.

Dowty, David R. 1979. *Word meaning and Montague Grammar: The semantics of verbs and times in generative semantics and in Montague's PTQ*. Dordrecht: Reidel.

Dryer, Matthew S., and Martin Haspelmath. 2013. *The World Atlas of Language Structures online*. Available at http://wals.info.

Eckhardt, Regine. 2012. *Hereby* explained: An event-based account of performative utterances. *Linguistics and Philosophy* 35: 21–55.

Embick, David. 2004. On the structure of resultative participles in English. *Linguistic Inquiry* 35: 355–392.

Embick, David, and Alec Marantz. 2008. Architecture and blocking. *Linguistic Inquiry* 39: 1–53.

Embick, David, and Ralf Noyer. 2001. Movement operations after syntax. *Linguistic Inquiry* 32: 555–595.

Ernst, Thomas. 2002. *The syntax of adjuncts*. Cambridge: Cambridge University Press.

Fine, Kit. 2000. Semantics for the logic of essence. *Journal of Philosophical Logic* 29: 543–584.

Fine, Kit. 2005. *Modality and tense: Philosophical papers*. Oxford: Oxford University Press.

Fine, Kit. 2014. Truthmaker semantics for intuitionist logic. *Journal of Philosophical Logic* 43: 549–577.

von Fintel, Kai, and Anthony S. Gillies. 2010. Must . . . stay . . . strong! *Natural Language Semantics* 18: 351–383.

Gehrke, Berit. 2015. Adjectival participles, event kind modification: The case of frequency adjectives. *Natural Language and Linguistic Theory* 33: 897–938.

Gehrke, Berit, and Louise McNally. 2015. Distributional modification: The case of frequency adjectives. *Language* 91: 837–868.

Giorgi, Alessandra, and Fabio Pianesi. 1997. *Tense and aspect: From semantics to morphosyntax*. New York: Oxford University Press.

Grimm, Scott, and Louise McNally. 2015. The *ing* dynasty: Rebuilding the semantics of nominalizations. In *Proceedings of SALT 25*, edited by Sarah D'Antonio, Mary Moroney, and Carol Rose Little, 82–102. Available at http://journals.linguistic society.org/proceedings/index.php/SALT/issue/view/132.

Grimshaw, Jane. 1979. Complement selection and the lexicon. *Linguistic Inquiry* 10: 279–326.

Grimshaw, Jane. 1990. *Argument structure*. Cambridge, MA: MIT Press.

Groenendijk, Jeroen, and Martin Stokhof. 1975. Modality and conversational information. *Theoretical Linguistics* 2: 61–112.

Hacquard, Valentine. 2006. Aspects of modality. PhD diss., MIT.

Hale, Kenneth, and Samuel Jay Keyser. 1993. On argument structure and the lexical expression of syntactic relations. In *The view from Building 20: Essays in linguistics in honor of Sylvain Bromberger*, edited by Kenneth Hale and Samuel Jay Keyser, 53–109. Cambridge, MA: MIT Press.

Hale, Ken[neth], and Samuel Jay Keyser. 2002. *Prolegomenon to a theory of argument structure*. Cambridge, MA: MIT Press.

Halle, Morris, and Alec Marantz. 1993. Distributed Morphology and the pieces of inflection. In *The view from Building 20: Essays in linguistics in honor of Sylvain Bromberger*, edited by Kenneth Hale and Samuel Jay Keyser, 111–176. Cambridge, MA: MIT Press.

Hallman, Peter. 2009a. Instants and intervals in the event/state distinction. Ms., UCLA.

Hallman, Peter. 2009b. Proportions in time: Interactions of quantification and aspect. *Natural Language Semantics* 17: 29–61.

Hankamer, Jorge, and Ivan Sag. 1976. Deep and surface anaphora. *Linguistic Inquiry* 7: 391–428.

Harley, Heidi. 2013. External arguments and the Mirror Principle: On the distinctness of Voice and v. *Lingua* 125: 34–57.

Harley, Heidi, and Rolf Noyer. 1999. State of the article: Distributed Morphology. *GLOT International* 4.4: 3–9.

Harwood, Will. 2011. There are several positions available: English intermediate subject positions. In *Proceedings of ConSOLE XIX*, edited by Enrico Boone, Kathrin Linke, and Maartje Schulpin, 215–239. Leiden: LUCL.

Harwood, Will. 2013. Being progressive is just a phase: Dividing the functional hierarchy. PhD diss., University of Ghent.

Harwood, Will. 2014. Being progressive is just a phase: Celebrating the uniqueness of progressive aspect under a phase-based analysis. *Natural Language and Linguistic Theory* 33: 523–573.

Heim, Irene, and Angelika Kratzer. 1998. *Semantics in generative grammar*. Oxford: Blackwell.

Henderson, Robert. 2016. Pluractional demonstrations. In *Proceedings of SALT 26*, edited by Mary Moroney, Carol-Rose Little, Jacob Collard, and Dan Burgdorf, 664–683. Available at https://journals.linguisticsociety.org/proceedings/index.php/SALT/article/view/26.664

Higginbotham, James T. 2007. Remarks on compositionality. In *The Oxford handbook of linguistic interfaces*, edited by Gillian Ramchand and Charles Reiss, 425–444. Oxford: Oxford University Press.

Hinzen, Wolfram. 2017. Reference across pathologies: A new linguistic lens on disorders of thought. *Theoretical Linguistics* 43: 169–232.

Hinzen, Wolfram, and Michelle Sheehan. 2015. *The Philosophy of Universal Grammar*. 2nd ed. Oxford: Oxford University Press.

Homer, Vincent. 2012. Neg raising and positive polarity: The view from modals. *Semantics and Pragmatics* 8: 1–88.

Huddleston, Rodney. 1974. Further remarks on the analysis of auxiliaries as main verbs. *Foundations of Language* 11: 215–229.

Iatridou, Sabine. 1990. About Agr(P). *Linguistic Inquiry* 21: 551–577.

Iatridou, Sabine. 2000. The grammatical ingredients of counterfactuality. *Linguistic Inquiry* 31: 231–270.

Iatridou, Sabine, and Hedde Zeijlstra. 2013. Negation, polarity, and deontic modals. *Linguistic Inquiry* 44: 529–568.

Inoue, Kyoko. 1979. An analysis of the English present perfect. *Linguistics* 17: 561–589.

Isard, Steven. 1974. What would you have done if... *Theoretical Linguistics* 1: 233–255.

Israel, Michael. 1996. Polarity sensitivity as lexical semantics. *Linguistics and Philosophy* 19: 619–666.

Jackendoff, Ray. 1972. *Semantic interpretation in generative grammar*. Cambridge, MA: MIT Press.

Julien, Marit. 2000. Syntactic heads and word formation: A study of verbal inflection. PhD diss., University of Tromsø.

Julien, Marit. 2002. *Syntactic heads and word formation*. New York: Oxford University Press.

Kamp, Hans, and Uwe Reyle. 1993. *From discourse to logic*. Dordrecht: Reidel.

Kamp, Hans, Uwe Reyle, and Antje Rossdeutscher. To appear. *Perfects as feature shifting operators*. Leiden: Brill.

Karttunen, Lauri. 1972. Possible and must. In *Syntax and semantics 1*, edited by John Kimball, 1–20. New York: Academic Press.

Kayne, Richard S. 1994. *The antisymmetry of syntax*. Cambridge, MA: MIT Press.

Klein, Wolfgang. 1992. The present perfect puzzle. *Language* 68: 525–551.

Klein, Wolfgang. 1994. *Time in language*. London: Routledge.

Klinedinst, Nathan. 2012. Intensionality and the progressive, Technical report, University College London.

Kratzer, Angelika. 1977. What "must" and "can" must and can mean. *Linguistics and Philosophy* 1: 337–355.

Kratzer, Angelika. 1981. The notional category of modality. In *Words, worlds and contexts*, edited by Hans-Jürgen Eikmeyer and Hans Reiser, 38–74. Berlin: Walter de Gruyter.

Kratzer, Angelika. 1989. An investigation of the lumps of thought. *Linguistics and Philosophy* 12: 607–653.

Kratzer, Angelika. 1991. Modality. In *Handbuch Semantik/Handbook Semantics*, edited by Arnim von Stechow and Dieter Wunderlich, 639–650. Berlin: de Gruyter.

Kratzer, Angelika. 1996. Severing the external argument from the verb. In *Phrase structure and the lexicon*, edited by Johan Rooryck and Laurie Zaring, 109–137. Dordrecht: Kluwer.

Kratzer, Angelika. 2000. Building statives. In *Proceedings of the 26th Annual Meeting of the Berkeley Linguistics Society*, edited by Lisa Conathan, Jeff Good, Darya

Kavitskaya, Alyssa Wulf, and Alan Yu, 385–399. Berkeley: University of California, Berkeley Linguistics Society.

Kratzer, Angelika. 2014. Situations in natural language semantics. In *Stanford encyclopedia of philosophy*, edited by Edward N. Zalta. 2014 ed. Available at https://plato.stanford.edu/entries/situations-semantics.

Kripke, Saul. 1959. A completeness theorem in modal logic. *Journal of Symbolic Logic* 24: 1–14.

Kripke, Saul. 1963. Semantical analysis of modal logic. *Zeitschrift für mathematische Logik und Grundlagen der Mathematik* 9: 67–96.

Landman, Fred. 1992. The progressive. *Natural Language Semantics* 1: 1–32.

Landman, Fred. 2008. 1066. On the difference between the tense-perspective-aspect systems of English and Dutch. In *Theoretical and crosslinguistic approaches to the semantics of aspect*, edited by Susan Rothstein, 107–166. Amsterdam: John Benjamins.

Leech, Geoffrey. 1971. *Meaning and the English verb*. London: Longman.

Lewis, David K. 1973. *Counterfactuals*. Oxford: Blackwell.

Lewis, David K. 1986. *On the plurality of worlds*. Oxford: Blackwell.

Llinás, Rodolfo. 1987. Mindedness as a functional state of the brain. In *Mindwaves: Thoughts on intelligence, identity and consciousness*, edited by Colin Blakemore and Susan Greenfield, 339–358. Oxford: Blackwell.

Löbner, Sebastian. 2001. The present perfect in German: Outline of its semantic composition. *Natural Language and Linguistic Theory* 19: 355–401.

Lundquist, Björn. 2008. Nominalizations and participles in Swedish. PhD diss., University of Tromsø.

Marantz, Alec. 1997. No escape from syntax: Don't try morphological analysis in the privacy of your own lexicon. In *Proceedings of the 21st Annual Penn Linguistics Colloquium*, edited by Alexis Dimitriadis, Laura Siegel, Clarissa Surek-Clark, and Alexander Williams, 201–225. University of Pennsylvania Working Papers in Linguistics 4.2. Philadelphia: University of Pennsylvania, Penn Linguistics Club.

Marr, David. 1982. *Vision: A computational investigation into the human representation and processing of visual information*. New York: W. H. Freeman.

McCoard, Robert W. 1978. *The English perfect: Tense choice and pragmatic inferences*. Amsterdam: North-Holland.

McNamara, Paul. 2014. Deontic logics. In *Stanford encyclopedia of philosophy*, edited by Edward N. Zalta. 2014 ed. Available at https://plato.stanford.edu/entries/logic-deontic.

Mittwoch, Anita. 1988. Aspects of English aspect: On the interaction of perfect, progressive and durational phrases. *Linguistics and Philosophy* 11: 203–254.

Moens, Marc, and Mark Steedman. 1988. Temporal ontology and temporal reference. *Computational Linguistics* 14: 15–28.

Moltmann, Friederike. 2018. Natural language and its ontology. In *Metaphysics and cognitive science*, edited by Alvin Goldman and Brian McLaughlin. Oxford: Oxford University Press.

Myler, Neil. 2017. *Building and interpreting possession sentences*. Cambridge, MA: MIT Press.

Nagel, Thomas. 1993. The mind wins! *New York Review of Books*, 4 March 1993, 37–41.

Narrog, Heike. 2012. *Modality, subjectivity, and semantic change: A crosslinguistic perspective*. Oxford: Oxford University Press.

Nauze, Fabrice. 2008. Modality in typological perspective. PhD diss., University of Amsterdam.

Owens, Robert E. 2001. *Language development: An introduction*. 5th ed. Boston: Allyn and Bacon.

Palmer, Frank. 1986. *Mood and modality*. Cambridge: Cambridge University Press.

Pancheva, Roumyana. 2003. The aspectual makeup of perfect participles and the interpretations of the perfect. In *Perfect explorations*, edited by Artemis Alexiadou, Monika Rathert, and Arnim von Stechow, 277–306. Berlin: Mouton de Gruyter.

Pancheva, Roumyana, and Arnim von Stechow. 2004. On the present perfect puzzle. In *NELS 34*, edited by Keir Moulton and Matthew Wolf, 469–484. Amherst: University of Massachusetts, Graduate Linguistic Student Association.

Parsons, Terence. 1990. *Events in the semantics of English: A study in subatomic semantics*. Cambridge, MA: MIT Press.

Perlmutter, David. 1971. *Deep and surface structure constraints in syntax*. New York: Holt, Rinehart and Winston.

Pfaff, Alexander P. 2015. Adjectival and genitival modification in definite noun phrases in Icelandic. PhD diss., University of Tromsø.

Pietroski, Paul. 2017. Semantic internalism. In *Cambridge companion to Chomsky*, edited by James McGilvray, 196–216. Cambridge: Cambridge University Press.

Portner, Paul. 1998. The progressive in modal semantics. *Language* 74: 760–787.

Portner, Paul. 2003. The (temporal) semantics and (modal) pragmatics of the perfect. *Linguistics and Philosophy* 26: 459–510.

Portner, Paul. 2009. *Modality*. Oxford: Oxford University Press.

Poser, William J. 1992. Blocking of phrasal constructions by lexical items. In *Lexical matters*, edited by Ivan A. Sag and Anna Szabolcsi, 111–130. Stanford, CA: CSLI Publications.

Potts, Christopher. 2007. The dimensions of quotation. In *Direct compositionality*, edited by Chris Barker and Pauline Jacobson, 405–431. Oxford: Oxford University Press.

Pylkkänen, Liina. 1999. Causation and external arguments. In *Papers from the UPenn/MIT Roundtable on the Lexicon*, edited by Liina Pylkkänen, Angeliek van Hout, and Heidi Harley, 161–183. MIT Working Papers in Linguistics 35. Cambridge, MA: MIT, MIT Working Papers in Linguistics.

Ramchand, Gillian. 2008. *Verb meaning and the lexicon*. Cambridge: Cambridge University Press.

Ramchand, Gillian. 2011. Minimalist semantics. In *The Oxford handbook of linguistic minimalism*, ed. by Cedric Boeckk, 449–471. Oxford: Oxford University Press.

Ramchand, Gillian. 2014a. Deriving variable linearization. *Natural Language and Linguistic Theory* 32: 263–282.

Ramchand, Gillian. 2014b. Structural meaning and conceptual meaning in verb semantics. *Linguistic Analysis* 39: 211–247.

Ramchand, Gillian. 2016. Event structure and verbal decomposition. Ms., University of Tromsø. To appear in *The Oxford handbook of event structure*, edited by Robert Truswell. Oxford: Oxford University Press.

Ramchand, Gillian. 2017. The event domain. In *The verbal domain*, edited by Irene Franco, Roberta D'Alessandro, and Ángel Gallego, 233–254. Oxford: Oxford University Press.

Ramchand, Gillian, and Peter Svenonius. 2014. Deriving the functional hierarchy. *Journal of Language Sciences*. Available at http://dx.doi.org/10.1016/j.langsci.2014.06.013.

Reichenbach, Hans. 1947. *Elements of symbolic logic*. New York: Macmillan.

Ritter, Elizabeth, and Martina Wiltschko. 2009. Varieties of Infl: Tense, location and person. In *Alternatives to cartography*, edited by Jeroen van Craenenbroeck, Hans Broekhuis, and Henk van Riemsdijk, 153–202. Berlin: Mouton de Gruyter.

Ross, John Robert. 1969. Auxiliaries as main verbs. In *Studies in philosophical linguistics*, edited by William Todd, 1: 77–102. Evanston, IL: Great Expectations.

Sailor, Craig. 2012. Inflection at the interface. Ms., UCLA.

Schachter, Paul. 1983. Explaining auxiliary order. In *Linguistic categories: Auxiliaries and related puzzles*, edited by Frank Heny and Barry Richards, 145–204. Dordrecht: Reidel.

Schwarz, Bernhard, and Rajesh Bhatt. 2006. Light negation and polarity. In *Crosslinguistic research in syntax and semantics: Negation, tense and clausal architecture*, edited by Raffaella Zanuttini, Héctor Campos, Elena Herburger, and Paul H. Portner, 175–198. Washington, DC: Georgetown University Press.

Sheehan, Michelle, and Wolfram Hinzen. 2011. Moving towards the edge. *Linguistic Analysis* 3: 405–458.

Simpson, Jane. 1983. Resultatives. In *Papers in Lexical-Functional Grammar*, edited by Beth Levin, Malka Rappaport, and Annie Zaenen, 143–157. Bloomington: Indiana University Linguistics Club.

Smith, Carlota S. 1991. *The parameter of aspect*. Dordrecht: Kluwer.

Sportiche, Dominique. 2005. Division of labor between Merge and Move: Strict locality of selection and apparent reconstruction paradoxes. Ms., UCLA. Available at http://ling.auf.net/lingBuzz/000163.

Stowell, Tim. 2004. Tense and modals. In *The syntax of time*, edited by Jacqueline Guéron and Jacqueline Lecarme, 621–636. Cambridge, MA: MIT Press.

Svenonius, Peter. 2004. On the edge. In *Peripheries: Syntactic edges and their effects*, edited by David Adger, Cécile De Cat, and George Tsoulas, 261–287. Dordrecht: Kluwer.

Svenonius, Peter. 2012. Spanning. Ms., University of Tromsø. Available at http://ling.auf.net/lingBuzz/001501.

Taylor, Barry. 1977. Tense and continuity. *Linguistics and Philosophy* 1: 199–220.

Truswell, Robert, ed. To appear. *The Oxford handbook of event structure*. Oxford: Oxford University Press.

Varasdi, Károly. To appear. Worlds, events and inertia. *Journal of Logic, Language and Information*.

Vlach, Frank. 1981. The semantics of the progressive. In *Syntax and semantics 14: Tense and aspect*, edited by Philip Tedeschi and Annie Zaenen, 271–292. New York: Academic Press.

Wasow, Thomas. 1977. Transformations and the lexicon. In *Formal syntax*, edited by Peter Culicover, Thomas Wasow, and Adrian Akmajian, 327–360. New York: Academic Press.

Werner, Tom. 2006. Future and nonfuture modal sentences. *Natural Language Semantics* 14: 235–255.

Williams, Edwin. 2003. *Representation Theory*. Cambridge, MA: MIT Press.

Wiltschko, Martina. 2014. *The universal structure of categories: Towards a formal typology*. Cambridge: Cambridge University Press.

Zamparelli, Roberto. 2000. *Layers in the Determiner Phrase*. New York: Garland.

Zanuttini, Raffaella. 1992. Syntactic properties of sentential negation: A comparative study of Romance languages. *Dissertation Abstracts International, A: The Humanities and Social Sciences* 52: 2536.

Zanuttini, Raffaella. 1997. *Negation and clausal structure: A comparative study of Romance languages*. New York: Oxford University Press.

Zimmerman, Thomas Ede. 2000. Free choice disjunction and epistemic possibility. *Natural Language Semantics* 8: 255–290.

Zucchi, Alessandro. 1999. Incomplete events, intensionality and imperfective aspect. *Natural Language Semantics* 7: 179–215.

Index

Linguistic Inquiry Monographs

Samuel Jay Keyser, general editor